# Practice Development for Professional Firms

# Practice Development for Professional Firms

Aubrey Wilson

**McGRAW-HILL Book Company (UK) Limited**

London · New York · St Louis · San Francisco · Auckland
Bogotá · Guatemala · Hamburg · Johannesburg · Lisbon · Madrid
Mexico · Montreal · New Delhi · Panama · Paris · San Juan
São Paulo · Singapore · Sydney · Tokyo · Toronto

Published by
McGRAW-HILL Book Company (UK) Limited
MAIDENHEAD · BERKSHIRE · ENGLAND

British Library Cataloguing in Publication Data
Wilson, Aubrey
    Practice development for professional firms.
    1. Professions—Marketing
    I. Title
    658.8   HF5415
    ISBN 0-07-084761-4


Library of Congress Cataloging in Publication Data
Wilson, Aubrey.
    Practice development for professional firms.
    Bibliography: p.
    Includes index.
    1. Professions—Marketing.   I. Title.
HD8038.A1W55   1984        658.8        84-9686
ISBN 0-07-084761-4

12345 BT 87654

Filmset by Eta Services (Typesetters) Limited, Beccles, Suffolk and
printed and bound in Great Britain by Butler & Tanner Ltd, Frome and London

This book is dedicated to my personal professional advisers and colleagues, not all of whom by any means approve what has been attempted, but from all of whom I have learned the art of the possible. Individually and collectively they have saved me and mine from physical, financial, legal and professional disaster; Iain Cuthbertson BDS, LDS, RCS, Norman Hitchcox RICS, Jonathan Douglas Hughes, L. G. Kingdom FRCS, Graham Lee LLB, David Levy, Richard Moore, Eric Newman FCCA, FFII, Ian Percy CA, Christopher Ratcliff MA (Cantab), DIP, AA, RIBA, Dr Stephen Spiro B.Sc., MD, MB, Harry Watson MC, RCVS, but most of all Dr Trevor Hudson BA, MD, B.Chir., without whom it could truly be said this book would never have been written.

# Contents

# Preface

Rather like geographical discovery the study of business and economic life shifts in emphasis as each area yields up its mysteries. Thus as the great exploration period of Central Africa came to an end interest and activities centred on the remoter areas of Antarctica. While it most certainly cannot be said that all is known that is to be known about any business activity, it is obvious that the study of the professions in relation to the publics they serve has gained in importance as researchers and practitioners alike turned away from the well trodden paths of management, industrial relations, innovation, corporate planning and the other esoterics of business.

When my previous book *The Marketing of Professional Services*[1] was published in 1972, its bibliography listed just four books concerned with professional activities and only one of these dealt with the question of practice development for professional firms. Today, over a decade later, the library shelves are awash with the outpourings of commentators offering a wealth of advice, techniques and advocacy—most of it regrettably of very little practical value. The majority of professional firms understandably have few or no skills in the arts of practice development and, what is more, many have no desire to develop or acquire them and some positively oppose their introduction and use. Thus the bulk of contributions have attracted either no significant audiences or following, or have been utilized within those activities which are called 'professions' although they might more unkindly be referred to as 'trade' or pseudo or semi-professions.

That this should be so becomes obvious from the fact that these fringe professions are not constrained in the methods by which they obtain clients and thus are free to adopt any techniques and to communicate any message that does not contravene accepted standards for business as a whole, not just the standards of their profession. Researchers and writers on the subject of services, as is demonstrated by their published work, while paying lip-service to the fact that services are not just intangible products, actually advise how services might best be offered to the various publics they are designed for by the adoption of marketing techniques and messages used for products. To attempt to offer services this way, as many failures have shown, is to build on a foundation so precarious as almost certainly to guarantee the structure will collapse.

It is however one thing to claim that there is a fundamental difference between offering professional services and providing goods, but it is quite another to demonstrate this difference. The distinction does not rest in the choice of methods which are used so much as in their careful adaptation to carry information and messages which are based on a far deeper and sensitive understanding of needs—in the very widest sense of that word—of the users of professional services and including those needs they are either incapable or unwilling to express. 'Evidence' for what are essentially expectations has to be relevant and has to be presented in ways which are unfamiliar if only because they are necessary to those who provide goods and among providers of many non-professional services. But above all, and in the final analysis, it will be the one-to-one practitioner–client relationship once achieved which will shape the conditions of successful practice development.

Thus the approach which a service adopts towards practice development depends heavily on its real or perceived or claimed status as a profession since the controls which can be exercised over members will also vary. What then is a profession? A catalogue of definitions contributes

1. Aubrey Wilson. *The Marketing of Professional Services*. McGraw-Hill (London, 1972).

nothing to the discussion except to illustrate just how widely views differ both within and outside those callings which are recognized by society as a whole rather than by its members as professions.

But despite definitional problems it is incumbent on an author to delineate clearly for whom his book has been written, so that a framework is needed as to the activities which are embraced by the subject of practice development for professional firms.

'In order to think clearly and systematically about anything one must delimit the subject-matter to be addressed by empirical and intellectual analysis. We cannot develop theory if we are not certain what we are talking about.'[2]

A statement such as this might presage the revelation of the philosopher's stone which would once and for all clearly define what is a profession. Alas despite such a portentous approach none of the many contributors to the studies which are prefaced with the above statement, succeeded in providing a wholly satisfactory definition of just what is a profession. Indeed in *The Marketing of Professional Services* the problem was not solved other than by the invocation of Says Law. 'If I says I'm a profession, I'm a profession.'

'There are certain vocations of ancient lineage which by common consent are called professions. . . . There are many other vocations which, though more recently and therefore less firmly established, are nevertheless usually granted professional rank: such vocations, architecture, engineering, chemistry, accountancy and surveying for example require mention.'[3] In fact Carr-Saunders identifies a further 23 vocations which he classes as professions and these include such obvious omissions from the quoted statement as dentists and veterinary surgeons. The argument as to precisely what is a profession is one which has defeated everyone including governmental investigative commissions and is not one which will advance an understanding of just how professional practices can be organized and operated to achieve the personal aspirations of the practitioners and the corporate aspirations of the practice.

For the purpose of this book the key audience is identified as those professions Carr-Saunders included in the quoted passage and a number to be found in his study of the professions. The unifying factor is that all of them conduct their work within a framework of controls which create very clear constraints to developing practices except by perhaps indirect methods or by sometimes recognizably devious means of avoiding the rules. Failure to observe the rules can and usually does lead to limited or total disqualification which in turn implies that an individual's earning ability rests on compliance. No one can prevent an advertising expert, a market researcher or a heating consultant from continuing to operate if he is expelled from or refused membership of the appropriate association. In contradistinction solicitors, doctors, pharmacists, veterinary surgeons, patent agents, and others are all professions controlled by statute and misconduct can lead to removal of the qualification and thus the legal right to practice. 'Ultimately only a statutory registered profession can hope to possess an ethical code which is strictly enforceable and guarantees legally to restrict a serious offender, thus protecting both clients and the profession.'[4]

These professions then are my prime audience but hopefully there will be much of value to those activities where voluntary restraints on methods of business seeking apply, as well as to those activities where only the good sense and responsibility of the practitioner are the guide as to what is and is not acceptable.

It is not the author's purpose to show practitioners how the rules which exist can be avoided

---

2. Eliot Freidson. 'The theory of professions: state of the art.' In *The Sociology of the Professions* (eds Dingwall and Lewis). Macmillan (London, 1983), p. 21.
3. A. M. Carr-Saunders and P. A. Wilson. *The Professions*. Cass (London, 1964), p. 3.
4. G. Millerson. *The Qualifying Associations*. Routledge & Kegan Paul (London, 1964), p. 156.

or subverted. Nothing that is written is intended to either breach the rules of practice the professions have adopted either in their letter or their spirit. The purpose is to show how practices can be developed within the framework of existing conditions (which of course vary between professions) and in a manner which is acceptable and compatible with the dignity and probity of the professions. It has a further purpose which is to warn of the impending relaxation of practice rules which is evident in all professions and world-wide and to enable practitioners to prepare themselves for the time when currently prohibited methods and messages will be permissible.

This book, which has attempted to incorporate the experience of working with the senior professions for many years, is intended as a wholly functional guide for professional firms and the practitioners within them seeking to develop their own organizations. It is founded on the important premise that resources, in the wildest sense of that word, for practice development will be extremely limited. It does not presume the availability of time, money, skills, which are poured into many consumer and industrial goods and services marketing.

The reader will have to adjust some of the material for the particular circumstances of his own profession and his own practice. Generalizations there must be, but they are related solely to professional services and thus are that much more adaptable for the individual profession. Every attempt has been made however to ensure that the circumstances of each profession have been considered. In this I have been fortunate in being able to have the manuscript checked by leading successful practitioners in virtually all the disciplines which have been included.

An explanation if not an apology is called for. Because different professions use different nomenclatures an author writing on professional services is faced with the task of qualifying every reference to the user of services by a whole series of different titles—clients, patients, cases, patrons, lessees, employers. The sheer tedium of constant repetition of the alternatives leads inevitably to the solution of calling all users of professional services 'clients' except where specific exceptions are necessary. For those professions which use terms other than 'client' it is hoped they will understand the reasoning behind the choice, will accept it and make the transmutation to their own nomenclatures.

This same situation must of course apply to the practitioners and organizations themselves. Some will be called 'practices'', some 'partnerships', some 'firms', some 'associates', some 'groups' and some 'organizations'. Again as a convenient shorthand the term 'firm' has been adopted except when reference is made to a profession where another title is commonly used. Individuals are referred to as 'practitioners' or 'professionals'. Their work may well be 'consultations', 'projects', 'assignments', 'matters', 'treatments', 'engagements' or 'contracts'. There is really no suitable generic term and the most appropriate noun is used within the context of the statement.

The other short cut concerns the vexed question of gender. The constant qualification of gender with 'him' and/or 'her' is just as boring as listing out different names for users or practices. The neutered 'person' is ugly. The male gender has been adopted throughout despite the notably increasing number of female professionals—a trend which can only enhance the acceptability and competence of the professions. The accusation of being sexist and moreover patronizing must be risked for the sake of brevity which it is hoped will not detract from the acceptability of the book to women who now grace all the professions.

No book can be said to be the sole work of its author and this one is exceptionally the result of considerable co-operation by many professional practitioners who advised me as the book developed. Many of them were kind enough to read the later manuscripts despite the time-consuming nature of this task and to make many suggestions to increase the relevance of the material to their own profession. My debt to them all is immense.

I particularly want to express my thanks to Lynn Shostack for her very ready agreement to permit me to use and adopt for my own purpose her highly original work in service marketing which has for me been an enormous stimulant to re-think my own ideas which might otherwise have tended to become inflexible and obdurate from too close a familiarity over too many years. I also want to express my gratitude to Professor Thomas Bonoma who allowed me to draw from his research more valuable information than I might ever have obtained on my own concerning the mysteries and esoterics of the corporate decision-making process. Dr Bonoma's work has provided a quantum leap in this most important area which has direct and important implications for professional firms. I feel privileged to be allowed to introduce the work of both Lynn Shostack and Dr Bonoma into the study of professional services and their users.

Throughout this book there are references to the importance of all support staff within professional firms; and the need for them as much as the practitioner to be client centred. I want to pay tribute to my own minute but vital support staff, in particular Jan Bennett who once again had the daunting task of trying to make sense out of manuscripts that were of cabbalistic obscurity and were highly idiosyncratic in their ordering. Transmuting the early drafts of this book into a manuscript which was a delight to publisher and printer was an achievement of considerable magnitude. It is a miracle she has performed for a second time for me. More importantly her unwavering good humour and continued interest despite considerable re-writing was an encouragement to make numerous changes many of which turned out to be of considerable importance. The fact the manuscript was delivered on time is also a tribute to Lynn Houston who rendered considerable assistance in preparing some of the later drafts for final typing.

The completion of this book is entirely the result of the constant encouragement of Dorothy Fincham, Senior Editor at McGraw-Hill. Her avid demands to see the book as it developed did much to keep me at my desk when I might have been tempted away. I am grateful, even if I did not always show it, for her constant interest and personal involvement in encouraging its completion.

In the preface of *The Marketing of Professional Services* I wrote 'In seeking to acknowledge the help and guidance of others, the risk inevitably exists that they will be held culpable for the faults of omission, commission, style and concept, when all they have sought to do is to remove the grosser errors. Thus my recognition of their aid is intended to indicate the extent of my debt to them and not to absolve myself from responsibility for that which has been written.'

This time the numbers involved have been greater, their tasks more onerous and perhaps the author has grown more obstinate over the years. Their triumph is therefore all the greater. It is truly regrettable that it will never be obvious just how much they contributed to the whole, both with their additions and deletions and their firm but gentle reminders of the need to be sensitive to the culture of the professions so that my comments and ideas would not create unnecessary alienations. If this and other dissonances have occurred the fault is mine alone.

Aubrey Wilson

# A workbook approach

In order to obtain maximum value from the book the following suggestions are offered to readers.

The book is organized in a way which it is hoped will enable those concerned with practice development to identify and concentrate on the issues of major concern to themselves. While the contents follow a logical pattern which parallels the practice development activity itself, many of the chapters are free-standing (but with considerable cross-reference) to permit them to be used in isolation. It is hoped by adopting this approach the practitioner will be able to confine his studies to those activities where more information and guidance is required, while at the same time being able to view the subjects within the total context of practice development.

Because the author has attempted to cover the subject of practice development in all its ramifications the result might seem daunting for those to whom the whole concept is unfamiliar. While the book is intended to be useful as an integrated text, it is also an attempt to include many single ideas which can be adopted by any practice as appropriate. The book contains a number of quick reference check lists as well as formats to enable ideas which are generated to be implemented quickly and with minimum difficulty.

In order to help the reader identify what is important to him and to move from consideration to implementation, at the risk of mutilating the book, it is advisable to mark all points and ideas which the reader wants to action. Different coloured markings can imply different priorities or tasks for someone else in the practice. Priorities, by the way, are not necessarily just those that have a time urgency. Any ideas which can be implemented immediately at low cost or no cost and without generating any difficulties should be acted on at once. A suggested *modus operandi* is as follows:

- Each of those items identified for action should be transferred to a copy of the *Action Plan*. This will then provide a simple, concise, easily monitored procedure.
- A definite target timing should be set for accomplishment of each task by the scheduled date or for monitoring its successful completion by others. Initiate the first action quickly so that a momentum is obtained.
- Set a date, or series of dates, when the results of the actions will be evaluated.
- Review the original action list after a designated period of time and then again at intervals to see if priorities have changed or whether items should be added or deleted.

As will be made clear in Chapter 5, 'Devising a practice development strategy and plan', every action which it is agreed shall be taken must be allocated by name, scheduled and monitored.

Action plan

| Action to be taken | Why | Who is to do it | How is it to be done | Must be completed by | Results and comments |
|---|---|---|---|---|---|
| | | | | | |

# Chapter 1.  Why practice development?

In the past the professions were fairly small groups of individuals and they served a small clientele. In those circumstances, it was relatively easy to maintain good communications between members of a profession and their public. The preservation of high ethical standards and the ability to respond to the clients' needs did not require elaborate machinery. Most of these things could be handled quite simply almost as though they were the affairs of a private club.

> Today the professions no longer serve a privileged minority. They meet the needs of, and depend upon, corporations, institutions and the public at large. Their clients are entitled to call upon them to discharge their duties, and these include assuring the client of the widest possible choice of professional advisers and the ways in which their services are rendered. Their tasks also involve the important obligation to provide a professional service which is efficient, answerable for its activities and which charges fees closely related to the actual cost of work performed. These services must be offered in a way and upon a scale that enables them to reach the much larger corporate and individual public which are now likely to need them.[1]

Moreover the state conferred on many of the professions a monopoly in certain activities. Only lawyers may be paid for transferring interests in land, only doctors may issue death certificates, only barristers may plead in some courts.

Both these factors—the consanguinity of practitioner and client and legal monopoly— either no longer apply or are unlikely to do so for another decade. The 'closed' and protected position of most professions is under increasingly critical surveillance.

The Monopolies Commission's report on professional services provides a reasoned view on the reality of the dangers of practice development or marketing and the possible advantages and disadvantages to the public. Therefore it is worth quoting at length:

> Except in small communities, the problems for the client of finding the appropriate professional services of all kinds are considerable. Professions which limit members' freedom to advertise may argue that, even if personal recommendation fails, a prospective client can consult a professional body and receive a list of recommended practitioners in the area. But an individual member of the public may not know whom to approach, especially when the body concerned does not advertise; nor are professional bodies necessarily well-informed (or, if they are, ready to impart information) about the range of the activities and specialisations of individual members. The fact that advice is sought from such sources as citizens' advice bureaux, post offices and banks only emphasises the need for more direct sources of information.
>
> Many of the means by which information might be conveyed to the public are proscribed or seriously limited for use by the professional practitioner. It is arguable that in many or most professions a substantial relaxation of some of these restrictions would bring benefits to the professions and the public which would far outweigh the dangers that might be thought to be involved

1. Sir Geoffrey Howe. Nigel Colley Memorial Lecture. Nottingham Law Society. May 1975.

to the integrity of the professions and the general quality of their services. Ignorance and lack of information on the part of the public can create distrust between the professions and the public; and this, it can be argued, is as great a danger to the professions' ability to fulfil their duty to society as any of the dangers feared by the professions.[2]

In all the professions it is stated that the quality of the service is the most effective method of practice development but at the same time it is asserted that the knowledge gap between the professional and the client is too great to allow the client to assess the quality of the service. 'The recipients' of expert services are not themselves adequately knowledgeable to solve the problems or to assess the service received.[3]

## Motivation

The main argument advanced today against professional service marketing seems to rest on the fact that it is thought that this will lead to unrestrained competition, and unrestrained competition could in turn induce price cutting, and price cutting would result in a lowering of standards of integrity and service. The concomitant of this is the fact that one of the characteristics of the profession, and indeed of most professions, is a dislike of commercialism, and marketing is seen as commercialism at its loudest and most abhorrent.

If the reasons were overwhelmingly convincing to the professionals it could be argued there is no need to reinforce them with the mandatory constraints which will be found in all the qualifying professions. By way of example the Law Society's Practice Rule 1 as it is stated at present could be interpreted as preventing a solicitor from doing just about anything at all to make his practice known.

'A solicitor shall not obtain or attempt to obtain professional business by

- directly or indirectly without reasonable justification inviting instructions for such business or
- doing or permitting to be done without reasonable justification anything which by its manner, frequency or otherwise advertises his practice as solicitor or
- doing or permitting to be done anything which may be reasonably regarded as 'touting'

Chartered surveyors are controlled with a simple and highly unequivocal rule. '. . . no member shall solicit instructions for work in any manner whatsoever'.[4] The medical profession makes its embargo in a similar if more comprehensive manner.

> The professional offence of advertising may arise from the publication in any form of matter commending or drawing attention to the professional attainments or services of a doctor, if that doctor has either personally arranged such publication or has instigated, sanctioned or acquiesced in its publication by others.[5]

Loss adjusters not only specifically prohibit 'Any approach either orally or in writing . . . made by a member or one of his staff with the aim of obtaining business' but also stipulate the level of hospitality which is permissible and ban heavy type insertions in directories.[6]

2. Monopolies Commission. *Professional Services: A report on the general effect on the public interest of certain restrictive practices so far as they prevail in relation to the supply of professional services.* HMSO Cmnd 4463-1/2 (London, 1970).
3. Dietrich Rueschemeyer. 'Professional autonomy and the social control of expertise.' In *The Sociology of the Professions* (eds Robert Dingwall and Philip Lewis). Macmillan (London, 1983), p. 40.
4. By-law 24(7) Royal Institution of Chartered Surveyors.
5. General Medical Council. *Professional Conduct and Discipline: Fitness to Practice* (August, 1983).
6. The Chartered Institute of Loss Adjusters. By-laws Part E.

While in the very recent past there has been some relaxation of the mandatory rules with, for example, solicitors, architects and quantity surveyors now permitted highly limited and controlled advertising, the 'no touting' constraints remain, for the moment, substantially intact.

However, superimposed on such specific restrictions as those quoted are more subtle but equally constraining factors. High among these is one which is only associated with success in practice development. That is, the attitude of other professional colleagues to the successful firm. For many professions where intra- and inter-professional consultation and co-operation is vital, for example, law, accountancy and architecture, it cannot be in clients' interest for anything to occur which may antagonize other professionals. Such lack of co-operation, however overt, can be significant in causing delays, creating or magnifying difficulties or even in escalating costs. Thus for any professional practice to be seen, whether justified or not, as aggressive in its pursuit of practice development, or even if not aggressive, simply successful, might well rebound in the long term and make development more difficult.

Far more fundamental to lack of motivation is the image of practice development, marketing or commercialism and the profession's self-image which may well clash. The former is regarded as 'brash', 'huxtering', 'aggressive', 'ungentlemanly', while the professionals see themselves as divorced from and above the haggling and wiles of the market place.

To these fundamental attitudinal constraints there can be added a number of others. Principal among these, and applicable world-wide to every senior profession, are the following:

- The quality of the service rendered is truly the best recommendation, and the only recommendation which can be offered without putting the public at risk.
- Since demand always exists there is no need to create it.
- The public must be protected from charlatans prevailing on them (and on businesses) to retain those who might serve them less well and disinterestedly than those who are modest about their personal attainments.
- Protection from unfair competition.
- Marketing in the form of practice development makes it difficult to maintain integrity and impartial detachment.

If these were correct, it would not be surprising that professionals do not want to be involved in the commercialism which practice development implies. Indeed, it cannot be denied that these arguments, and many more besides, are not without merit, but to the public they display evidence of a greater concern with the professionals for themselves than for their clients.

There may well be a deep-seated revulsion for the market place. But practice development can be performed with grace and sophistication. Approaches need not be loud, aggressive, crass or intrusive. The practice of marketing is itself a sophisticated art and discipline, and the widespread confusion between marketing and selling has led to a totally incorrect view of what marketing comprises, and from this view has come its almost complete rejection by the professions.

It is, of course, all a matter of scale and approach. Since Jacob marketed his mess of pottage of Esau, the exchange of goods and services between people has been characterized by the use of persuasive methods to convince one of the parties that the exchange, on whatever basis agreed, will provide satisfaction. To quote a leading American marketing teacher, Professor Theodore Levitt,[7] the question must be asked how often it is not just coincidental that the

7. Theodore Levitt. *Innovation in Marketing*. Pan Books (London, 1972), pp. 13–14.

needs of the buyer are satisfied when the needs of the seller are also met? The important thing within the context of marketing professional services, however, is that the distaste for selling has rubbed off on all marketeers. The reason is not difficult to see. To begin with, marketing and selling are seldom properly distinguished. They are in the eyes of practitioners the same thing—'touting'. There still hangs over all selling transactions a scarcely veiled suspicion that they are an attempt to obtain money from the unwary buyer by some trickery. This is because there is a natural and irremovable difference of interests between seller and buyer, based largely on the view that the seller is more expert, better informed on the subject of the sale, than the buyer who is an amateur. The confusion between bad selling and good marketing is widespread, and a major reason for the rejection of any form of practice development by professionals.

Establishing a bridge between selling (or even the slightly more acceptable 'marketing') and the professional must be achieved if the practice development is to be accomplished. To succeed, the person charged with practice expansion must believe in the 'product' and in what he is doing. It is also necessary to satisfy the almost universal human need to be appreciated, and achieve an acceptance that he makes a useful contribution both to society and to his firm. Without this motivation, professional service marketing will continue to take refuge behind real or pseudo-professional ethical barriers to justify the non- or anti-marketing approach, while the deeper reasons remain happily hidden, since they are too uncomfortable to face.

## Practice development—who benefits?

Acceptance that practice development is relevant to all the professions will never occur until they are convinced that both they and their clients will benefit from whatever form of communication takes place. The incompatibility of professional practice and marketing is seen to be axiomatic. It is, therefore, for all senior and regulated professions[8] at least, not regarded as a matter for discussion. The nature of the professional/client relationship is said to be such that any question of actively seeking business would disturb the trust and confidentiality of the relationship to the detriment of both parties. If this proposition is indeed true, then not only would the marketing of professional services be ineffective, but it would destroy the very 'product' being marketed.

It must be conceded that professional services are not always suitable for the unrestricted rigours of the market place, if only because the lay client cannot necessarily distinguish or monitor the services provided. Some paternalistic surveillance by the qualifying associations may be necessary to maintain standards. Nevertheless, the professions cannot expect to be insulated, legally or through the cabbalistic smoke screen they sometimes raise, from the pressures and scrutiny of modern economic life.

In a completely free competitive market for the supply of services, the natural expression of consumer choice should lead automatically to the most satisfactory organization, and so to the commensurately cheapest price. How far is this model applicable to professional services?

The fears expressed by many professionals concerning their relationship with their clients, if they have any real basis at all, do not offset the undoubted benefit to the public which would stem from a better knowledge and understanding, not only of the services but of the relative expertise, interests and experience of the individual practitioners.

---

8. Because there is no generally accepted definition of a profession, membership of a qualifying association can be taken as one, but by no means the only, criterion for a professional or professional practice.

A widely held definition of marketing devised by Professor Philip Kotler is 'satisfying human and corporate needs', or 'satisfaction engineering'. That is precisely what it is; the operation of a business (or practice) in a way that provides satisfaction, both to the clients and the practitioners, and it is difficult to argue that this should not be a desideratum of all professionals. There is nothing unprofessional in customer or client satisfaction engineering. Organizations of every type, including non-profit organizations, depend on goodwill to survive, and must learn how to sense and meet their public's or customers' needs effectively. This truism applies in equal measure to all professional services because, whether it is admitted or not, professionals must (and do) sell to survive.

It is a truism that both parties in any transaction should perceive a benefit. If the wider dissemination of knowledge concerning professional practices would benefit the public and competition, then the practitioners should themselves see an advantage in the adoption of marketing techniques to expand their practices

## Five forces

There are five reasons why practice expansion is now, or shortly will be, vital for every firm, not just as means of expansion, but also to prevent the loss of existing clients and business.

1. *Survival* The professions have not survived unscathed from world recession. Those who rely on business clients to provide the main flow of their work have seen a decline in their numbers or the volume of work. Even the demand for a statutory service such as auditing has stagnated if not actually diminished in response to a reduced population of commercial concerns and fewer successful start-ups. In the private sector the quality of life for many has worsened, caused by unemployment, early retirement or perhaps far less rapid advances in position and salary than would have occurred in more prosperous times. The services that these clients purchase are also adversely affected.

   It is axiomatic in business that organizations have the greatest difficulty in staying on a plateau of activity. They tend either to move forward or to regress if only because the activities which support a given level of fee income or revenue cannot be so finely tuned that they will produce precisely the same, or even approximately the same, results each year. Every practice is caught in a never-ending process of losing clients for perfectly valid and acceptable reasons. People marry, die, move away, acquire changed responsibilities and possessions; companies expand, merge, re-locate, close down. To stay at the same level of fee income, at the very least firms must replace these 'natural' losses and other losses whatever their cause. Thus it might be said that only in the case of the exceptional firm or practice and exceptional circumstances is expansion not a key factor in survival of the majority of firms.

2. *Competition* Clients of the traditional professions are being increasingly, and indeed energetically, wooed by non-qualified competition, by other professions whose traditional boundaries are no longer seen as barriers and by products which substitute for services.

   The small or one-man practitioner cutting fees and corners is an irritation but a minor danger. There are however massive and powerful commercial organizations intent on moving into the activities of the established professions. These latter organizations have the skills and resources to achieve successes on a scale that must spell, if not disaster, then grave risks, for many practices. Banks and building societies are already pointed strongly in this direction and are seeking through political pressure the legal right to take over many other professional activities currently barred to them. Equally, if not on such a considerable scale, stockbrokers, management consultants, and even retailers, the latter with dental, optical, medical and property services, will make inroads.[9] There is some pressure from solicitors to be allowed rights and audience in courts where barristers currently hold a monopoly.

As threatening perhaps is the competition which is emerging from product substitutes for services which turn what was previously a personalized service, by highly qualified professions, into a 'do-it-yourself' activity. In medicine blood glucose monitoring devices for diabetics make them independent of medical monitoring; in accountancy tax planning software, it is claimed, will save companies millions of pounds every year at a capital cost of less than £1000. The savings will come from what is currently part of accountants' revenue.

3. *Inflation* Increased revenue that is not ahead of inflation means stagnation, decline and ultimate demise. Even accountancy practices which might be thought more than most professions to be aware of the ravages of inflation have been found, when looking at their own progress, not to have taken into account its impact. A 50 per cent increase of fees between, say, 1978 and 1983 is in real terms a drop in revenue of 20 per cent. While the level of inflation world-wide will continue to vary, it is unlikely in the foreseeable future that it will cease to be a matter for the most careful scrutiny in both appraising performance and setting target.

4. *Technology* In all the professions technology is creating profound changes in traditional methods. Many of these changes represent both threats and opportunities to be grasped. Threats such as the non-qualified—legal assistants, para-medicals, architectural technicians—substituting for the qualified whose skills they can emulate with the aid of technology are very real. In medicine, agriculture and pharmaceuticals chromosome analysis kits take such analysis out of the laboratory into routine use.

Thus new technologies will, in many instances, change the content of the traditional services provided and the way in which they are rendered. Interactive communications network, the ubiquitous computer and word processor will induce fundamental changes in both administrative and operational procedures and will raise the level of client expectations in terms of efficiency and cost. Those practices that do not keep abreast of changing technology will find themselves increasingly adversely affected by more progressive and aggressive competitors. Technology may represent a far bigger threat to many professions than the adoption of practice development techniques.

5. *Changing client attitudes* The humility which typified many clients—private and commercial—in the face of the apparently overwhelming expertise of the professional is vanishing fast. The respect once accorded as of right to the professions has been eroded both by changing social attitudes and education and by the inability of the professions to conduct their affairs in privacy. Government inquiries and supervision, consumer protection bodies and investigative journalism, much of it of the sensational kind, the means of rapid mass communication have done much to remove both the mystique and the authority of many of the professions. After all, venality makes more interesting reporting than altruism! Clients now ask questions that previously they could not have formulated or were too intimidated to do so, such as 'what will it cost?' Those who cannot ask for themselves have plenty of well-meaning and sometimes not so well-meaning bodies and pressure groups to ask the questions on their behalf. The professions cannot treat such manifestations of growing client awareness and adversarial attitudes with the lofty disdain of the past. There will always be those professional firms and individuals who will make the

9. A competitive scenario for the next decade is given by Graham Lee. 'Future shock—a midsummer night's dream.' *The Law Society Gazette* (London, 28 October 1981).

effort to be 'nice people to deal with' and these are the ones to whom the public will turn and who will then benefit from changing attitudes.

The argument that most professions already work to capacity is a dangerously deceptive excuse for not developing a practice. Today's business is not necessarily indicative of tomorrow's volume or profitability.

But in a positive sense practice development, while having as one of its main purposes increased fee income, also has other highly desirable objectives. An improved 'mix' or work which has a greater compatibility with the firm's skills, resources, interests and specializations will lead to a number of highly desirable results for the firm and practitioner:

- Greater profitability thus the realization perhaps earlier than might otherwise have been possible of both personal and practice aspirations.
- Greater work satisfaction which will provide intellectual stimulus and the opportunity for considerable personal self-expression.
- Better career opportunities thus making the firm attractive to higher calibre recruits as well as helping to retain both professional and support staff.
- Improved services to clients through an understanding of their needs which enables the firm to ensure that the services it offers are wholly compatible with them.

Given these changes taking place in all the professions in the United Kingdom and the world-wide liberalization of codes of practice, most particularly in the USA in the wake of the Bates case,[10] it is not now a question of whether professionals should adopt the marketing concept to assist in practice expansion, but whether they adopt it to survive and how well they undertake the tasks involved.

There is a very small body of knowledge, and little in the way of educational or training material to guide professionals through the marketing procedures. This is a gap which must and will be filled and which this book seeks to make a small contribution towards closing.

10. John Bates, an attorney practising in Phoenix, Arizona, challenged ruling of the State Supreme Court that an advertisement for his legal clinic violated the disciplinary code of the State Bar of Arizona. On appeal to the Supreme Court of the United States it was ruled that restrictions on advertising by lawyers violated the free speech guarantee of the First Amendment of the Constitution. Thus the door was open for lawyers to use normal marketing techniques. This ruling led to the New York Regents who control all the professions in New York State except lawyers to permit professions to advertise. Similar relaxation through the United States resulted.

# Chapter 2.  Understanding service businesses

The adoption of practice development techniques is greatly assisted by an understanding of both the elements which comprise a professional service, or indeed any service, and the problems specific to offering the services. The fundamental problems faced by any practitioner charged with the task of profitably expanding his practice can be summed up simply:

1. Physical display of the service itself is impossible although the outcome can sometimes be shown, e.g., architectural services but not many of the range surveyors' services. Thus surrogates for the service must be used.
2. Demonstration without rendering the service cannot be offered and accepted, e.g., accountancy, medicine.
3. The law of warranty will not apply in most cases and guarantees are inordinately difficult to offer and to claim because rarely do absolute standards of performance exist.
4. Samples, like demonstrations, and because of the lack of physical display, cannot be made available.
5. Packaging except in the most superficial sense is inapplicable.
6. There is no patent protection for services.

Even the most cursory examination of these limitations will show that they appear to eliminate a very large number of business expansion techniques which are available to producers of goods and indeed to many non-professional services.

The situation is however far less constrained than might at first appear to be the case. All the problems relate to the concept that services are said to be intangible, not durable, cannot be tested, production and consumption must be simultaneous and the user has to participate in the 'production' of a service. These however are far from being absolutes. Indeed they are not even applicable at all to many types of professional services, let alone consumer/industrial/commercial services, despite the academic adherence to such neat distinctions.

There are of course always degrees of intangibility, durability, testability and client participation.[1] Because of this it is possible to treat the problem of expanding a professional service at different levels, influenced however by the extent to which such services either in themselves or their outcome are indeed tangible, durable, testable or involve their users in terms of commitment and participation in the production of the service.

The six problems listed above, deriving from the peculiar characteristics of service, provide apparently valid reasons and additional reasons to those given in Chapter 1, 'Why practice development?', for not actively offering services to the various publics of a practice. An

1. These concepts and their implications are discussed in some depth in Aubrey Wilson. *The Marketing of Professional Services*. McGraw-Hill (London, 1972).

understanding of the concepts which are held to be immutable but which are in fact manipulatable will lead to actions which can be adopted to expand a practice as well as removing some of the de-motivation which is engendered in individuals who feel themselves to be operating within a rigid system.

## Intangibility

While there is almost invariably some physical element in services, there is also a service element in products which will vary in accordance with the product and its market. Thus a professional service may be intangible but its rendering is highly tangible since it essentially comprises people, infrastructures and what has been termed physical evidence of the service necessary to enable the service to be delivered. The situation has been extremely well explained and illustrated in what is called the 'molecular' approach.[2]

> Product/service combinations that form larger market entities can be quite complex. Since they are dynamic and have highly interrelated elements, it is useful to view them in an organic way, rather than as static bits and pieces. In fact, product/service combinations can be viewed very much like 'atoms' connected in unique 'molecular' configurations.
>
> The molecular analogy has considerable merit. First, it allows full consideration of service elements as well as product elements. Second, it offers a framework for identifying and visualising all the parts of any complex market entities. Finally it suggests the behavioural hypothesis that re-arrangement or alteration of any element, whether by design or accident, will change the overall entity, just as changing the bonds or atoms in a molecule creates a new substance. This latter hypothesis has significant implications for both the planning and management of complex market entities. Thus scientific analysis can be applied in marketing to build models and to show structure and relationships. The system for doing so is called molecular modelling.

Within the context of practice development this molecular modelling approach has great practical significance. The augmentation of a professional service, which is substantially intangible with a physical component, can make the total service and thus the firm, that much simpler to offer and can, to some extent, avoid the major problems which arise from intangibility.

As examples, a legal service which provides safe keeping and retrieval for clients' important documents or a contract R & D firm with computer based data loggers for collecting information on production plants in order to devise ways to improve their efficiency both provide important pieces of hardware.

In Figure 2-1 the entities which are of course generic are arranged from product dominance to service dominance. At the far end of service-dominant complexity might be found legal services which are nevertheless a conglomeration of services having little product content. At the other end might be educational self-instruction material. While such material might be purchased to provide a benefit (i.e., training or knowledge) no important services are purchased along with the material other than the now indirect services of devising the material and distributing it.

However, within an entity there can be many variations. If only surgery and diagnostics are included within medicine, the service element dominates and would be further to the right of the diagram. If the service was physical medicine, where prescription drugs are a major part of the patients' expectation and the doctors' methods, then it would be slotted more to the left. Using education as a further example Socratic teaching, wherein knowledge is conveyed

2. Lynn G. Shostack. 'How to design a service'. *European Journal of Marketing*, **16** (1) (Bradford, 1982). The author is deeply indebted to Lynn Shostack for her additional comments and suggestions for this section of the chapter.

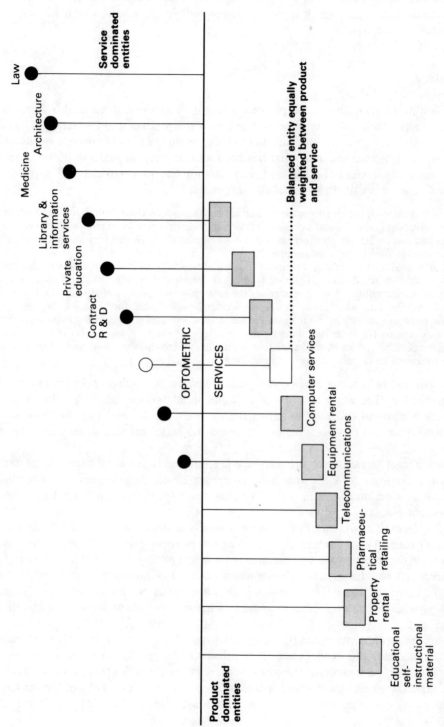

**Figure 2-1** Scale of elemental dominance[3]

3. In order to relate Lynn Shostack's approach to the precise problems of practice development for professional services, her models have been adjusted from their original consumer/commercial subjects to a professional service.

10

verbally or through demonstration, would represent a pure service as against the self-instruction material which is almost a pure product. It is not without significance that professional as opposed to other services cluster in the service-dominated section of the diagram.

Figure 2-2 shows the components of dentistry services to illustrate the varying product/service elements in different types of treatment. The circles represent the pure service and the squares the product element. All of these are given as the same size but in actuality, measured by any standard (e.g., sales or fees, extent of usage, frequency of usage), preventative consumables will far outweigh the service element in preventative dentistry, while in conservation the service will be much greater than the consumable elements.

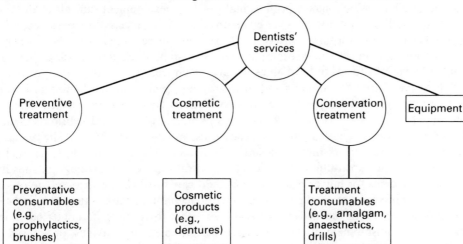

**Figure 2-2** Elemental dominance sub-scale

It was suggested earlier that professional services comprise the pure service, the physical support system and 'evidence'. This 'evidence' is physical objects which play a critical role in verifying the existence or the completion of the service. Lynn Shostack identifies two types of 'evidence'. Those she terms 'peripheral' and 'essential'.[4]

For an example of 'peripheral' evidence it is possible to use architectural services. The physical output of an architect in the form of drawings, specifications and reports reflects the architect's thought processes and creativity. The drawings and other documentation are evidence that the service is being or was performed but it is not this physical evidence which the client purchases even though it is virtually indispensable to the service. What is purchased is the thought and creativity and the documentation is the vehicle which expresses it until the structure is satisfactorily completed.

Essential evidence cannot be possessed by the client. Nevertheless it may be so dominant in its impact on the service purchase and use that it must be considered virtually an element in its own right. The client who purchases contract R & D may receive peripheral evidence in the form of a proposal but the existence of certain types of equipment, perhaps highly accurate laser levelling equipment for checking surface conditions and shape of large callendering equipment in paper mills, has a major impact on the client's perception and even choice of the service or service firms. Neither peripheral nor essential evidence are surrogate for the service, although they maybe perceived as such but they are certainly not purchased for their own sake.

4. G. Lynn Shostack. 'The importance of evidence'. *The American Banker* (New York, 25 March 1981). This subject is covered in more detail in Chapter 10, 'How the individual practice is selected'.

From the foregoing it can be seen that 'pure' services are largely an academic fiction and that the physical element in any professional service has an important function in the formation of perceptions and images and of course in the message which is to be conveyed to the clients and prospective clients of the service. The practice development implications of the intangibility aspect of professional services and resultant actions are discussed in later chapters.

## Durability

The second attribute which makes professional practice development difficult is 'durability' which like tangibility is not nor can ever be an absolute. The concept that services cannot be stored has been breached in many instances. That they can be stored in terms of staffing to meet maximum demand is a simple example, they can also be stocked in the sense they can be substituted by various forms of hard and software which will provide the service or a service substitute; at one extreme computers and their programs which can mechanize and simplify many accountancy, legal and design services to perhaps coin operated medical diagnostic equipment. There are what Theodore Levitt[5] has termed hard, soft and hybrid technologies which make a service either a durable or at least less insubstantial. The off-shelf insurance policy and unit trusts are examples of soft technologies. Hard technologies, as might be expected, refer to the substitution of services by hardware, the electrocardiogram substitutes lower paid technicians for higher paid doctors; credit cards and cash dispensers are products replacing labour intensive manual procedures. Hybrid technologies are exampled by pre-order shipment of perishables or fuel deliveries based on weather forecasting, computer based least-cost routing for transhipment of goods to achieve economies, time savings, or security.

The examples are given only to show the dangers of assuming absolutes rather than relativities in terms of intangibility and durability.

## Testability of services

Testability is another attribute which, like 'intangibility' and 'durability', is only applicable in a number of cases and not in every instance but which has important implications for practice development.

There is little doubt that many professional services are only testable in a qualitative sense. The implications of this for practice development are all pervasive since favourable purchasing decisions can only be based on user expectations and on past experience, neither of which are necessarily or ever reliable guides.

Because it is not usually possible to apply guarantees and warranties to many professional services the reassurance the user of services seeks, overtly or covertly, cannot be given with any degree of certainty or perhaps honesty. No solicitor would offer a guarantee of the outcome of any litigation, no accountant can positively assure a client on the acceptance of tax returns by the authorities, no doctor can pronounce that without a shadow of doubt the cure will be total and even an architect is unlikely to be too happy in an unequovical assurance that his design is disaster proof.[6]

Moreover because 'satisfaction' is so inexact a term, what is seen as 'satisfaction' by one

5. Theodore Levitt. 'Production-line approach to services'. *Harvard Business Review* (Cambridge, Mass., September/October 1971).
6. Geoffrey Scott. *Building Disasters and Failures*. Construction Press (Hornby, Lancaster, 1976).

recipient of a professional service can just as easily be regarded as a disastrous performance by another. An assessment of a professional service by a user can and usually is based as much on how close the service as received conforms to his expectations, irrespective of the reality of those expectations, as on the intrinsic quality of the service delivered. There is always a need to know which resources and which activities under the control of the firm or the professional have an impact on expectations and realization. Thus to add to the variability in the rendering of a service caused by the human element, there is also the variability of the perception of the quality of services.[7]

## Production and consumption are simultaneous

In one sense at least the difference of opinion which exists between practitioners of marketing and the academic world is a semantic one. How instant is 'simultaneous'? Is taking a brief or instruction rendering a service at all, however vital a part it may play in the ultimate delivery of the service? The architect's service is delivered long after the instructions are given. Many financial services are conducted at arms length and often by purely mechanical means usually over a period of time wherein there is no client involvement. The exceptions are many.

This particular phenomenon of services is closely linked to the belief that they cannot be stocked if they have to be produced and consumed at one and the same time. If, as has been and will again be shown, services or some element of them can be 'stocked', then many of the proven techniques for marketing goods and non-professional services will also be shown to be applicable if sensitively adopted.

## User involvement in production

The last attribute to be considered in laying a base from which the use of marketing techniques in practice development can be considered, although used in a different way from goods and other services, refers to the user's involvement in production. Here it must be said that this is indeed a concomitant of services although the actual production contribution can be and is in very many cases so superficial as to have little significance.

To receive an entertainment service may require no more contribution on the part of the user than to sit in front of a television set; to retain an architect to design and supervise the construction of a building will demand liaison and indeed supervision. The client's involvement will appear to rule out standardized professional services and the economies of scale. While it is not suggested that these latter are necessarily preferable to personal services, they do represent alternatives that may well have advantages to the client not the least in reducing the cost of services—a key point which will be referred to later.

Certainly in the USA there has been an explosive growth in off-the-shelf insurance policies, packaged and unalterable except through the selection of other packages; mutual funds instead of one-at-a-time stock selection; fully systematized production line yet personalized income tax preparation service on a walk-in basis.[8]

There is a world-wide ambiguity in that despite some spectacular failures there is a stong technology-led push to reduce user involvement in the service production process while at the

7. Christian Gronroos. *Strategic Management and Marketing in the Service Sector*. Swedish School of Economics and Business Administration (Helsinki, 1982), p. 60.
8. Theodore Levitt. 'The industrialization of service'. *Harvard Business Review* (Cambridge, Mass., September/October 1976).

opposite pole more and more service companies are seeking a greater participation by the user: financial services, particularly banking, is an example.

The introduction of technology into the professions, now moving apace world-wide, will undoubtedly create considerable changes in the practitioner–user relationship. If adopted and used correctly such changes will be productive of better services and better client relationships.

## People and infrastructures

The claimed problem attributes of services have been examined and hopefully substantially demolished because, if it is accepted that they are correct, then there is no possibility of practices being expanded through the use of marketing techniques. Belief in the attributes as stated by the theoreticians must lead to marketing despair in that practice development cannot occur because the techniques available are just not suitable for an activity which is intangible, unstockable, non-testable, instantaneously consumed and requires the presence and activity of the user at all times it is being delivered. It can be seen that reality is a very long way from theory or rather incorrect theory. The polemics are of little concern to the practitioner. What is important is that they should not believe that professional services even with no legal or perceptual constraints are unmarketable in the usual meaning of that word.

Services are essentially people intensive and people have to have a physical infrastructure to enable them to render the service. The client perceives a total service and does not deliberately separate out the infrastructure from the people unless one or the other is outstanding in a favourable or unfavourable way. In presenting the professional service company to its publics the need for a compatibility between the physical aspects of the service and the personnel is paramount. At the simplest level it would be an unwise client who, because he liked the staff, would risk investing with a financial institution known to be in difficulties. Such a preference would not overcome the fear of losing his money. Conversely, no matter how strong the asset base, with many alternatives available, clients will not patronize an organization where they have a strong antipathy to its personnel.

## Demand interactions

However, while the infrastructure is likely to or can be made to remain at a given level of quality and appearance, this cannot be said of people who will vary in the level of service they give both on different occasions and as a reaction to various types of clients and situations. Thus it is neither possible nor sensible to regard professional services as capable of rendering a fixed level of satisfaction to clients, setting aside that 'satisfaction' itself is a highly variable factor both between people and over any period of time. Additionally, into the highly dynamic mix must be added two more variables; demand level for any particular service within a practice and the impact of one client on another.

A sudden and heavy demand for veterinary services in the form of vaccination against a threatened parvovirus epidemic could casue some decline in the quality of diagnostic services as the capacity becomes overloaded and less time can be devoted to apparently non-urgent requirements. Thus what might be seen on one day as an efficient caring veterinary practitioner or practice, might appear on the next day to be less responsive, sympathetic or even skilled. This is the effect of the impact of the demand for one service within the same profession on another.

Similarly a sudden influx of clients for the same service, for example, representation for compensation claims arising out of a particular development, can create an adverse impression as clients 'queue' for service.

A study of consumer services has revealed other phenomena which are also applicable to professional services for both private and commercial clients and these must be considered before setting out methods of practice development.[9] These phenomena relate to practices as a whole and not to the individual services they provide.

The complexity of the service system as compared to products is exacerbated by the fact that in professional services' practices, a large part of the activity is 'invisible' to clients. The clients generally only see a small part of the organization and are either unaware or indifferent to both the infrastructures and personnel which support the 'invisible' part of the practice. The result is that two incorrect perceptions ensue.

1. The cost of all professional services appears to be high when related to the visible part of the organization. The charging rate for a consultant, for example, is never broken down to show the actual salary cost, support costs and overheads any more than a product price reveals raw materials, labour, packaging, production and transport costs or distributors' margins. The difference is that the buyer of a product has more than an expectation on which to base his assessment of 'value for money' and, additionally, in many instances will have comparable competitive product prices as an approximation to give reassurance.

   Because professional services are frequently perceived as 'expensive' first-time users may be deterred. Certainly the image of high cost sends all clients in search of alternative ways of meeting their needs where any option exists. The implications are obvious and they represent a fundamental problem in all practice development which must be appreciated and countered in ways which are explained in later chapters and most particularly in Chapter 7, 'Professional services and client needs', Chapter 12, 'The importance of images and perceptions' and Chapter 14, 'The role of fees in practice development'.

2. Errors which occur in the 'invisible' part of the practice are difficult to explain and excuse. The old dictum 'never tell your clients your problems . . . they've got their own' is never more true than in service business. Additionally, however, errors in the 'invisible' segment are usually not detected and corrected as quickly as those which happen in the 'visible' area. Thus problems are aggravated.

## Core and satellite services

A second phenomenon is that few professional services are totally specialized. Personal care services (medicine, dentistry, opticians) are examples of specialization. However in medicine, for example, specialization is taken to the extent that practitioners concentrate on some often very narrow aspect of their calling and in veterinary the practice may deal only with any farm animals, small animals or even a single genus such as horses. Most other professions however have a strong central service and add-on satellite services have been developed which are intended both to enhance the central service and to be profit making in their own right. Examples are numerous (see Figure 2-3).

However, clients have neither the ability nor the desire to understand the relationship between the core and any other services the practice offers. Failure in any service—basic or add-on—will reflect on the whole practice even if the link between the different services is

---

9. John Bateson. 'Do we need service marketing?' *Marketing Consumer Services: New Insights.* Marketing Science Institute (Boston, Mass., 1977).

| Profession | Core service | Examples of satellite services |
|---|---|---|
| Solicitors | Legal representation and advice | Insurance<br>Taxation<br>Mortgages |
| Accountants | Auditing | Financial advice<br>Tax planning<br>Management consultancy<br>Inter-firm comparisons |
| Banking | Providing, holding, transferring, money products | Payroll administration<br>Night safes<br>Trusteeships<br>Safekeeping<br>Travel facilities<br>Mortgages |
| Architects | Structure design construction and supervision | Viability studies<br>Town planning<br>Interior design |
| Chartered surveyors | Measurement, planning, valuation development, management of land, buildings and minerals | Project management,<br>Computer consultancy,<br>Contracting insurance<br>Loss adjusting/assessing |

**Figure 2-3**  Core and satellite services

tenuous.[10] Thus if a solicitor's litigation department is perceived as ineffectual, inefficient or uninvolved, the client will almost certainly consider that other departments—matrimonial, non-contentious, unfair dismissal, landlord and tenant—are likely to be afflicted with the same drawbacks.

In summary, the practitioner has to be aware of the peculiar phenomena which are a fundamental part of professional services and must devise his practice development activity to take account of them and to react sensitivily to them:

- Risk of a perceptual gap between expectations from a service and the reality of its delivery.
- Problems of presenting a professional service to its various publics.
- Variability of speed or quality of service caused by the interaction of clients on each other and on the services rendered.
- 'Visibility' (to the client) of the only part of the activity which comprises the service and the service firm.
- Perceived high cost of services.
- Inter-relationship of services within a practice and their impact and effect on each other.

## Service quality

It would be totally inappropriate in attempting to describe and explain how the professional service system operates not to make reference to the 'quality' of services. With one notable exception academicians and practitioners have failed to define 'quality' in a way which could guide management decisions. The term is described as if it were a variable in itself and not a function of a range of resources and activities.

10. P. Eiglier and E. Langaard. 'Services as systems: marketing implications'. *Marketing Consumer Services: New Insights* (Marketing Science Institute, Boston, Mass., 1977).

To state that service firms will have to develop service quality to be able to compete successfully in the future is meaningless unless one can (i) determine how service quality is perceived by consumers and (ii) determine in what way service quality is influenced and which resources and activities have an impact on service quality.[11]

Gronroos is unequivocal in his belief that quality of service depends on the two variables of *expectations and perceptions*. Both are of considerable importance to the practitioner since many of the factors which impact on these variables can be controlled or influenced. What the user of a service receives in his interaction with the service firm is clearly important to him and his evaluations of the quality of the service. This is termed 'technical quality'. There is then the question of how the service is received; the impact of one client on another; the attitude of the professionals and the support staff. This is the functional quality of the service.

While the technical quality is capable in many circumstances of being evaluated objectively, the assessment of the functional quality is always highly subjective. The perceived service is the result of a mixture of service dimensions and it is when the client's perceived service is compared to the expected service, the assessment of service quality emerges.

The situation is illustrated in Figure 2-4.[12]

For the practitioner therefore Gronroos's approach has very important activity implications in terms of practice development, all of which will be considered in the further chapters of the book.

For example, 'expected service' will be based substantially on the outcome of practice development methods—personal and non-personal—messages, referrals and very substantially images, all of which are dealt with in depth in Chapter 12, 'The importance of images and perceptions', Chapter 13, 'The referral (recommendations) system,' Chapter 16, 'The use of personal contact' and Chapter 17, 'Non-personal methods of practice development'.

A highly practical approach to ensuring that the service as it is delivered is as close to expectation as possible has been suggested.[13] The technique called 'blueprinting' comprises as

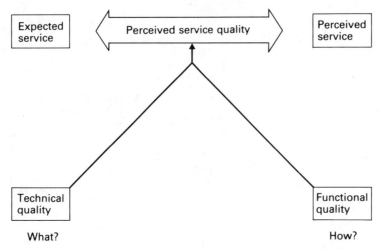

**Figure 2-4**  Technical quality and functional quality of service

11. Christian Gronroos. Op. cit., pp. 56–66.
12. Ibid.
13. Lynn G. Shostack. 'Designing services that deliver'. *Harvard Business Review* (Cambridge, Mass., January/February 1984). This article provides useful models of 'blueprints' as examples of how the system works.

a first stage the mapping of the processes that constitute the service. Second, the points at which failure can occur are identified thus enabling fail-safe procedures to be introduced to identify and correct any errors. The third stage is to set a time frame. Because all services are heavily time dependent and time is usually the main cost determinant, a standard execution time should be established. Finally, a profitability analysis is needed to help measure performance and control uniformity and quality.

Understanding service businesses has as its concomitant understanding how clients regard and use a service. The two are inseparable and to regard either in isolation can lead to less than effective practice development strategies and activities.

# Chapter 3.  Creating a client-centred practice

The advantages to be gained from a consistent programme of practice development have already been stated and it has been implied that success requires more than the acquisition of the appropriate commercial skills—it also needs as a pre-requisite, strong motivation from everyone within a practice. Such motivation can only emerge and be encouraged if there is a commitment at the most senior levels within a firm. Achieving this is rendered especially difficult both because of the content of most professional training and because of the comparisons which professionals make between the historic developments of their own disciplines and that of commerce.

## Conditioning factors

Professional training in most of the senior professions, whether intended or not, has a strong elitist element and considerable emphasis is placed on the incompatibility of professional and commercial practices and standards.

The very young professional, recently released from the rigours of training and indoctrinated and enthusiastic for the status rewards of newly acquired qualification, is very unlikely to be the precursor of changes in attitude towards practice development. The older professional may well have a conscious or unconscious objection to changes if they require a reconsideration of the standards and codes which have been accepted without question over the years but which may well now be anachronistic in the present conditions and incompatible with the attitude of private and business clients to the professions.

The perceived incompatibility of commercial methods, most particularly marketing and its component elements such as personal selling, advertising and public relations, with professionalism is based as much on history as on current activities. The development of the professions has been along a very different path from those activities which are regarded as 'trade', 'commerce' or 'business'. The three stages of professional development are:

- Achievement of legal recognition.
- Adherence to a self-imposed code of ethics.
- Recognition by society as a whole which transcends national origin, political, social or economic backgrounds.

Not all professions have accomplished all three stages but activities which strive for professional status and recognition pursue these objectives consciously or unconsciously.

In contradistinction the historical development of 'trade' has been very different and along a widely divergent path. The days of *caveat emptor* are not wholly past. Thus there still hangs over all transactions a scarcely veiled suspicion that there is an attempt to obtain money from the unwary client or customer by some trickery. This is as was pointed out by Professor Theodore Levitt many years ago because there is a natural and irremovable difference of interests between the vendor and the buyer based largely on the view that the former is more expert, better informed on the subject of the transaction than the buyer who is an amateur. When a client or customer is dissatisfied, he assumes that some facts that would have helped him make a wiser decision, particularly in the case of professional services, have been withheld. Thus the client can hardly be criticized for exaggerating the extent of the apparent duplicity by which he was misled or at worse cheated.

Given the contrasting background of training and history it can be seen that for a practice to become client centred, a very considerable change of attitude is required. This is likely only to be initiated successfully at the top or middle seniority of management levels.

It is these people who will first appreciate the need and desirability of practice development but it is the most senior members of a practice who must institute the changes needed and have a genuine enthusiasm for so doing. If however they are not to lose the support of their most vital and indeed possibly only significant asset—people—then they must be capable of communicating both their enthusiasm and their reasoning for embarking on a policy of practice development based on client-centred activities and policies.

This means that they have to be convinced that there is nothing unprofessional in 'client satisfaction engineering' which is what practice development is about. Professionals, both as individuals and in their practices, depend on client goodwill to survive and they must develop a sensitivity to their needs and how they can best be met.

It was an industrial psychologist discussing these desiderata of good communications and good relationships with clients and prospective clients who said:

> Responsibility for demonstrating that our credentials really mean something and will produce genuine benefits for the clients constitutes a selling proposition that we must recognise. In short if we can't sell our credentials in the sense of demonstrating that they stand for something far more substantial than the elegant initials after our name, then we are failures not only as salesmen but as professionals as well. As professionals possessing professional skills we still have not only the requirements, but the obligation of actively and energetically selling these skills. They won't sell themselves! We have to sell them. And if we have to sell them, it is better that we do so on a conscious explicit basis rather than on an unconscious, implicit, hit or miss basis.[1]

Although this was said many years ago, it remains true today.

What in practical terms does being client centred entail? These can be summed up under four headings:

- Sensing needs.
- Responding effectively to enquiries.
- Seeking opportunities to provide additional services.
- Satisfying needs through the provision of high quality services at commensurate fees.

Practice development starts with the realization that it is necessary to operate in a way that satisfies clients—a lesson learned in consumer goods marketing many decades ago and in industrial marketing more recently, perhaps in the 1950s and 1960s. The marketing concept, for that is what it is, can be most readily appreciated by describing it as a way of conducting the affairs of the firm, or the individual practitioner so as to create client satisfaction. That is, it is necessary to view the professional service through the eyes of the client in terms of what he, the

---

1. Warren J. Wittreich. 'Selling—a prerequisite to success as a professional'. (A paper presented at a conference in Detroit, Mitch., 8 January 1969.)

client, regards as 'satisfaction' and acting and motivating everyone within the practice to be client centred.

Being client centred, however, does not mean that the needs of the firm are totally and always subordinated to the needs of the client. The marketing concept does not entail abandoning the requirements of the firm in terms of job satisfaction, types of clients served or business undertaken or the myriad other things which together make up the total operating activity and environment. 'The firm that is at the mercy of its clients deserves sympathy and nothing else' wrote one marketing commentator which is a realistic view of the balance to be achieved in adopting a client-centred policy.

## Sensing needs

One of the few skills professional practitioners and marketing practitioners share or require in common is the ability to sense a client's needs even those he cannot always express himself. All professions are problem solving but not all problems, as will be shown in Chapter 7, 'Professional services and client needs', necessarily indicate which is the correct profession for the client to approach. This aside, a client's needs frequently go well beyond the disciplines of the profession being consulted. They can vary from the tangible in the form of physical support systems (infrastructure) to the socio-psychological requirements. Moreover the client's needs may be less than obvious to the client himself. New legislation and innovation in methods, systems, products and other services may well indicate to the professional adviser a client situation demanding services which the client himself cannot perceive. By way of examples only: a legal decision that a letter of intent is not a commitment has implications for both the corporate and private clients who may not know of the decision; the revelation that the interaction of some insulating materials with atmospheric conditions can create either toxic or noxious gases places an obligation on architects and surveyors to advise clients of the risk which they may not know exists.

Another aspect of sensing a client's needs may well be related to the availability of the service in time or geographical terms. An emergency service, accessibility of professionals outside normal working hours, the existence of a local office or the willingness or ability of the professional to come to the client rather than expect the client to come to him could be very real requirements which are not exposed.

A client's needs may be definable in explicit terms but they may well be totally perceptual and the significance of perceptions and images is dealt with at length in Chapter 12, 'The importance of images and perceptions'. A company about to 'go public' will almost certainly require the service of well-known professional advisers and practitioners, accountants, solicitors, merchant banks. Many a local, provincial or suburban practice which has assisted a business in growth to public company stature has found itself arbitrarily abandoned in order that prestigious names appear in the offer documents. Indeed it might be said that professional practices that do not grow alongside their corporate clients are almost certainly bound to be disadvantaged in the long run since the clients' needs in some form or another are not being met. To a lesser extent this also can apply to private clients who obtain some satisfaction or reflected prestige by consulting leading practitioners or firms in a particular discipline.

## Responding effectively to enquiries

For new clients a critical point in the development of a relationship exists, paradoxically, at the very first moment of contact. Just how a prospective client is received, either by telephone or personal contact, has an all-pervasive influence on whether the relationship does develop or develops on a basis which is satisfactory for both parties.

While for prospective clients, effective enquiry handling is obviously a crucial first step in creating a satisfactory client–professional relationship, it is also important for established clients. In some respects it might even be of greater significance in that established clients might well feel entitled to a very high degree of intelligent attention by virtue of their on-going relationship with the practice or individuals.

Dealing effectively with enquiries includes prompt and efficient telephone or reception techniques, intelligent identification by support staff of the most suitable member of the firm to deal with the enquiry, ensuring a rapid response from the appropriate person, correct client interrogation and problem identification and then a clear statement of the next steps to be taken and by whom. Where the enquiry cannot be dealt with by the appropriate person at once, then it is important that it is routed effectively and rapidly and that a method exists to ensure that it is received and acted on. Practical methods for ensuring effective enquiry handling are dealt with in later chapters.

While it is easy to set out the rules for handling enquiries, it must be said that such rules throughout all sectors of business are more honoured in their breach than in their observance. In this respect the professions organized in the smaller practices or individually are probably superior than business in general. For the larger practices the sins of omission and commission are numerous and largely unnecessary and unforgivable. No individual, professional firm or business can claim to be client centred if clients cannot have their enquiries dealt with rapidly, efficiently and pleasantly.

## Seeking opportunities to provide additional services

If, as the professions claim, the best advertisement for a service are its satisfied clients, then the best opportunity for increasing demand for the practice or an individual's services are the self-same clients. Thus sensing clients needs may well provide the opportunity for providing additional satellite services which are compatible in terms of skills and perception with the core service. (See Chapter 2, 'Understanding service businesses', pages 15–16.)

The most effective route to practice development and expansion for many professional firms and individuals may well be to obtain more revenue from existing clients. Since this will generally not be possible by increasing the use of the basic service—clients will sensibly not 'buy' more services than they can usefully or profitably consume—the key must be additional services. While there is a strong case for high specialization such as occurs in parts of the medical profession, there is an equally good case for 'one stop' professional services as can also be seen within the medical profession in the development of family health centres and in the American diagnostic clinics, emergency centres and health maintenance organizations. In financial services there has been a considerable trend to 'one stop' services such as banks and building societies are attempting to provide.

However, between the extremes there is considerable potential for most professional service firms to provide a wider range of appropriate services to existing clients. It not only confers all the advantages of practice development already referred to—increased revenue, profitability, work satisfaction, career opportunities—but for many clients it can be a highly desired convenience. Chapter 6, 'Deciding the service offering of the practice', deals at length with the technique of creating an optimum range of services.

22

## Satisfying needs through the provision of high quality services at commensurate fees

Practice development, to be successful, is wholly dependent upon the provision of services which are perceived to be of the quality required by the client and at a fee which is regarded as fair. In all professional services the greatest and most frequent sources of disagreement between client and practitioner rests on the client's perception of 'quality' and 'fair fees'. Neither can be subjected to totally objective criteria so that there is always considerable room for dissatisfaction on both sides.

If the client's perception of 'quality' and 'fair fees' is out of line with reality, almost invariably the professional has only himself to blame for permitting this situation to exist. Most professionals try consciously not to allow the client's expectations to rise to an unreasonable level, but all too often client and practitioner speak different languages, and what can be a muted expression of hope by one might easily be transformed into a wild hyperbole by the other. Moreover there can be wide fluctuations of perceptions over time and as the matter evolves. An amusing but nevertheless all too true interpretation of clients' changing attitudes within an American context is shown in Figure 3-1.

Satisfaction, it was stated in the previous chapter, is a function of how close the results of the application of a professional service are to the client's expectations. The closer they are the greater the likelihood of the fees being regarded as 'fair'.

There is total accord between the professional's training and his inclinations to place the facts, uncoloured, before the client and the marketing man's objective of ensuring the client has a clear conception of what it is that he will eventually be paying for. Their objectives are identical in that they both require an informed client so that there will be minimal risk of *post facto* disaffection or disappointment.

There are few airline passengers who do not understand why a first class airline ticket costs more than a stand-by economy class ticket, but not many clients can make the same distinction between one level of professional service and another or between one practitioner and another. Thus the need to ensure that there is complete understanding on what the service when rendered can and will achieve is of considerable importance.

The problem is intensified however by the fact that it is virtually impossible to compare many professional services even within the same discipline. Even such an apparently mechanical process as the conveyancing of property can in a single city, as one recent survey showed, vary by as much as 75 per cent in the fees charged. It is difficult, if not impossible, for the client to see why such a large difference can exist when the services offered are seemingly identical. There are many reasons why they are not identical but these reasons may have little or no meaning to the client who essentially is purchasing a result—a conveyance with good title—and nothing else.

To be client centred the practitioner must be sensitive to the quality–price equation which is inherent in all client relationships. The success of practice development will hinge on the client's perception of value for money—something which will re-emerge again and again throughout this book.

## The marketing concept

What has been enunciated would be recognized in business as the end result of applying the marketing concept. The marketing concept is a philosophy not a system of marketing or an organizational structure. It is based on the belief that the individual's or firm's objectives are

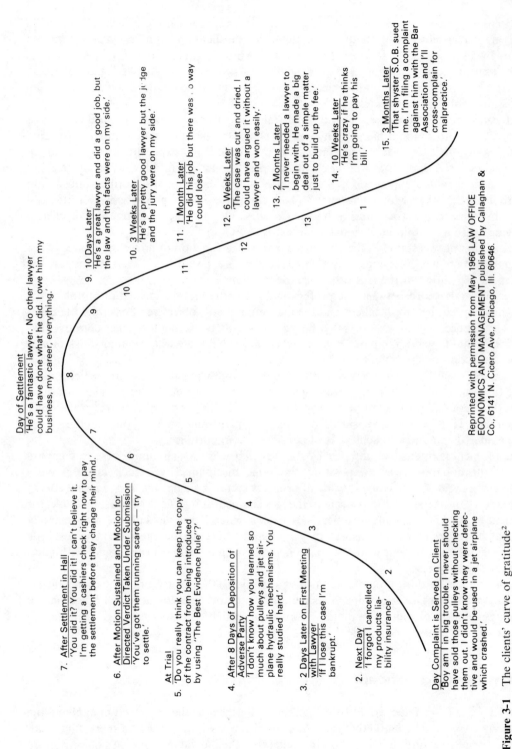

**Figure 3-1**   The clients' curve of gratitude[2]

2. Reprinted with permission from May 1966 *Law Office Economics and Management.* Callaghan & Co., 6141 N. Cicero Ave., Chicago, Ill. 60646. © 1966 Callagham & Co.

best achieved by identifying, anticipating and satisfying a client's needs and desires—in that order. It is an attitude of mind that places the client in the very centre of the professional's activities and inevitably orients them towards the client and avoids the tendency of professionals to turn introspectively towards their own skills and interests.

Practice development (or marketing) is the actual process of integrating and co-ordinating all those functions which serve to identify and anticipate needs, communicating these needs to the professionals who must satisfy them, creating among clients the awareness of the benefits of the service and the actual 'delivery' of the service to the client.

The marketing concept has some nine sub-concepts which have very practical implications.

1. *Deciding the 'mission' or business of the practice* Firms tend to define their purpose too narrowly and as a result do not always see opportunities open to them. Asking 'what business are we in?' and obtaining a correct answer is the first practical step in developing a practice. It is two decades since market research companies re-defined their business as 'problem solving' not 'fact finding' and, as a result, enhanced the use of research and with it their own businesses considerably. Insurance companies have long established they are in the 'peace of mind' and 'responsible citizenship' business.

   While deciding the business purpose of a practice is not easy, because there may be several answers to the same question, it is nevertheless the starting point. Accountancy firms have moved a long way from their auditing core to offer a 'full line' of business services ranging from executive search to management consultancy. Today many of them adopt not the 'business adviser' role but the 'business colleague' role, a difference which is more than semantic. Financial institutions in all the developed countries offer, or are in the throes of offering, 'one stop' financial services where client needs can be satisfied at a single source—credit cards, leasing, real estate, investment, management, trusts and many other services. From perhaps just holders, transfers and providers of the money product they now see their role as more in the nature of financial chain stores or warehouses.

2. *Identifying suitable targets* Identifying the target clients in terms of common character- istics and needs will enable the limited practice development resources of the firm to be concentrated on those types of clients most likely to help them achieve their objectives. The idea that all clients are equally desirable, irrespective of the volume or type of work they provide or the income or profit they generate, can lead to massive wastage not just of practice development activities but also the very professional skills which are offered. Chapter 5, 'Devising a practice development strategy and plan', will explain this sub- concept in depth and how it impacts on practice development activity.

3. *Client attitudes, behaviour and need analysis* In creating and meeting the demand for professional services, knowledge of and attitudes of clients may be formed on impressionistic evidence. Folklore rather than fact can hinder the development of the services offered, prevent accurate segmentation criteria and differentiated appeals being devised. Increas- ingly, firms recognize that knowledge of a client's attitudes, activities and requirements are not yielded without some form of enquiry. Industry, national and individual archetypes are a poor guide for developing elegant approaches. Accurate and up-to-date information is a prior condition for the successful practice development and is perhaps the one aspect which is rarely disputed. The need for data on clients, on the competition and on the environment, whether their collection is formal or informal, dominates and influences every aspect of the practice development plan and the application of every tool available.

   While it is commonplace in the USA for professional service firms to seek client opinions on how well their service and personnel performed, it is unusual in most other countries. Yet this is a quick, low cost method for obtaining reliable actionable data. An example of client questionnaires is given in Appendix A of Chapter 17, 'Non-personal methods of practice development'.

4. *Differentiated advantages* Every firm and individual who is actively engaged in the provision of professional services has some unique competence resource or facility which distinguishes the individual or practice from all others. Only relatively rarely is a professional service chosen in a totally random manner. The basis for choice may be trivial or may be fundamental, real or perceptual, but a distinction between those who offer what are perceived as similar services is almost invariably made because of some preference for an aspect or a combination of aspects of the offer. Every firm must consider what elements in its resources, capabilities, experience, or reputation will create special and unique values in the minds of its clients. There is no suggestion of searching for a pot of gold at the end of the rainbow. A differential advantage will exist except under the most unusual circumstances.[3]

Because services cannot be patented there is little opportunity to achieve a lasting differentiation by some innovative aspect, although short-term and valuable advantages can be developed. Differentiation is likely to occur through personnel, 'packages' of services, the way which information on the practice is presented, benefits offered, clients served, referral sources, location, availability and perhaps the creation of an attractive ambience.[3]

5. *Differentiating the practice—development methods* Differentiated techniques for practice development are required to distinguish each practice offering the same services. When all practices in a given discipline appear to the potential client to be identical, then the choice will be arbitrary such as picking a name from the classified telephone directory. Differentiation has as its purpose to ensure that the particular practice is perceived as favourably distinguishable from all others offering similar services. Varying approaches will be needed for each client type because not every segment of a market for a given service will respond to the same approach or methods. Marketing financial services, for example, can be effectively carried out through the use of intermediaries of various sorts which themselves can create a differentiation. It would be difficult to use intermediaries in management consultancy and virtually impossible with such services as loss adjusting, or assessing arbitration and taxation consultancy. Banks may have been able to develop unique merchandising techniques for their services, but this is inappropriate for medicine. The presentation of the service, the frequency of approaches to prospective clients and/or exposure, the time and place of practice development activities, all require careful aligning to the target segments and their needs.

6. *Selecting appropriate, permissible and acceptable methods for contacting clients* The communication channels are diverse and the methods of reaching, explaining to, and convincing potential clients complex. Personal contact and public relations are just two methods, press and direct mail two media, from perhaps a range of 20 obvious possibilities and 30 less obvious ones.[4] Many methods and media are rejected by professional service companies as too brash, too costly, or too ineffectual, without any real consideration of their relationship to the firm's services and markets. This unnecessary reduction of alternatives reflects a distaste for marketing rather than a considered view of what is appropriate and permissible. Extreme examples drawn from the most strident parts of the consumer goods industry's communication methods are used to confirm the opinions of the inappropriateness of many techniques (e.g., posters, audio/visual techniques, display, gifts and competitions).

---

3. The practical application of this concept of unique competence or facility is demonstrated in Chapter 10, 'How the individual practice is selected'.
4. See Chapter 16, 'The use of personal contact', and Chapter 17, 'Non-personal methods of practice development'.

The various tools of marketing should not be judged by either their title or their association with consumer goods marketing. While it is conceded that many will be totally antipathetic to the professionals engaged in practice development and possibly to their clients, others will be found, if examined objectively and free from their image connotations, to have a direct applicability as later chapters will illustrate.

7. *Integrating the practice development activities*  Despite the small scale, in comparison to other businesses, of the practice development activities, there can nevertheless be a cancelling out effect unless the various techniques adopted are integrated both with each other and over time. The role of the co-ordinator has been compared to that of a conductor of an orchestra. The analogy is not a good one since most usually the conductor while integrating and co-ordinating the musicians is usually interpreting someone else's composition. The practice development task within professional service firms will usually include that of devising the strategy and tactics as well as ensuring its efficient implementation. In the context of the marketing concept, efficiency must embrace timing and integration of the various elements that comprise practice development and also with the other activities of the firm.

8. *Continuous information feedback*[5]  The information-gathering process, formal or informal, is continuous in all firms. Most product businesses use their salesmen, research departments, outside research organizations, advertising agencies, and informal contacts to monitor changes in their environment and their own performance. Professional service companies tend to be more casual about collecting these vital data.

   Information must be collected, integrated and stored in a common data bank and collected from externally and internally originated information which is required for the effective operation of the organization. However, it is vitally important that collection, integration and storage should be purposeful, and that the information should be easily retrievable when needed and as appropriate available to all levels of management.

9. *Market and marketing audits*  'Audits' in this context have three applications. First, to measure the changes in the structure of the environment in which the firm operates—its markets. Second, to evaluate and, where possible, measure the effect of the use of any particular method, medium or message used—marketing. Third, to enumerate and evaluate the resources a firm may possess or acquire that are available for practice development—resource realization.

   To expand profitably, periodic, reliable audits of achievements, resources, opportunities and threats are needed. Basic business philosophies, as well as important marketing aspects such as those described and explored in this book, require a regular and careful examination. **Market** audits, however, do tend to be used to monitor the course of the battle rather than to influence its outcome. As interesting as such an application for an audit may be, it is unlikely to add to the capability of the firm. The need to know what change is required, when the change is needed and the ability to make it when it is most opportune or before it is too late is important both for the continued existence of the firm and its expansion.

   **Marketing** audits are somewhat different. The internal marketing audit is an examination of available resources used, unused, underused or wrongly used, with the purpose of putting them to work effectively. It refers to the measurement or evaluation of the various methods which are applied to expand the practice. While it is difficult in every sphere of business to pinpoint the effect of any one method, message or media, at the very least it is important to know whether any effect at all is being produced and whether such an effect is positive or negative.

5. The 'information resource' is dealt with in Chapter 4, 'Preparing for practice development'.

Information concerning all three audit types—markets, marketing and resources—is necessary to ensure that the marketing concept does not become just one more business cliché but is, as it should be, a realistic, down-to-earth framework within which the practice can become totally client centred.[6]

## Marketing problems of practice development

These desiderata set by the marketing concept were perhaps conceived before there was the present understanding of the service system. They take little account of the specific problems listed at the beginning of Chapter 2, 'Understanding service businesses', and facing anyone concerned with marketing services but most particularly professional service. The implications of the six issues listed in Chapter 2, 'Understanding service businesses', page 8, are best understood before embarking on a practice development policy since they go some way to explain the differences in the choice of methods and the nuances as between the marketing of goods and services and practice development for professional firms.

| Limitation | Effect |
| --- | --- |
| 1. There can be no physical display of the service | Surrogates in the form of tangible evidence are required and it cannot be assumed that clients will necessarily make the perceptual link |
| 2. Demonstrations are not possible | While commercial or domestic services such as dry cleaning can be demonstrated, it is not practical and usually not permissible to demonstrate a professional service: for example, Hobday's Operation on a horse |
| 3. Warranty | Warranties either do not apply or are difficult to apply because there are no absolute standards. While professional negligence and legal protection do exist, the giving of warranties or guarantees for the quality or outcome of a service is as unwise as it is unrealistic |
| 4. Samples | Because services are intangible sampling is no more possible than is demonstration |
| 5. Packaging | Packaging can only relate to what are highly marginal aspects of professional services; documents, reports and software and these only have a minor image impact |
| 6. Patent protection | Services cannot be patented so that the most innovative of services can be copied immediately and without reference to the originator |

As a consequence of these factors a number of marketing methods which might otherwise have had some application to practice development are immediately removed from consideration. Thus the choice of strategies, methods and messages is circumscribed in a special way. The practice developer will require above average creativity to devise methods which are as acceptable to clients as to his professional colleagues given that these problems exist.

6. A detailed instruction on how to conduct an internal marketing audit will be found in Aubrey Wilson's *Marketing Audit Check Lists—a guide to effective marketing resource realization*, McGraw-Hill (London, 1982) and in J. Naylor and A. Wood. *Practical Marketing Audits*. Associated Business Programmes (London, 1978).

# The communication process

It will be obvious from the foregoing that practice development techniques will produce very little unless the methods of communication with the actual and potential clients and the information which is conveyed reach them by an acceptable method and in an acceptable form. The communication task is easily summarized. It is necessary first that the firm should be known or 'visible' to its potential and inactive clients. The next level is to ensure that the communication targets, whoever they may be, understand the information given, about the services, practices, members, reputation, experience, resources and facilities. This too will not ensure the practice will be selected and used by clients. A further barrier to be overcome requires that the potential clients understand the relevance of the message to their own situation and can appreciate the benefits which will ensue from the adoption of the service. Finally they have to be convinced of the truth of the information. Then and only then will a favourable decision occur at the final level. None of the stages are ever omitted in any decision to affect a practice:

- From unawareness (of the practice).
- To awareness (visibility).
- To comprehension (understanding of the information).
- To relevancy (appreciation of benefits).
- To conviction (belief in its accuracy).
- To favourable decisions (action).

There is however no law of gravity which pulls the potential client or customer downward through these various levels towards the ultimate decision. There are instead methods and techniques for ensuring effective communication at each level which are discussed later. However, countervailing forces are at work which tend to drive the client upwards away from the decision. These countervailing forces are those of competition both within a profession and from outside, memory lapse, and among a commercial client's, attrition, that is changes of personnel and policies. The situation has been best illustrated as shown in Figure 3-2.

The diagram (Figure 3-2) encapsulates very effectively the total task of practice development. It can be said with absolute certainty that it is impossible to obtain a favourable decision if the practice fails at any one of the levels illustrated. Without 'visibility' there can be no question of understanding, without understanding there is no chance of establishing relevancy and without an acceptance of relevance the belief stage cannot be achieved. Thus all four levels must be penetrated before a favourable decision can occur. The task of the personnel charged with practice development is therefore to:

- Create awareness.
- Develop understanding.
- Demonstrate relevance.
- Achieve belief.

The practical implications of this continuum can be illustrated indicating, but only by way of example, what methods might be adopted to ensure the movement of the practice message through each stage to the final favourable decision. A model might look like that shown in Figure 3-3.

The remainder of this book is dedicated to setting out how practice development for professional firms operating under conditions of mandatory and self-imposed restraints can be accomplished without demanding skills usually not found in professional practices or in any way seeking to circumvent the rules or breach the dignity and integrity of the professions.

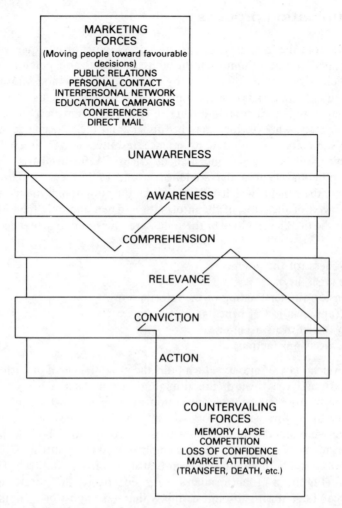

**Figure 3-2**  The communication process[7]

7.  Adapted from A. H. Colley. 'Squeezing the waste out of advertising'. *Harvard Business Review* (Cambridge, Mass., September/October 1962).

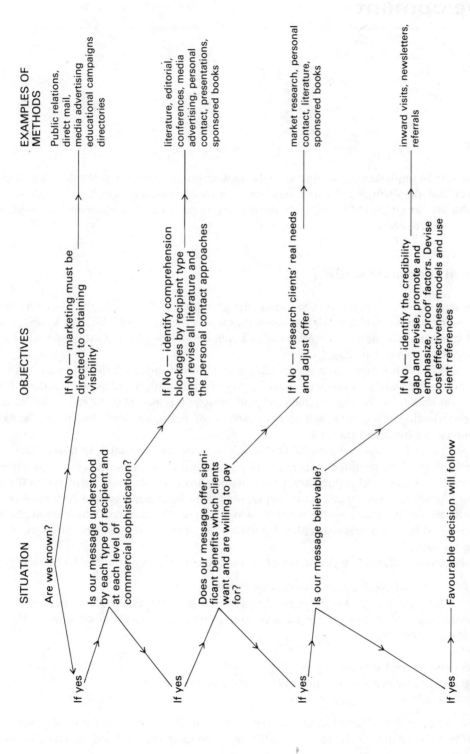

**Figure 3-3** Path to a favourable decision

# Chapter 4.  Preparing for practice development

The first step in implementing a practice development programme is not the devising of the plan itself but the identification and evaluation of those resources which are available or acquirable and which should be built into the plan to ensure maximum effectiveness—needless to say *cost* effectiveness.

## Internal resource audits

Practice development depends on the availability of resources to achieve the objectives and there is no gainsaying in almost all professional practices there is a total lack, or an apparent lack, of appropriate human resources as well as a considerable dearth of information on which a development plan can be based.

Plans will be neither practical nor profitable if they do not utilize all the resources—in the widest sense of that word—that can be devoted to their preparation and implementation. It is perfectly possible to devise elegant, detailed plans which on paper meet the full requirements for practice development and yet will never be used or will be applied badly because of the lack of resources to carry them through.

All professional firms have resources which can be incorporated into the practice development but these resources either remain unidentified or so committed that it is impossible to re-direct them to other purposes without damaging the service itself. To prepare a sound basis for a practice development programme, which is to be introduced and continued on a systematic and disciplined basis, the very first step is to audit the resources which are available or which could be made available either by acquisition of the resource or re-direction of an existing resource.

For the purpose of practice development, resources can be grouped under seven headings:

- People—with their skills, interests and experiences.
- Information—internal and concerning the environment in which the firm operates.
- Infrastructure and hardware—word processors, computers, mechanized and electronic equipment, premises, etc.
- Finance.
- Clients and referral sources.
- Images and perceptions of the practice and its personnel.
- Services available.

There are of course others but identifying and evaluating these will be of only indirect value. Planning is not likely to be assisted by becoming too detailed in consideration of resources. It is proposed to review briefly the types of and applications for major resources areas and then relate the method of identifying the information and then to an existing programmed test that will give considerable assistance to an inexperienced 'auditor'.

## People resource

Services are a 'people' business and therefore it is sensible to start with a listing of all personnel and their qualifications, skills, experience, contacts and interests and it is also necessary, however subjective judgements may be, to assess attitudes to practice development. It is useless, unwise and in the end dangerous to impose on both professional and support staff tasks which they find incompatible or unacceptable for whatever reason. Thus the core of practice development personnel will be those within a practice who believe that such activities are desirable for all the reasons given and others or who are at least agnostic. These identified personnel, irrespective of their position within the firm's hierarchy, should be given clearly defined roles both in the creation of the practice development strategy and/or its implementation.

The key appointment must be the designation of a senior member of the firm to accept responsibility for the programme. Such an appointment requires, apart from the necessary enthusiasm for the task and ability to convey this enthusiasm to others, diplomacy, the energy to sustain the plan once it is adopted, self-discipline not to be diverted from it, the ability to motivate others and to maintain this motivation in the face of inevitable disappointments and indeed often outright antagonism within the practice, and, let it be said, those very features once ascribed to the good salesman—empathy and ego drive. 'Empathy' is the power of projecting personality and responding to situations and 'ego drive' is a personal need to succeed in whatever task is accepted. This key appointment of the practice development leader is the equivalent in commerce to the appointment of a marketing (not a sales) director. It is around this person the team will be built and thus the strong emphasis given to the importance of appointing a person most suited for the task is justified.

In one type of professional service the practice developer will be at least partly self-designated; this is the senior clerk in barristers' chambers. While everyone within chambers, individually and collectively, will have an influence, the senior clerk does have a very important role to play in ensuring the development of good relations with their solicitor clients and prospective clients.

To ensure that the scope of the task is appreciated by the incumbent and that standards of performance exist, it is necessary to prepare an outline description of the appointment. Such a description will be most effective if it specifies the following issues:

- Purpose of the position.
- The essential characteristics of the environment (including mandatory and self-imposed constraints) within which the incumbent must operate.
- Key financial and resource dimensions.

Essentially it should be a description of the *activity* not of the person who is to fill the role. The task specification, to be most practical, should concentrate on the purpose of the appointment not the means to its achievement and critically focus upon the essential features of the activity and the results to be obtained in a specified time. A good specification will be sufficiently flexible to allow for some changes. The methods for achieving the results are the items that are quickly overtaken by events. Needless to say the most successful descriptions are those which have been agreed between the person charged to undertake the activities and the chief executive or senior partner (see Figure 4-1).

The following information should be recorded at the beginning of each description, preferably in a standardized format.

- *Indicative task title*
- *Person designated*
- *Identification of person to whom the designated person is to report (and who will have agreed the task description)*
- *Identification of the person who carried out the job analysis*
- *Date*

1. Purpose
The purpose section requires an accurate, concise and undetailed statement of why the activity exists. Its primary purpose for being part of the firm's organization.

2. Dimensions
Measurable areas upon which the task has either direct or indirect impact. It would normally include such items as: other personnel involved in the task and managerial relationships; quantitative targets such as fee income, profit, ratio of new to repeat business and new and old clients, budgets, operating expenses, personnel costs, other significant money values.

3. Accountabilities
Accountabilities are fairly broad statements of what the tasks are required to accomplish. They usually incorporate end results from the following areas:
- establishing objectives
- organization structuring and apportionment of staff
- planning, communicating and directing the attainment of objectives
- achieving results
- promoting innovation
- motivation gain
- developing people
- developing and maintaining internal and external relationships

4. Nature and scope of position
The nature and scope of the position should provide a clear, concise narrative about the tasks and includes:
- role and place in the practice
- environment in which the tasks must be accomplished
- major areas of concern and activities
- organization of subordinate activities and composition of supporting staff
- working relationships—internal and external
- nature of the required technical, managerial and human relations, know-how related to the service provided
- problems and basic challenges in the tasks
- freedom to think and act

In order to draw together these facets an example of a practice development task specification is given in Appendix A.

**Figure 4-1**   Format for task specification[1]

In most practices, it is unlikely that there will be more than one or two people available for full-time practice development and therefore the team will have to be built from members of staff able to contribute limited time. These are part-timers in the sense that they are currently fully employed in their professional or other capacity but will allocate designated time inputs to the development task. The problem is not so acute with support staff and it should be possible without difficulty to recruit the services of appropriate people on a full-time basis or again devoting part of their time to the practice development activity.

This statement may seem highly impractical for many professional service firms which most frequently are operating under considerable time pressure. However, what is known in

1. Adapted with permission from John Rawlinson's 'Writing job descriptions'. In Michael Rines (ed.) *The Best of Marketing* Volume 2 *People and Practices*. Leviathan House (London, 1975), pp. 24–25.

industry as a 'job content analysis' will frequently reveal that the very people required to provide time inputs into practice expansion are also the ones undertaking tasks which others with equal but different talents can well carry out for them, thus leaving time for accepting other tasks.

This audit of human resources is concerned not only with the available skills, in practice development terms, but also with what time can be released to utilize them. As a preliminary to devising a practice development plan, an important first step therefore is to assess, if needs be by a job content analysis study, just what time/skills can indeed be released. A self-analysis over a typical period of say four to six weeks will reveal this by breaking each day down into small units (say one hour) and re-ordering the time spent on those activities which are not the essence of the professional's skills. For example, a solicitor interviewing clients, a veterinary practitioner's time spent in the surgery, a loss adjuster's site visit are all essential parts of the professional's work. However, making appointments, information retrieval, purchasing supplies, para-legal and para-medical activities, office management and so on are activities high on the list for delegation. Although self-analysis of job content can be both boring and sometimes daunting, it is only of a short duration and has a value out of all proportion to the investment in the activity. A simple format will make recording easy and it is, after all, probably very little different in principle for the effort required to record and collate 'billable' time in many professions.

The Law Society, for example, recommends breaking time down into five-minute units. An example of this is given in Appendix B. For the purpose of task specification for practice development, such a fine breakdown is probably too detailed. A more simple format will be found in Appendix C.


## Information resource

Many professional service firms ignore one of the most important and usable resources for practice development, and one which they frequently possess in abundance. This is information. While it is recognized there may be a lack of information concerning the environment in which they operate, there is within firms a wealth of information which provides a sound factual basis for planning, at least so far as their existing clients are concerned, but which can often reveal important information on prospective clients. However, the addiction of marketing experts to obtaining market size and market share is one that ought not to concern practice development personnel. For most professional services it suffices to say the market is 'big enough' and the market share of no significance as compared with absolute revenue or profit which can be attained.

Information can be divided into two groups: desk or secondary research and original field research. Within the former group is the information already inside the firm, although not perhaps in an immediately usable form. The latter group represents that which must be obtained by external enquiry, usually marketing research. In fact external marketing research is only a rarely required function since data needed for devising an expansion plan can almost invariably be generated from within the firm with a far higher degree of accuracy than can be achieved by the use of external sources.

The types of internal information which can be (or should be) easily extracted are various forms of analyses. For example fee analysis, which can be broken down by types of services performed, by types of client, sources of new business, geographically, over time, achieved by individual professionals, and many others. The value of these types of data is obvious in that by way of example, if certain types of assignments are more profitable than others or provide greater work satisfaction or career opportunities, then clearly this gives a purpose to the practice development objectives. Similarly, if an analysis of client types shows that a certain type of client, perhaps corporate rather than private, international rather than local, large rather than small, appears to find the firm's services satisfactory, then the profile of the type of client which the firm must focus on becomes clear.[2]

Similarly, internal data can reveal key cost ratios or correlations, historical trends and even actual data which may indicate the point in time when a client may require further services.[3]

Appendix B in Chapter 5, 'Devising a practice development strategy and plan', lists some of the more common and useful categories of internal information, their reporting frequency, standards for comparison and use. It is essentially a model and each firm would need to adjust to its own specific requirements.

Usable information however is not confined to the type mentioned. To the purely quantitative data the following documentation will always assist in the preparation of a practice development plan:

- Organization chart (formal and informal) showing lines of authority, reporting and responsibility.
- Brochures or other printed material (own and competitors).
- Newsletters and other non-specific forms of client and prospective client communications.
- Enquiry records, showing source through which enquiries reach the firm and their outcome.
- Journals received.
- External statistics received.
- Complaints analyses.

The list is not complete and must be specific to the individual practice but lack of any of these or other items may well itself indicate a planning input requirement and subsequent action.

Information is unquestionably a most valuable marketing resource and there is less and less excuse for any professional service firm not to make full use of it, with the advent of low cost computers and programs and of other electronic equipment in offices which is penetrating down to the one man practice. However, information technology can itself lead to problems in that there is too little discrimination in extracting and storing information that has a direct and important contribution to make to practice development. The major dangers are:

- Too much information of a non-actionable type.
- Too little information on data which are immediately usable.
- Too great a dispersal through the practice to the extent that even simple data cannot be obtained easily.
- Information obtained too late to take action or avert problems.
- Information suppressed by those who may regard it as inimicable to their own interest.
- Data presented in a form that requires further processing to make it usable.
- Failure to distinguish fact and opinion.[4]

## Infrastructures and hardware resource

The hardware inventory is perhaps the simplest part of the internal resource audit. More

2. A profiling technique is described in Chapter 11, 'Identifying potential clients'.
3. Examples of internal analyses and their use will be found in Aubrey Wilson's *The Assessment of Industrial Markets*. Associated Business Programmes (London, 1973).
4. John Naylor and Alan Wood. *Practical Marketing Audits*. Associated Business Programmes (London, 1978), p. 86.

difficult is the assessment of what hardware is needed. A feasibility study to determine the cost effectiveness of any particular piece of equipment or system is outside the scope of this book but it does not make it less important. Assistance in feasibility studies for hardware can be obtained usually without charge from any supplier of such equipment. The professional must never cease to appreciate that the supplier is attempting to sell both the concept and *his* equipment. A computer supplier is not likely to extol the virtues of a simple word processor as an alternative or vice versa. The concept decision might best be assisted either by an independent specialist or by other similar firms which have already taken the appropriate purchase and can base their views on experience received.

While the level of co-operation is frequently high between practices which are competitive, but even where it is not, it is not difficult to obtain the assistance of identical practices not geographically or service 'product' competitive. For example, a solicitor practising in Bournemouth is not likely to compete with one in Leeds; an architect specializing in major international projects is unlikely to compete with one concerned with housing associations. In both examples the nature of the work is sufficiently similar, while not being competitive, to give valid analogies for decision making.

Additionally, many of the collegial organizations are themselves undertaking studies and giving technical advice to members and even negotiating favourable purchasing arrangements—services which both the individual and firm can take advantage of to augment and improve their hardware resources.

## Financial resource

As with hardware, finance is outside the scope of this book but it is nevertheless a vital resource that must be assessed in terms of requirements for practice development. That is not simply if there is enough finance to fund the additional work obtained by the successful expansion of activities but also if such funds are sufficient to support the practice development activity itself.

Where practice development of funds requires finances beyond the resources of the firm, a full-scale search of the many sources available should be undertaken. Financial support schemes (particularly governmental ones because they are associated with job creation and regional developments) tend to be written off as inappropriate. This is a mistake that can lead to lost opportunities.

Certainly in the UK, in the EEC and in other countries there are numerous sources of funds or at least tax advantages which can be utilized to assist in the acquisition of finance, or the better utilization of available funds. These range from investment allowances, tax- or rate (local taxation)-free 'holidays' to outright grants and 'soft' loans. Many private organizations operate schemes, some specializing to the extent of concentrating on finance for a particular profession.[5]

## Client and referral resource

Clients are unquestionably a major resource of a professional service company and can be

---

5. Three useful guides to sources of funding are G. Walker and K. Allen, *Industrial Aids in Britain*. Centre for the Study of Policy, University of Strathclyde (Glasgow, Annual). *Blay's Guide to Regional Finance for Industry and Commerce* (Chalfont St Peter, Bucks, Annual). *Finance for New Projects in the United Kingdom*. Peat Marwick and Mitchell (London, 1983).

used as such. In Chapter 6, 'Deciding the service offering of the practice', reference is made to expanding activities with existing clients by increasing the volume of demand which utilizes existing services and also by offering such clients new and expanded services. These are perhaps the easiest and most profitable methods of obtaining new business. The question must always be asked in preparing for a planning exercise 'Can we increase our revenue from existing clients?' Clients are, after all, in one profession's terminology the 'goodwill' element in a business which has a monetary value but only because it has a marketing value.

But clients, at least satisfied ones, have a further considerable importance. They are a source of referrals which for professional companies almost certainly represent the most frequent and effective form of new client acquisition. For the professions where marketing or practice development is banned or subject to stringent and rigid controls, referrals can represent well over 90 per cent of the sources of new business. Thus clients who also act as referrers represent a double resource.

A pre-planning requirement therefore is to identify key clients in terms of the revenue they generate or may be capable of generating and also in terms of the referrals and introduction they may be able to give the practice.

But aside from clients there are also influential sources of referrals who themselves will never be clients. For many professions high on the list will be bank officials who are often consulted by their own clients for advice on other professionals such as solicitors, accountants and stockbrokers; doctors are asked to recommend specialists, para-medical personnel or practices or even pharmacists; architects advise on different types of surveyors, interior designers, valuers and so on. If information on sources of referrals is not documented so that it is impossible to identify precisely from where recommendations are generated and by whom, then it is a first important step to adjust records to identify such important and influential groups and people. Chapter 13, 'The referral (recommendations) system', concentrates on this subject.

## Images and perception resource

It is not only the consumer in the supermarket who is influenced by images and perceptions. He remains just as motivated by images in the more rarefied field of professional services as in commercial and domestic services. These same comments apply equally to corporate clients. The fact that Chapter 12, 'The importance of images and perceptions', is devoted to this one aspect of practice development indicates its importance. A firm's or an individual's image and the public's perception will have a dominating role in decision making and images can work just as easily against a firm as for it. Difficult as it may be, part of the audit of resources must include information on the image of the practice and its members and the meaning to its potential and prospective clients. It is as well for the firm, before formulating its plans, to take as objective a view as it can of the way it might and should appear to those who use or could use it service. In this respect limited market research using postal questioning and interrogation of clients when a matter is completed can be highly revealing and indicate immediate steps to be taken to improve or adjust images. Chapter 17, 'Non-personal methods of practice development', contains an Appendix showing examples of questionnaires which can be used.

It must be borne in mind however that no professional service can completely free itself from the image of the profession as a whole. Thus accountants might well be seen, as the managing partner of one major firm stated, as 'dull, unadventurous and detached'. Lawyers universally have a poor press. Rarely are they mentioned in the media except with reference to some breach of the rules of practice or unacceptable behaviour. Chartered surveyors, associated as they so frequently are with estate agents, fare little better. Doctors are all too frequently accused of arrogance, a lack of real involvement with the patients and sometimes negligence.

It is of course difficult, even for a major firm, to disassociate itself totally from the image of the profession as a whole. However, within that image—good or bad—the individual firm or sole practitioner, can develop an acceptable image, which must be based on reality and which to some extent can cancel out any negative perceptions the prospective client may have of the profession as a whole. The image of a firm or individual and the perceptions a client holds of it or them is an intangible but none the less substantial resource that can make a major contribution to the success of the firm.

## Services range resource

Within a practice the availability of a range of services derived from the skills and interests of those employed as well as the other resources such as hardware and software, can be an important resource in distinguishing the firm in a favourable way. High specialization, such as is common in parts of the medical profession and management consultancy activities, can be of great actual and perceptual value. Equally the 'full line' practice has in the very range of its services an exploitable resource. Once again it is necessary to refer forward to Chapter 6, 'Deciding the service offering of the practice', which deals with the development of new or extended services where a capability may be inherent within the firm or acquirable and which could or would be used by clients if a knowledge of their existence and availability existed.

One of the basic elements which comprise the practice development includes 'service strategy'. Before devising an appropriate plan it is obviously important to identify what services exist or can be made to exist as a pre-condition in establishing the posture of the firm relative to the services it wishes to provide.

## Check list approach to resource identification, evaluation and realization

This brief overview of resource identification may make it appear that the task is onerous, time consuming and requiring the type and level of skills not normally found in a professional service firm. None of this is true. The work involved can be considerably reduced and simplified by adopting the check list approach. These are a series of sectionalized interrogation formats which can be selected for dealing with any particular aspect of a practice. Within the sections are precise questions, the answers to which will yield actionable answers.

In order to assist in this first stage of expansion planning and ultimately implementation readers are referred to a complete programmed text[6] which will guide the auditor through the procedures required and will enable almost all the information needed to be obtained or at the very least identified. The value of the check list approach is that it saves the auditor having to re-invent, re-order or re-write what has been done many times before by others, it gives an insight into the thinking and experience of others in the same field and it ensures that no important item is forgotten. Check lists are a starting point (not a stopping point); a logical notation of aspects of the firm's operations which impact directly and importantly on practice development strategy.

6. Aubrey Wilson's *Marketing Audit Check Lists—a guide to effective marketing resource realization*. McGraw-Hill (London, 1982).

Although the text referred to contains over 1000 questions it would be a very rare circumstance indeed where more than perhaps one-quarter of these would be required. In a typical professional practice resource audit the whole enquiry can be completed in one day.

To use the programmed text successfully the following summary explains the procedures which are fully set out in the book itself:

- Collect the documentation already referred to.
- Eliminate all non-applicable sections of the text.
- Delete all non-relevant questions in the remaining sections.
- Answer all questions within the capability of the auditor drawing out the actions implied with recommended courses of action.
- List others within and external to the practice who need to be consulted to complete audit.
- Decide whether to take individual replies or operate as a group.
- Write in the suggested courses of action arising from the response of others.
- Extract all action points and categorize according to urgency, likely cost, ease of implementation, etc.
- Allocate each task by name, schedule it by date or elapsed time, agree monitoring procedure.

The last point requires extra emphasis. Completing a resource audit does not automatically imply that the appropriate actions will be taken. To be certain that the resources will be fully realized, it is important to ensure that every action decided is allocated to an individual or group, that the time for its completion is scheduled and promulgated and that someone has the task of monitoring that the task is satisfactorily completed by the due date. Allocate, schedule and monitor are the key words for guaranteeing action, a statement which has already been made and will be repeated elsewhere to emphasize its importance.

The audit is not a substitute for action, nor should it be permitted to delay decision taking. Its purpose is to ensure that in formulating the practice development plan full use is made of all appropriate resources at all times.

# Appendix 4A.   An example of an appointment description for a practice development leader

| | |
|---|---|
| *Title:* | Practice Development Partner |
| *Reporting to:* | Managing Partner |
| *Purpose:* | To direct the development of practice expansion programmes which will achieve the firm's objectives of fee income and profitability, types of clients and work, new services and facilities for clients |
| *Fee income objectives:* | £2.5 million by 198? |
| *Budget:* | £100,000 |
| *Staff:* | One full-time assistant, one secretarial assistant. Contributions from individual partners and support staff to be specified on a time input basis |

## Principal accountabilities

1. Ensure that challenging, yet realistic objectives are developed for all the firm's services.

2. Develop a team which in quality, depth and creativeness assures excellent current performance and provides effective succession to key task positions.

3. Ensure complete understanding and acceptance of practice development policies and programmes within the firm.

4. Ensure acceptable performance for each service in relation to agreed objectives and standards.

5. Evaluate the accomplishment of each service against objectives and ensure that proper changes in approach and emphasis are made to meet changing client and competitive situations.

6. Appraise the effectiveness of any external bought-in services (e.g., newsletter editors, brochure designers, public relations) and recommend changes as appropriate.

7. Ensure that complete internal and market intelligence is effectively received, analysed and disseminated so that opportunities are maximized.

# Appendix 4B(i). Example of weekly time sheet[7]

♻ **Centre-file Limited**

THE LAW SOCIETY'S COMPUTER SERVICES FOR SOLICITORS

CONFIDENTIAL TIME SHEET

| SUBSCRIBER NUMBER | RT | TIME RECORDER CODE | DATE |
|---|---|---|---|
| S | 2 1 | | |

TIME RECORDER NAME

| | CLIENT MATTERS | DAYS | | | | | | | DATE | CLIENT MATTER No | BASIC TIME Hrs \| Min | OTHER TIME Hrs \| Min | TOTAL Hrs \| Min |
|---|---|---|---|---|---|---|---|---|---|---|---|---|---|
| 1 | | | | | | | | | | | | | |
| 2 | | | | | | | | | | | | | |
| 3 | | | | | | | | | | | | | |
| 4 | | | | | | | | | | | | | |
| 5 | | | | | | | | | | | | | |
| 6 | | | | | | | | | | | | | |
| 7 | | | | | | | | | | | | | |
| 8 | | | | | | | | | | | | | |
| 9 | | | | | | | | | | | | | |
| 10 | | | | | | | | | | | | | |
| 11 | | | | | | | | | | | | | |
| 12 | | | | | | | | | | | | | |
| 13 | | | | | | | | | | | | | |
| 14 | | | | | | | | | | | | | |
| 15 | | | | | | | | | | | | | |
| 16 | | | | | | | | | | | | | |
| 17 | | | | | | | | | | | | | |
| 18 | | | | | | | | | | | | | |
| 19 | | | | | | | | | | | | | |
| 20 | | | | | | | | | | | | | |

| REMEMBER | THE CHARACTER CONVENTIONS | | | TOTAL |
|---|---|---|---|---|
| Numeric | 0 1 2 5 8 | | | |
| Alphabetic | Ø 1 Z S B | | | 25252 |

25252

| SUBSCRIBER NAME | |
|---|---|

7. Reproduced by permission of the Law Society, London.

42

# Appendix 4B(ii).  Daily time record[8]

| FEE EARNER CODE | DATE | FEE EARNER NAME |
|---|---|---|
| | | |

| before 9 am | | |
|---|---|---|
| time taken | work done | client code |
| | | |
| | | |
| | | |
| | | |

| start time | work done | client code |
|---|---|---|
| 9 00 | | |
| am 05 | | |
| 10 | | |
| 15 | | |
| 20 | | |
| 25 | | |
| 30 | | |
| 35 | | |
| 40 | | |
| 45 | | |
| 50 | | |
| 55 | | |
| 10 00 | | |
| 05 | | |
| 10 | | |
| 15 | | |
| 20 | | |
| 25 | | |
| 30 | | |
| 35 | | |
| 40 | | |
| 45 | | |
| 50 | | |
| 55 | | |
| 11 00 | | |
| 05 | | |
| 10 | | |
| 15 | | |
| 20 | | |
| 25 | | |
| 30 | | |
| 35 | | |
| 40 | | |
| 45 | | |
| 50 | | |
| 55 | | |

| start time | work done | client code |
|---|---|---|
| 12 00 | | |
| 05 | | |
| 10 | | |
| 15 | | |
| 20 | | |
| 25 | | |
| 30 | | |
| 35 | | |
| 40 | | |
| 45 | | |
| 50 | | |
| 55 | | |
| 1 00 | | |
| pm 05 | | |
| 10 | | |
| 15 | | |
| 20 | | |
| 25 | | |
| 30 | | |
| 35 | | |
| 40 | | |
| 45 | | |
| 50 | | |
| 55 | | |
| 2 00 | | |
| 05 | | |
| 10 | | |
| 15 | | |
| 20 | | |
| 25 | | |
| 30 | | |
| 35 | | |
| 40 | | |
| 45 | | |
| 50 | | |
| 55 | | |
| 3 00 | | |
| 05 | | |
| 10 | | |
| 15 | | |
| 20 | | |
| 25 | | |
| 30 | | |
| 35 | | |
| 40 | | |
| 45 | | |
| 50 | | |
| 55 | | |

| start time | work done | client code |
|---|---|---|
| 4 00 | | |
| 05 | | |
| 10 | | |
| 15 | | |
| 20 | | |
| 25 | | |
| 30 | | |
| 35 | | |
| 40 | | |
| 45 | | |
| 50 | | |
| 55 | | |
| 5 00 | | |
| 05 | | |
| 10 | | |
| 15 | | |
| 20 | | |
| 25 | | |
| 30 | | |
| 35 | | |
| 40 | | |
| 45 | | |
| 50 | | |
| 55 | | |

| after 6 pm | | |
|---|---|---|
| time taken | work done | client code |
| | | |
| | | |
| | | |
| | | |
| | | |
| | | |
| | | |
| | | |
| | | |
| | | |
| | | |
| | | |
| | | |
| | | |

## CLIENT CODE ALLOCATION

| DATE |
|---|
| |

| FEE EARNER NAME |
|---|
| |

| | client matter | chargeable time |
|---|---|---|
| 1 | | |
| 2 | | |
| 3 | | |
| 4 | | |
| 5 | | |
| 6 | | |
| 7 | | |
| 8 | | |
| 9 | | |
| 10 | | |
| 11 | | |
| 12 | | |
| 13 | | |
| 14 | | |
| 15 | | |
| 16 | | |
| 17 | | |
| 18 | | |
| 19 | | |
| 20 | | |
| 21 | | |
| 22 | | |
| 23 | | |
| 24 | | |
| 25 | | |
| TOTAL CHARGEABLE TIME | | |
| TOTAL OF OTHER TIME | | |
| TOTAL FOR THE DAY | | |

8. Reproduced by permission of the Law Society, London.

# Appendix 4C.  Time report

TIME RECORDING

TIME REPORT (Time in multiples of quarter days)

| SURNAME +<br>INITIALS | STATUS | WEEK-<br>ENDING |
|---|---|---|
|  |  |  |

| Project | Client name/matter | Int. Acc.<br>Code | MON | TUES | WED | THURS | FRI | TOTAL |
|---|---|---|---|---|---|---|---|---|
|  |  |  |  |  |  |  |  |  |
|  |  |  |  |  |  |  |  |  |
|  |  |  |  |  |  |  |  |  |
|  |  |  |  |  |  |  |  |  |
|  |  |  |  |  |  |  |  |  |
|  |  |  |  |  |  |  |  |  |
|  |  |  |  |  |  |  |  |  |
|  |  |  |  |  |  |  |  |  |
|  |  |  |  |  |  |  |  |  |
|  |  |  |  |  |  |  |  |  |

| Int. Acc.<br>Code | Internal Activity Details | MON | TUES | WED | THURS | FRI | TOTAL |
|---|---|---|---|---|---|---|---|
| 2 |  |  |  |  |  |  |  |
| 0 |  |  |  |  |  |  |  |
| 0 |  |  |  |  |  |  |  |
|  |  |  |  |  |  |  |  |
| 3 |  |  |  |  |  |  |  |
| 0 |  |  |  |  |  |  |  |
| 0 |  |  |  |  |  |  |  |
|  |  |  |  |  |  |  |  |
| 440 |  |  |  |  |  |  |  |
| 640 |  |  |  |  |  |  |  |
| TOTAL (both sections) |  |  |  |  |  |  |  |

# Chapter 5.   Devising a practice development strategy and plan

'It is better to leave the future open to error than to leave it open to chance.'

Peter Drucker

It is always unwise to discuss the creation of a practice development strategy and the appropriate planning system for its implementation divorced from the context of the firm's total activity. To do so is to create an unreal, indeed a dangerous, situation. In a professional practice the total activity which is the equivalent to corporate strategy of a company can be defined as the pattern of objectives, purposes or goals and major policies and plans for achieving these goals, stated in such a way as to define what business the firm is in or is to be in and the kind of practice it is or is to be. Practice development decisions and their methods of implementation are only a sub-section of the firm's total planning activity and they must be compatible with that activity. It is important that they are seen this way.

While the strategies are considered in isolation in this chapter their inter-connection with, and relevance to, the firm's overall plans must be constantly kept in view.

## Strategies and tactics: a differentiation

Considerable confusion exists between strategy and tactics. It is confusion that occurs in almost all business activities. Military definitions (strategies are the deployment of forces in a war situation to defeat an enemy in pursuit of goals prescribed by leaders of state) and political definitions (the application of national resources to accomplish national goals) provide a starting point for distinguishing strategic and tactical plans and actions. In a business, strategy might be defined as the creation and implementation of plans, devised to accomplish long-term objectives and, as such, they are likely to induce major changes in the relationship between the firm, its clients and the competitive environment. Tactics are concerned with activities directed to achieve short-term objectives.

However, 'short' and 'long' terms are relative to total time spans, and can be interpreted in many ways. For some activities, if defined on a time continuum, it becomes arguable as to whether they are, in fact, strategic or tactical.

The individual practice development functions, with the exception of new 'service' development, tend to be applied tactically rather than strategically, since they are usually directed to achieve short-term aims; the fee scale objectives may be to obtain a firmer foothold among a particular client type; the merchandizing to develop revenue for a specific part of the service 'mix'; and the public relations campaign to obtain credibility in a particular activity. Even if all three were directed to obtaining more business in the long term, they remain tactical in that long-term fee or profit objectives may themselves be directed to achieve the strategic objective of, say, a given return on investment.

The concept of practice development strategy differs somewhat in the way it is undertaken from the way it is propounded in marketing literature. It tends to break down into two or three generally accepted groupings: (a) segmentation, the selection of the targets; (b) the 'mix' of communication tools and methods, that is the combination of various activities; and (c) the 'mix' of services. Service 'mix' it can be argued, is a separate strategy but its impact on the practice expansion is so pervasive that a strong case can be made out of its inclusion as one of the basic components. The advantage of treating it as part of the overall strategy and not separately is that it makes compatibility with the total plan that much more certain.

The most difficult of questions to resolve is inherent in the very blurred lines between strategic and tactical decisions; that is, should the long-term strategies be adhered to or should adjustment be made in the light of the reality revealed by the short-term tactical operations? There can be strong arguments for resolutely pursuing the stated objectives through the selected strategies and for rational adjustment to reach attainable targets. While it is absurd not to make adjustments in the light of changes which have occurred, it is equally unwise to abandon long-term strategic targets and policies in response to each variation from the anticipated results or the agreed approaches. Because tactics are essentially short term and flexible, it is these that should be modified to ensure the master strategy can be maintained so long as the objectives remain realizable. The adjustment in tactics will inevitably alter the communication 'mix' which must always be most sensitive and responsive to change.

## Practice development plan

Strategies and their components can be considered in a most practical way within the context of the planning document. The complexities of planning have all too often been over-elaborated by those with a vested interest in planning. There has also grown up the myth that within small organizations planning is an unnecessary, time-consuming and expensive luxury that is made superfluous because of the short lines of communication and considerable flexibility inherent in small organizations. Both these extreme views are invalid for the professional practice. Planning is fundamentally a simple process and is really only concerned with taking decisions at a moment in time that will position a firm where it wishes to be at another moment in time.

There are a number of options a firm can adopt. They can be summed up as either 'adaptive', that is reacting to external and internal changes as they occur—a totally opportunistic approach, or they can follow a pre-determined course which attempts to influence favourably a number of key variables.[1]

While there is no denying the success of many firms and individuals who have an undefinable but instinctive reaction to situations, for the majority of people a plan is a far less speculative method of ensuring a profitable direction to any attempts to expand a practice. Indeed, even the instinctive and entrepreneural practitioner would benefit from some form of structuring of his visceral methods into an ordered and methodical approach. Thus planning is not a substitute for management decisions, risk taking or flair but a way of extending the value of these and of ensuring that the firm is sensitive to and influential within the environment in which it must operate.

1. John Winkler. *Winkler on Marketing Planning*. Associated Business Programmes (London, 1974), pp. 46–47.

The headings for an easily implemented plan can be reduced to some seven aspects. More sophisticated and complex headings are almost invariably unnecessary.

1. **External situation analysis**  List relevant and significant facts about the clients, competition, economic, technical, social and governmental trends impacting on the demand for the service and the services themselves.
2. **Problems, opportunities and vulnerabilities**  From **external situation analysis** above identify issues which are problems to be avoided or opportunities to be exploited.
3. **Objectives**  Statement of purpose of the plan in quantitative and qualitative terms and over a stipulated time period.
4. **Strategy**  The general approach to the achievement of the targets (usually three to five year plan).
5. **Tactics**  Methods, tools, message, media to be adopted for the achievement of the objectives (usually a 12 month plan).
6. **Resources (budgets)**  Specify resources (including financial) required to fulfil the plan's objectives or apportion fixed resource to each section of the plan.
7. **Evaluation and control**  Methods for assessing effectiveness of tactics and controls for adjustment.

The re-cycling of objectives, opportunities, strategies, tactics and resources to the point at which an optimum position is achieved, may seem to be inordinately time consuming and difficult. If it is incorporated into a system which is itself logical and uncomplicated the whole process can be set in train without it becoming an activity in its own right—always a danger—or drawing away time and skills which could be applied more usefully or profitably elsewhere in the practice.

## 1. External situation analysis[2]

This need be no more than a profile of the factors which impact on practice development. A full market audit is not required but there should be at least an overview of the dispositions within the environment in which the firm operates or wishes to operate. Everything of course depends on the amount of information available, since many professional firms' activities are on a very local basis and there is little likelihood of detailed data being available at this micro level.

The type of information which is easily obtainable and assimilable is nevertheless likely to cover a considerable spectrum of activity and, as such, needs to be carefully considered as to its role in the strategy development and the plan itself. The acquisition and analysis of information which makes no direct contribution is wasteful of time, money and talent and is de-motivating. Therefore the planner needs to be highly discriminating in his demand and search for information.[3]

Information is a most valuable resource and nowhere does it make a greater contribution to the expansion of the practice than its utilization in the firm's plans. By way of example the type of information and data that is likely to be relatively easily and quickly obtainable and, as importantly, assimilable is as follows. Many of the items listed may require explanations. These will be given in the appropriate chapters to follow but notably Chapter 8, 'Professional

2. The external situation must of course be aligned to the resource analysis specified in Chapter 4, 'Preparing for practice development', to give an accurate situation analysis.
3. See Chapter 17, 'Non-personal methods of practice development'. Market research, pages 213–15.

services and the commercial client', Chapter 9, 'How a professional service is selected', Chapter 10, 'How the individual practice is selected', Chapter 12, 'The importances of images and perceptions' and Chapter 16, 'The use of personal contact'.

- Data derived from internal and desk research analyses (see Chapter 4, 'Preparing for practice development')
  - numbers and trend in population of potential clients
  - frequency and timing of utilization of the firm's services.
- Data derived from client and prospective client contacts such as
  - requirements for services (by types and quality of service)
  - desirable service features
  - methods used by clients for locating suitable practices
  - factors considered in the choice of a professional adviser
  - methods of purchasing the service (commercial clients)
  - critical factors for service
  - referral sources used
  - benefits sought
  - job functions of decision makers (commercial clients)
  - identification of key clients and key referral sources
  - methods of communications and media to which potential clients are exposed.
- Data derived from competitors and from own and clients' experience of their activities
  - numbers of direct and indirect competitors
  - any advantages held by competing firms—staff quality and numbers, location, links with clients, fees, range of services, warranties, financial strength, reputation and image, etc.
  - any weaknesses of competitive firms
  - estimate of competitors' market share by client types
  - extent and quality of practice development
  - extent to which competitive firms are known to the relevant publics.
- Data derived from the market conditions
  - trends likely to stimulate or inhibit demand for specific services
  - general level of quality of personal and corporate life
  - changes in technology impacting on clients, prospective clients and the firm
  - legislation affecting type or strength of demand
  - availability to the firm of specific skills at cost-effective salary levels
  - impact of government activity and legislation
  - public's attitude to the profession as a whole
  - effect of changes in the composition of the service range.

This is a simplified outline list and every firm will need to develop its own based on the specific service and markets as well as the objectives of the practice and its personnel.[4]

## 2. Problems, opportunities and vulnerabilities

Few firms have any difficulty in identifying problems although they are not always so successful in identifying the more fundamental ones. Opportunities and vulnerabilities are

4. The check list referred to in the previous chapter (footnote 6), Aubrey Wilson's *Marketing Audit Check Lists*, is broken down into numerous function-related sub-headings and will give the strategist and planner a much more detailed structure for selecting useful information items, op. cit. particularly Lists 1, 4, 6, 8, 13, 16 and 17.

more difficult to focus on. Clearly a book devoted to the principles of practice development cannot be specific in identifying each issue. It can only point to ways of ensuring that this important step in strategy development and realization is not overlooked and that the findings are incorporated into the strategy and the plans.

Two techniques, both developed by SRI (Stanford Research Institute) of Menlo Park, California, provide simple and quick methods for obtaining the profiles needed and have the further advantage of involving others in the firm besides the strategist/planner with the obvious benefits this in turn implies. Additionally, these techniques will make a contribution to completing the 'external situation analysis' referred to above.

The first of the techniques is known by the acronym of SOFT (*S*trength *O*pportunity *F*ault *T*hreat) and simply requires members of the practice to identify single issues under each heading listed in Figure 5-1 with references, sources and facts and asking for a range of possible actions or resource requirements. This will usually produce a consensus of views but even a single statement can make a valuable input previously overlooked. Any patterning of response should provide action indications to exploit or avoid a situation.

(PLEASE USE ONE FORM FOR EACH POINT RAISED)
THE FOLLOWING IS ONE FACTOR IN OUR FIRM'S FUTURE

1. NAME _____ JOB TITLE _____

2. THIS ISSUE REFERS TO A: (TICK ONE ONLY)

    STRENGTH ☐        OPPORTUNITY ☐

    FAULT ☐        THREAT ☐

    IN OUR (TICK ONE ONLY)

    FEE AND/OR NON-FEE EARNING STAFF ☐

    ADMINISTRATION AND/OR MANAGEMENT ☐

    CLIENTS ☐

    LOCATION OR PHYSICAL FACILITIES ☐

    RANGE AND/OR QUALITY OF SERVICES ☐

    OTHER (SPECIFY) _____ ☐

3. DESCRIPTION OF STATEMENT OR POINT

4. REFERENCES, SOURCES OR FACTS

5. RANGE OF POSSIBLE ACTION OR RESOURCE REQUIREMENTS

**Figure 5-1**  SOFT analysis

The second technique is 'vulnerability analysis'.[5] Vulnerability analysis substitutes a precise and disciplined methodology for emotional or even hysterical reactions to emerging threats or, at the opposite extreme, a 'don't let's look, it might go away' philosophy.

The concept of vulnerability analysis is simple. It commences with the identification of those factors, circumstances, resources which must exist, or not exist, for a firm to operate successfully. At its simplest and using a 'people resource' as an example, if there were no new

5. This summary is based on the work of Douglas A. Hurd, *Vulnerability Analysis in Business Planning*, SRI (Menlo Park, California, 1977) and Douglas A. Hurd and E. Riggs Monfort, 'Vulnerability analysis: a new way to assess future trends'. *Planning Review* (Dayton, Ohio, November 1979). The author is grateful to the originators of the technique and to SRI for permission to adapt and reproduce it.

entrants into a profession, a practice must eventually cease. Thus a supply of suitably qualified personnel is (or could be) an underpinning of that practice.

Some 12 critical factors have been identified, not of all which apply to professional services, and of course there may be others specific to professional services which have not been identified.

(a) *Needs and wants*—traditionally applied almost exclusively to clients but necessarily must be extended to stakeholder's groups in firms.
(b) *Resources*—refers to all people, physical assets, materials and services employed in running a practice.
(c) *Relative costs*—the relationship of a firm's key cost elements with those of competitors.
(d) *Client base*—this relates to the number and composition of the client base.
(e) *Technology*—this concerns technologies which impact on the services in the way they are performed and by whom performed.
(f) *Special abilities*—the ability of one firm significantly to outperform its competition in certain ways.
(g) *Identifying symbols*—logos and other means whereby the client's services are identified.
(h) *Artificial barriers to competition*—various laws and regulations which eliminate markets or exclude competitors.
(i) *Social values*—those clusters of social values which create demand for specific services.
(j) *Sanctions and supports*—the enabling permission or public endorsement given to professions by governments and other groups.
(k) *Integrity*—the basic trust a client places in a service.
(l) *Complementary products*—products and services which are essential to the performance of the services.

The firm must identify which of the underpinnings relate to its own activities. It certainly will not be all or indeed many of those listed. The key test is whether, if the identified underpinning were removed, the practice would cease to be able to operate, or could only be operated under the most adverse and unsatisfactory conditions.

The next stage is for all those engaged in the vulnerability analysis exercise to identify the threats which could attack the underpinnings. Here the imagination need not be bounded by what is likely so much as by what is possible.

Individuals are invited to consider each threat and to locate them on a grid in terms of the likelihood of their occurring (horizontal axis) and the severity of their impact (vertical axis). Figure 5-2 illustrates one person's assessment of ten different threats.

A consensus is then taken of each threat by grouping on to one matrix the judgements of the individuals involved in the exercise. If there are wide disparities of views, each person is asked to give the basis for the position he has allotted the threat, and, through re-cycling, a Delphi forecast is produced. The same grid is used both for the individual personal assessments and the consensus results.

The grid containing the consensus for each threat can then be segmented to isolate them so that the appropriate actions can follow. Figure 5-3 divides the grid into three sections. Threats in Crescent 'A' require immediate, urgent avoiding strategies. Crescent 'B' threats must be subject to contingency planning so that if they move either upward making them more dangerous or to the right whereby the risk of their occurring becomes greater, no delay will occur in dealing with them. Crescent 'C' calls for monitoring of any threats within it to be ready to reconsider their significance and any actions necessary should their position change.

Vulnerability analysis is a simple exercise and combined with the SOFT analysis will give a reliable profile for this second stage of strategy formation and market planning.

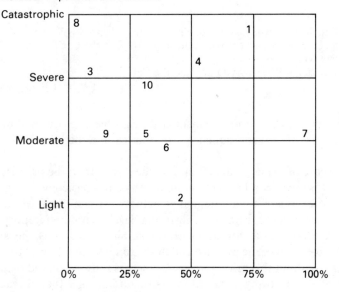

**Figure 5-2** Vulnerability analysis—threat assessment (showing one person's assessment of 10 different threats)

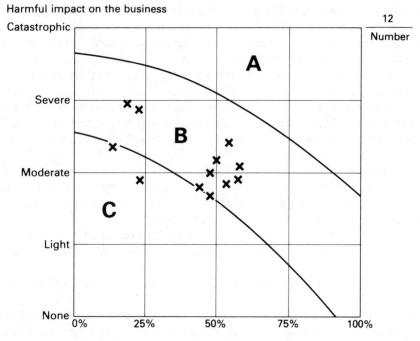

**Figure 5-3** Vulnerability analysis (showing composite of evaluations for sample threat)

51

# 3. Objectives

'Would you tell me, please, which way I ought to go from here?'
'That depends a good deal on where you want to get to' said the Cat
'I don't much care where' said Alice
'Then it doesn't matter which way you go' said the Cat.

*(Alice in Wonderland,* Lewis Carroll)

Nothing could be more true. Without realistic and clear objectives the method and the route to their achievement is of no consequence, since it cannot be known if they have been accomplished.

Objectives, the core of managerial action, provide direction to the practice development by defining targets. Objectives can be stated in many ways, but basically they group into time or scope dimensions, or relate to a designated activity within the firm. Objectives can be expressed for any functional area or organizational level considered important as well as for the firm itself. A pre-requisite for developing suitable strategies is the acceptance by all concerned of the objectives of the practice and of the route to be followed to achieve these over a given time scale. Without this prior agreement, there is little likelihood of any strategy being successful or of objectives being achieved in a structured rather than a reactive manner.

The setting of objectives is best accomplished in four stages, but the importance of a disciplined approach to objective setting and of devising a system which will achieve them, cannot be overstated.

The first stage is to decide precisely what business the professional service firm is in. The importance and relevance of this step was emphasized and explained in Chapter 3, 'Creating a client-centred practice', page 25. The merchant banks, which have grown over two centuries from their origins of being merchants and bankers financing the world-wide movement of goods, may now see their role in an environment where tranditional lines of demarcation in financial services are becoming increasingly blurred as either greater specialization in traditional fields, for example trade-related financing, short-term lending and corporate finance and investment advisory services, or they may offer aids for achieving higher financial productivity which covers a very much wider spectrum. The conceptualization of the content and application of the services offered is fundamental to objective setting. A generic definition of the services offered is a necessary precondition to establishing practical objectives and targets as well as for market planning.

Next, the broad objectives of the firm must be related to key-result areas, that is those in which success is vital to the firm, and which can be measured, preferably against quantified objectives. Revenue generated by each practitioner, improved profit performance or wider geographical coverage are examples of key-result areas.

This is followed by the setting of sub-objectives to accomplish the practice's broad objective—for example, higher fee volume, wider client base, and the development of new services.

The final stage is the use of the designated key-result areas to serve as yardsticks for the sub-objectives.

The last two steps are re-cycled until specific objectives have been created for all those involved in practice development including the lower levels of management. Sub-objectives must be checked for inconsistencies and conflicts, horizontally with sub-objectives of other parts or activities of the firm and vertically with the broader objectives.

It is always easiest to commence with the general objectives which will emerge easily from the external situation analysis and review of problems, opportunities and vulnerabilities.

Quantification and detail are more simply and realistically added as the plan is developed. Examples of specific objectives are:

- Increase fee income to £... by 19??.
- Identify and concentrate on key clients.
- Introduce new services to account for ? per cent of fee income by 19??.
- Improve conversion rate of enquiries to quotations (or presentations) to assignments.
- Widen knowledge of the practice to targeted 'publics'.
- Increase the number of clients for each (or specified) service(s).
- Extend and increase activity of referral sources.
- Develop services with anti-cyclical demand characteristics.
- Achieve improved image profile.
- Reduce identified vulnerabilities.
- Improve ratio of new to repeat instructions.
- Identify blockages to progress.
- Increase billable time by ... per cent.
- Improve ratio of commercial to private clients.
- Open ... new offices by 19??.

The implication so far is that all objectives have the same time span. This is clearly impractical, and while they can be divided between the overriding purpose of the organization and the sub-goals which make up the hierarchy of objectives, they will require to be classified into short-, medium- and long-term goals. Just what these time spans mean in weeks, months or years depends upon the scope of the overall plan but, typically, short term will be within 12 months, medium two to three years and long term up to five years. The level of speculation beyond five years, given the inaccuracy of forecasting in present turbulent times, makes detailed planning beyond five years unrealistic. However, all plans should be 'rolling' so that the five year 'end of plan' period is constantly moved forward and the programme adjusted in accordance with any changed internal and ambient conditions and resources.

All objectives should be ambitious enough to stretch the capacity, capabilities and energy of those within a practice charged with expanding it and who will be held responsible for the successful achievement of the plans. Equally they must not be so unrealistic as to be demotivating in the sense that they are unachievable and therefore not worth striving for.

## 4. Strategy

It is not sensible to define specific strategies which can be taken either wholly or piecemeal and applied to any particular service or circumstance. What is required is an understanding of precisely what comprises practice development strategies and their different types. A grasp of these essentials enables them to be developed and implemented. Then, within its framework, it is possible to define appropriate tactical inputs and apply the correct combination of practice development tools. Thus practice development or marketing strategy—there is no difference despite the nomenclature—has three basic elements:

- Segmentation—the division of the total potential for the practice's offerings into homogeneous sub-segments sharing some common characteristics which enable the firm to concentrate its limited practice expansion resources on those segments most likely to fulfil its objectives.

- Service range—the group of services (core and satellite—see Chapter 2, 'Understanding service businesses') which it is necessary or desirable to offer to maximize the utilization of the firm's skills and experience and to achieve its objectives.
- Communication and content—'messages' to be used to convey to clients and prospective clients information on the practice and to develop favourable perceptions of it which are needed for clients to make decisions on the choice of professional advisers.

These basic elements of strategy influence and in turn will be influenced by a number of variables which move around the central strategy. It can be compared with a planetary system (see Figure 5-4).

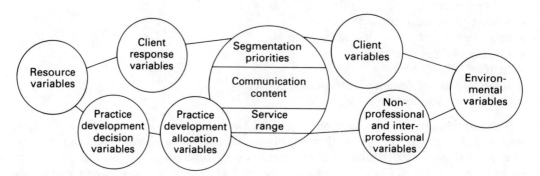

**Figure 5-4** The strategy 'planetary' system

These variables are:

- Client variables: the number of actual and prospective clients, their decision motives, needs and attitudes.
- Environmental variables: economic activity, social trends, governmental activities and technical innovations.
- Competitive variables: policies of other firms and other professional services offering similar and substitute services.
- Practice development variables: any factor under the control of the practice which may be used to increase revenue. These could include the 'mix' of services offered and the communication 'mix'.
- Practice development allocation variables: division of the firm's efforts among its different services, segments and geographical areas.
- Client response variables: fee income response to alternative levels, allocations and 'mixes' of practice development effort.
- Resource variables: availability of resources—personnel, finance, information, clients and referral sources, equipment and facilities, services offered.

The adoption of a practice development strategy requires the co-ordination of all marketing activities with a common objective—meeting the needs and wants of the clients. Nevertheless, the direction of a firm's activities to the satisfaction of these needs must be compatible with its resources and objectives, and it is this restraint which significantly alters the approach of practices offering similar or substitutable services in identical markets.

It is always worth while checking the strategy, once established, against clear criteria which will be wholly or partially applicable to all professional service firms and individual practitioners. A suggested list is:[6]

- Is the strategy identifiable and has it been specifically stated within the organization so that all participants understand it?
- Does the strategy fully exploit opportunities?
- Is the strategy consistent with the competence, skills, interests, qualifications and resources which the firm currently possesses or are projected?
- Are the major provisions of the strategy and programme for its implementation internally consistent?
- Are the risks involved feasible in financial and personal terms?
- Is the strategy compatible with the personal values and aspirations of key professionals in the firm?
- Is the strategy compatible with any desired level of contribution to the private or business community?
- Does the strategy give a strong stimulant to organizational effort and commitment?

A fuller check list covering more detail of the planning process will be found in Appendix A at the end of this chapter.

The three elements of strategy are now considered separately:

## Segmentation

The definition of a segmentation given above is best appreciated from a simple model. Each circle in Figure 5-5 represents the 'universe' and the dots the actual and prospective client groups the service is aimed at. Circle (a) treats the total potential as homogeneous, recognizing no differences between each unit in it. This is an unbelievably wasteful approach given that the units in it are unlikely, as is implied, to be similar. Circle (b) approaches the market as though every unit was unique in some way and there is no commonality between them. This is equally wasteful. Circle (c) divides the universe in the example given by income groups thus enabling the service, if it was for instance a financial one, to direct its offering to the group which is most appropriate: (1) in the circle might be the mass market; (2) the middle market; and (3) the wealthy individual market. A portfolio management service would clearly be of the highest value and attraction to wealthy individuals, less so for the middle market and of no value at all for the mass market.

Circle (d) creates another division, this time by age group: (i) might be under 40 and (ii) over 40. Again portfolio management is likely to be more attractive to the older age groups both because of accumulated resources and because of a greater prudence in investment likely to occur with maturity. Circle (e) is a double segmentation dividing the potential both by income class and age group. Top priority segment for a portfolio management service would now be the 'over 40 wealthy individuals', circle section (ii) 3, followed by the 'under 40 wealthy individuals', circle section (i) 3, with perhaps the over 40 middle income group third, (ii) 2. From this description it can be seen how it is possible to focus sharply the message on specified groups and to use the media, message and methods appropriate to them.

Apart from enabling the practice to concentrate on those types of potential and active clients which will most likely enable the firm to fulfil its objectives, there are two further basic purposes of segmentation. First, to differentiate the services from all others, thus creating a special and selective demand for the services differentiated, and, second, to offer what is a

6. Adapted from E. P. Learned, C. R. Christensen, K. R. Andrews and W. D. Guth. *Business Policy—Texts and Cases.* Irwin (Homewood, Ill., 1969), pp. 22–25.

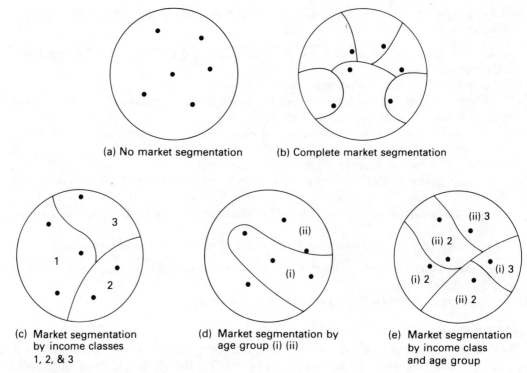

(a) No market segmentation

(b) Complete market segmentation

(c) Market segmentation
by income classes
1, 2, & 3

(d) Market segmentation by
age group (i) (ii)

(e) Market segmentation
by income class
and age group

**Figure 5-5** Examples of segmentation criteria

direct appeal to particular segments of the total market which at present purchases services according less closely to its requirements than the differentiated service. The criteria for segmentation will vary from firm to firm, but the starting point must be the identification of the firm's strengths and resources (see Chapter 4, 'Preparing for practice development'), since a segmentation strategy not based on strength cannot succeed. The other major consideration is 'need identification'. At some point the two must meet if segmentation is to work. It may be necessary to build strengths and resources to fill the need or to seek to educate or persuade the clients of professional services or practitioners to modify their needs to make the services offered acceptable.

While it is perfectly possible for a service firm or individual to prosper within a single and narrow segment, for most there will be a number of segments with differing degrees of attractiveness. These must be ordered in priority so that resources can be concentrated on the top-priority groups, moving to lower priorities only when penetration of those more highly rated has been achieved.

The advantages of intelligently applied segmentation policies are that they enable a firm to focus firmly on its target clients' group and to direct its practice activities to the group. The benefit to the service firm is optimization of resource use and in image terms is considerable.

Figure 5-6 lists a number of suggested criteria for consideration by any practice. It is emphasized that the list is far from complete. Moreover the final segmentation will usually be a combination of a number of criteria. For example a structural surveyor might define his target group as 'large organizations with multi-site operations'. These might be multiple stores or transport depot operators. Thus the criteria used are (a), (d), (f) and (h). A patent agent might seek business from large firms with a strong innovative history in a specified technology. He would therefore be using the parameters created by (c), (e), (f), (h) and (i).

| | Business clients | Private clients |
|---|:---:|:---:|
| (a) Geographical | x | x |
| (b) Demographic | x | x |
| (c) Operational methods of clients | x | |
| (d) Form of organization of clients | x | |
| (e) Specialization of the practice | x | x |
| (f) Size of client company | x | |
| (g) Extent of use of services | x | x |
| (h) Client activity/occupation | x | x |
| (i) Psychographic factors (life style) | x | x |
| (j) Benefit sought | x | x |
| (k) Seasonal utilization of service | x | x |
| (l) Size/value of matter or project | x | x |
| (m) Reasons for purchasing the service | x | x |
| (n) Activity function of decision maker | x | |
| (o) Referral source | x | x |
| (p) Need for full range of services | x | x |
| (q) Frequency of use | x | x |
| (r) Type of client problem | x | x |
| (s) New/old clients | x | x |
| (t) Age/sex/ethnic/religious/socio-economic group | | x |
| (u) Family size | | x |
| (v) Education | | x |

**Figure 5-6**  Segmentation bases

*Key clients*

The segmentation approaches suggested above clearly apply to potential clients rather than to existing clients. For existing clients the segmentations have been pre-empted which does not imply they are necessarily the best ones for the firm. With most business enterprises there are always clients or customers with little potential and who are either serviced with sub-normal profitability or even at a loss. Divestment of such clients is a difficult decision for historic business reasons and often, in professional services, for personal reasons. The ruthless shedding of unprofitable clients is never recommended both because it can be demoralizing for the professional staff and word-of-mouth comments can produce adverse perceptions of the professional firm. A decision to eliminate such clients may be better fulfilled by attribution rather than execution.

Every practice must, to operate effectively, identify its 'key' clients. These are either individuals or companies which bring to the practice the types of business or situations it seeks, with a frequency and at a level of profitability regarded as satisfactory. The simplest way to identify a key client is to calculate what impact the loss would have on the practice's business. If the effect on fee income is significant, then the client is indeed a key one. Obviously any practice development resources the professional firm may have are best directed to such firms recognizing at the same time that key clients represent a vulnerability as well as an opportunity.

It is obvious but worth stating that too small a number of clients, no matter how profitable or satisfactory they may be, exposes the practice to considerable risk when, as will inevitably happen over however long the period may be, one of such a group of clients either ceases to have need of the practice (removal, death) or changes their professional advisers. A static position relative to key clients is dangerous since it is also the harbinger of decline.

For key clients there must be retention planning which implies, apart from devoting more practice development resources to those clients, expansion of the services they could use (more of existing services or else new services) and the use of such clients as referral sources.

One of the most effective ways of ensuring client retention, and which in no way breaches professional rules on soliciting business, is to devise and maintain a reminder system which, with modern office aids, can become a very low cost, highly efficient practice development tool. What are the issues and matters about which clients would welcome reminders or advice? For some professions this is a valuable aid to the client as well as to practice development—medicine, law, accountancy, veterinary practitioners and many types of financial services—while for others the technique is not feasible—architecture, surveying, loss adjusting and assessing actuarial services. Each practice can best judge for itself just how far the reminder system will work for it and how appropriate it is for its clients. Where it is relevant it will be found that in many cases it will provide an on-going communication vehicle.

When a matter is ended and the file closed it is the work of moments to note and feed into the system the appropriate time when further activity may be needed. Clients never resent a *single* reminder (more could be interpreted as solicitation) and such activity demonstrates both the involvement and efficiency of the practice.

*Other clients*
There will of course be other clients whose loss, while not causing any critical problems for the firm, would nevertheless be considered more than averagely disadvantageous. These clients and those who are currently unimportant but hold potential will also require nurturing but perhaps at a lower level than those of identified key clients. The apportionment of scarce practice development resources between these two groups cannot be a single mechanistic decision but must be dynamic and responsive to changing conditions within the practice and among the clients themselves.

Profit and loss must be seen as including the opportunity costs of devoting resources to firms of this type and the yield such resources would produce if applied to clients with higher potential prospects.

The decision as to which clients have future potential is entirely judgemental and each firm must accept that it will not always make the correct categorization. The important thing is for it to be right more frequently than it is wrong and this will be achieved only if there is a lively awareness within a practice of the client's situation, activities and plans.

A quick check list for client retention policy relative to segmentation priorities is as follows:

**Client retention check list**

- Is client retention important?
- What percentage of total fees comes from existing clients?
- How is it known if a client is non-active or lost?
- If the answer to the first question is 'yes' but answers 2 and 3 cannot be given without further investigation, what is the reason?
- What information is kept on existing clients?
- How is it gathered?
- Who uses it?
- How often?
- Is information kept up to date? How frequently and by what method?
- What methods can be used to maintain, monitor and improve client relations?

## Range of services

The second component of the marketing strategy is the service range; that it is precisely what services should be offered. While, for example, it was unthinkable 30 years ago that an accountancy firm would provide anything other than accountancy activities, the development of management services (e.g., consultancy, executive search) capability by a number of accountancy practices is now accepted as a logical, if sometimes controversial, addition to their service 'mix'. Similar developments in banking and architecture can also be easily identified. The introduction of a range as opposed to a single service, whether through opportunistic growth or as a deliberate and planned policy, is always a significant strategic decision.

It is perhaps in deciding the range of services to be offered that the core and satellite service concept explained in Chapter 2, 'Understanding service businesses', becomes clearer. While the basic purpose of the practice must never be compromised the augmentation of that basic service is an important part of the strategic development.

The inter-relationship of segmentation and service range policies is obvious since the availability of a given service may pre-empt the segmentation decision and the opposite is also true. The development of an appropriate service strategy is dealt with in depth in Chapter 6, 'Deciding the service offering of the practice'.

## Communication content

The decision on the audience to be addressed will have been taken when the segmentations have been agreed. The third element in the strategy is the decision concerning what types of 'message' or information will be conveyed to the target audiences. These 'messages' will have the strongest influence on clients and prospective clients' perceptions of the practice; its competences, personnel, experience, attitudes and other image factors which in turn will have a pervasive influence on the numbers and types of clients who will be attracted and held. The 'message' will position the firm within the profession, area or activity it is involved in so that a 'message' which does not attract the target audience can be said to have failed.

Positioning is a strategic decision of seminal importance. It will influence not only how successful the firm will be with its chosen audience but just what methods and media would be appropriate to adopt. Moreover it is not just the content of any message which will form the perceptions but the way which it is presented. There are, after all, many ways of expressing the same thing which may attract and convince one client but can have the opposite effect on another.

The form and content of the information the practice wishes to convey has to be settled as a strategic, not a tactical, issue and its inter-relationship with the segmentation and service range decisions is obvious. All must be compatible.

The information that is conveyed to the potential and actual clients will, of course, vary by the profession or discipline, the firm's objectives and other factors. However, it can be said with certainty that ideally the 'message' should clearly convey the benefits which will accrue to the user of a service by the selection of that service and the particular practice. Any decision to use a professional firm, knowingly or not, will be based on the client's perception of the benefits he will receive as well as the normal economic consideration of the alternative use of the moneys involved. The 'message' is after all crucial in expanding a practice since it has to register with the potential client, has to be understandable, relevant and believable, but above all it has to convey to the prospective client enough favourable information to move him towards the decision to retain the practice. This is explained in Chapter 7, 'Professional services and client needs'.

## 5. Tactics

Tactics, as has already been emphasized, are concerned with short-term goals and while these may be related to the three basic strategic issues, segmentation, service range and communication content, they tend, so far as professional practices are concerned, to be concentrated on the incorporation, timing and use of communication methods and media.

The choice for professional service companies in many disciplines is very much more limited than for non-professional services or products but none the less remains wide and will be considered in detail in Chapter 16, 'The use of personal contact', and Chapter 17, 'Non-personal methods of practice development'. Among the many methods which may be adopted to expand a practice, at least some of the following are available to all professions and a good number of them to most professions, even those where strict control is exercised. The most frequently used techniques in the majority of professional practices are in italics.

| | |
|---|---|
| *Personal contact* | *Directories/year books* |
| Telephone contact | *Financial incentives and aids* |
| Media advertising | Reciprocal arrangements |
| *Public and press relations* | *Direct mail (including newsletters)* |
| *Merchandising techniques* | *Distribution (branch networks)* |
| *Brochures* | Sponsorships (events, books, academic) |
| Fee strategies | Audio/visual material |
| 'Full line' of services | *Inter-personal network (referrals)* |
| Support services | Secondments |
| Marketing research | Competitions |
| *Presentations* | Educational campaigns |
| Client training | *Inward visits* |

The more important of the methods listed are described and their relevance, with examples of their use in professional services, will be found in Chapter 16, 'The use of personal contact', and, Figure 17-1 of Chapter 17, 'Non-personal methods of practice developments'.

The tactical decisions to be made concern which techniques will be used, when they will be used, how they will be used and where they will be used. These decisions, of course, emerge from the basic strategic decisions and have to be totally compatible with them in the sense that they will achieve not only the objectives set for the practice as a whole, but also the tactical goals such as greater 'visibility' at a given moment in time or under some specific circumstances.

## 6. Resource (budgets)

The final decision on which methods should be utilized will be based on a number of factors, not the least of which will be the resources available. Chapter 15, 'Guidelines for the choice of practice development methods', reviews the considerations involved as well as budgeting methods, Figure 15-2. A model of fee/budget ratio will be found in Figure 15-3.[7]

In Chapter 4, 'Preparing for practice development', it was stated that an audit of internal resources available for practice development was necessary. Some of these resources were listed and explained but in summary they can be stated as:

- People—skills, experience, interests, qualifications, contacts.
- Information—internal and environmental.
- Infrastructure and hardware.
- Finance.
- Systems.
- Clients and referral sources.
- Images and perceptions of the practice.
- Range of services available.

If this audit has been undertaken then an inventory exists and the decisions to be taken can be related to how much and at what period in time they can be released for practice development purposes.

It is here that the overall needs of the firm must be aligned to the requirements for practice development since it cannot be sensible to denude it of resources required for other parts of its operation.

There is one resource input about which it is possible to be precise, indeed dogmatic. This concerns the appointment of a person within the firm to be responsible for practice development activities. Such an appointment is without question necessary if practice development after an initial burst of enthusiasm is not to atrophy. Whether the appointment is to be a full-time activity or an agreed part of that person's available time is a decision for the individual practice to make. Either way the appointment has to be made, a job specification written (see Chapter 4, 'Preparing for practice development', Appendix A for guidelines on specification writing) and action initiated with regular progress checks.


## 7. Evaluation and control

Some measurement of total performance, as well as of the performance of components of the practice development activity, is required. The final part of the practice development plan is the incorporation of methods for evaluating the unfolding progress of the plan and for controlling or introducing variances.

There is little point in setting up complex monitoring and detailed measuring systems if there is no intention of attempting to control the phenomenon reported. Performance must be seen as comparative, that is: comparison with the stated objectives and how far they have been achieved; comparison with the methods devised to achieve the objectives and how these methods have been realized; comparison with competitive performance; and, finally, comparison with the performance of the market as a whole. It is not without significance that measurement (or monitoring) and control are almost invariably grouped together in books on marketing. They are insolubly linked because control cannot be effective without standards of performance.

---

7. An extremely useful guide to budget setting and resource allocation although needing adjustment to professional service activities will be found in John Stapleton's *How to Prepare a Marketing Plan*, 2nd edn. Gower Press (Farnborough, 1974), Section 13, pp. 172–183.

Aside from the achievement of objectives there are other criteria for developing and for evaluating standards of performance. They group conveniently under the headings:

- Profit.
- Costs.
- Market share.
- Fees earned.

While in large concerns the marketing department can often be treated as accountable for profit or loss in its own right, it would be rare to find such an arrangement applying to practice development in the professional service firm. Nevertheless, the contribution activities to develop the practice make to total profitability requires assessment, if only because of the essentially variable nature of practice development costs. The ability of a firm to measure profitability in its operations, as distinct from the total profitability of the firm, will vary with the firm's size, the complexity of its operations, and the range of services offered. For small practices, there is ample evidence to show that the administrative and accounting methods it is necessary to install to measure and control performance are often out of all proportion to the results achieved. For professional services' firms (and not ignoring the need for at least an outline idea of profit contribution), measurement and control may be achieved through cost control.

Cost control is a necessary operating objective of any firm. One way in which it tries to achieve its profit objectives is to administer its expenditure to get the maximum results from the cost it incurs. Practice development activities, which stem from the strategy, must be subject to cost accounting procedure to enable management to make periodic comparisons of costs in terms of the specific origins of these costs. The statement can be used both as a standard of performance and as an instrument of cost control. A comparison of costs over a period of time, and also with averages for the profession as a whole (where these are available) is one of the more conventional ways to approach the measurement and control of performance.

A frequently used standard of measurement of the success of any practice development strategy and overall effectiveness is market share; the use of this criterion is not without its critics. A decline in a total market may leave a company with a smaller fee volume, but the same or even increased percentage of total business available. Another objection is that market share analysis ignores the profit element of the operation. The fact that market share analyses do not incorporate profit studies means that they cannot be combined with profit/cost analyses in attempts to achieve some correlation. The advantages of market share studies as a measure of performance, aside from the fact that they are relatively simple and easy to understand and provide a common basis for comparing one firm with another, are that in appraising performance they largely avoid the problem of accountability for forces over which the service firm has no control, and thus relate largely to the firm's performance and effectiveness in whatever conditions exist.

But knowing market share requires knowing market size, usually an expensive marketing research enquiry, the results of which are not proportionate to its cost. Market share as a measure of performance does not, for most professional service firms, have any real significance and since, as has been commented earlier, it can usually be said of the market as a whole it is 'big enough', the cost of obtaining and monitoring market share is generally not commensurate to the use to which the data can be applied, particularly when there are better indicators of performance.

It is probably a combination of factors rather than a single aspect which for the individual firm will provide the optimum method for assessing the effectiveness of its practice development activities. However, there will have to be considerably more information on the size, structure, and trends of markets for individual services before measurement of performance will reach even the fairly crude standards achieved by the goods-producing industries.[8]

Obviously the reporting system must be capable of revealing the situation otherwise there can be no adjustment of activity or of the plan itself. Both the requirement for a touch on the tiller or a desperate grab at the wheel demands detailed recent and accurate information on just how the practice development is progressing and how individuals and techniques are performing. Each firm will need to develop its own signals. For example, in the short term, using the average time between an enquiry and a commission or instruction and the percentage of conversion to actual business as a comparison will indicate an imminent downturn or upturn in business. Where available inter-firm comparisons and professional norms may be a practical guide. For some practices there will be reliable 'lead–lag' indicators. New housing starts, which provide business for solicitors, financial institutions, possibly surveyors, estate agents as well as many trades, may be a macro indicator of demand.

A full check list of control information with suggested frequency of collection and dissemination, standards and methods of indicating variance as well as internal circulation can be adapted for the purpose of professional practices and will be found in Appendix B of this chapter. Control programmes which results from the implementation of the strategy, like control of any other management activity, should be a dynamic process responding to changes as they occur. In short, it is the continuous process by which management makes certain that the strategies are adopted, implemented, guided, or restrained to achieve the goals which they have been devised to attain. It cannot be effective if practised in a one-off or reactive way.

However, watching the results of a practice development plan unfold will not assist the situation unless a contingency plan exists against anticipated variances. Such a plan should identify actions which must be introduced in the short, medium or long term to exploit or avoid the consequences of any deviations from the plans or the assumptions on which they are based.

That is not to say that every variance must be countered. It is unwise to adjust the plan for short-term fluctuations or aberrations. It is the trend that must be observed closely and when confirmed acted on.

## Re-cycling the plan

The identification and evaluation of resources, whether they are fully exploited or not, will have been undertaken in the early stages of constructing the plan. It is now necessary to see if the most efficient use of the existing resources will enable the plan to be carried to fruition or if new resources be required. The decision facing the firm at this point is whether to re-cycle the objectives to bring them within the capability of available resources or to adjust the resources themselves.

One crude but useful check on the realism of objectives as compared to resources can be quickly applied by using what is termed 'gap analysis'. That is a surprise-free projection of present fee income or profit as compared to the hoped for results in, say, 5 years. The firm can forecast that if it continues to operate in the existing manner, its revenue (or profit) will probably reach a given level. This is illustrated in Figure 5-7. By superimposing the objectives

8. Further comments on market research related to size of markets will be found in Chapter 11, 'Identifying potential clients', pages 126–7, and Chapter 17, 'Non-personal methods of practice development'.

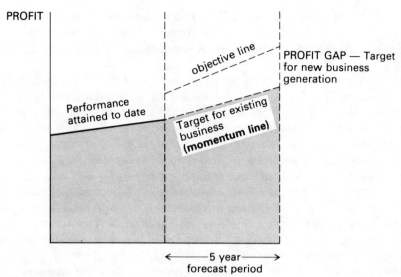

**Figure 5-7** The 'gap' analysis

on the projection it will indicate the extent to which business must be obtained to fulfil the target and also if the resources required to achieve the target level are or can be made available.

The same 'gap' analysis will also serve to alert firms to actions which must be taken if a deteriorating situation is to be countered (see Figure 5-8). A projection of present business under conditions of competition for work and for staff, inflation and changing technology and for the other on-going threats to any profession may indicate a downward trend in fees. The gap may relate to the practice holding its own rather than expanding.

As with all forecasting there can be no exactitude or certainty. It was rightly commented by

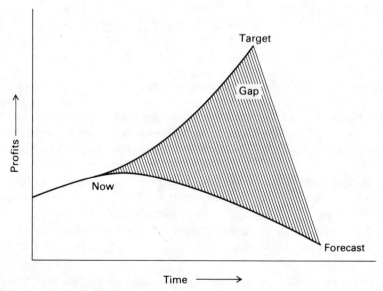

**Figure 5-8** 'Gap' analysis. Declining market

**64**

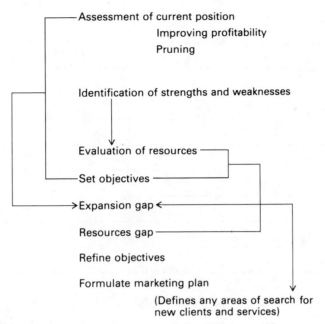

Assessment of current position
Improving profitability
Pruning

Identification of strengths and weaknesses

Evaluation of resources

Set objectives

Expansion gap

Resources gap

Refine objectives

Formulate marketing plan
(Defines any areas of search for
new clients and services)

**Figure 5-9**   The re-cycled plan

Herman Kahn that the only surprising thing about a surprise-free forecast is that if no surprise occurs! Obviously continual monitoring of the internal and external situation will be required if both target and resources are to remain realistic. The situation is summed up in Figure 5-9.

## Implementation

Creating a practice development strategy and incorporating it into an action plan must be an early activity for any firm seriously intent on expanding its business or even in maintaining its present position. It is however an immutable rule of planning no matter what the subject may be that plans atrophy unless the three important steps already referred to are incorporated into the planning process:

- Allocate.
- Schedule.
- Monitor.

Because within all practices personnel are under considerable pressure both from day-to-day requirements and unplanned circumstances and emergencies, there is always a valid reason for not undertaking an additional task whose outcome can only be evaluated in the medium or long term. There is a sort of Gresham's law of planning which says 'Today's events drive out tomorrow's activities'. A discipline must be introduced and the first rule of that discipline is that those who have volunteered or been instructed to perform any given task must do so.

Second, acceptance of a task does not ensure it will be completed by the required date. All tasks should be scheduled with a desirable and an absolutely final date for completion. The reality is that most people will not achieve the first or even second date, but nevertheless the

| Target group | Objective | Activity/ Media | Budget | Person responsible | Plan dead-line | Period | | | | | | | | | | | | Date of issue |
| | | | | | | Time-schedule | | | | | | | | | | | |
| | | | | | | Jan | Feb | Mar | Apr | May | Jun | Jul | Aug | Sep | Oct | Nov | Dec |
| | | | | | | | | | | | | | | | | | |
| | | | | | | | | | | | | | | | | | |
| | | | | | | | | | | | | | | | | | |
| | | | | | | | | | | | | | | | | | |
| | | TOTAL | | | | | | | | | | | | | | | |

**Figure 5-10**  Marketing action plan

| Report section Identification | Recommended actions | SUGGESTED TIME IMPERATIVES | | | | ACTION SEQUENCE | | |
| --- | --- | --- | --- | --- | --- | --- | --- | --- |
| | | At once | Short term (say 6 months) | Medium term (say 12 months) | Longer term (say 2 years +) | By whom | By when | Monitor |
| | | | | | | | | |

**Figure 5-11** Marketing action plan

67

existence of date will concentrate the mind and in the end produce the results if only because constant excuses are embarrassing to the professional.

Quality must of course be satisfactory. Just completing a required action is not necessarily a mark of its quality. The person whose task is to monitor must ensure that the work in hand has been undertaken and completed in the way it was envisaged.

*Allocating, scheduling* and *monitoring*. They cannot of course guarantee the plan will come together at the right time or will be of a high quality, but they do at least ensure that major mistakes are avoided.

Two planning formats are given in Figures 5-10 and 5-11. Suitably enlarged for actual use they will give a daily, weekly or monthly reminder of progress to the planner and those involved in the plan.


## Profile of the practice developer

The implication is, and all experience has proved it, unless there is a clearly defined function, usually allocated to one person, to lead the practice development activity, then it will either not occur, occur sporadically or ineffectually. If a policy decision is taken to develop and implement a practice development plan, then that decision must also include the appointment of a senior, authorative member of the firm to devise and implement the expansion plan. If this person is not himself the most senior in the practice, then he must be seen to have the unwavering support of the chief executive or senior partner and of all the stakeholders in the practice.

The practice development manager, officer, leader, or whatever title he may be given, is almost certain to be unsuccessful unless he has an enthusiasm and strong motivation for accepting and carrying through the assignment. Such motivation is of greater consequence than skills or experience in the activity. The latter are far more easily acquired than the former. It is relatively simple to learn the techniques but changing individuals' values is a task of far greater complexity.

Leading a practice development activity is not necessarily a full-time occupation. In the majority of cases there would be no need for the appointee to lose contact or terminate his involvement in professional work. What is required is self-discipline to ensure that any attachment to professional activities does not make inroads on the time which should be devoted to practice development activities.

The practice developer will regard himself rightly as a manager of his own personal service business within the firm. He will see himself in the dual role of maximizing profitable operations and at the same time satisfying his own personal aspirations.

Because the practice developer will be entrepreneurial as well as managerial he will concentrate on profitable clients and potentially profitable clients not just obtaining more business.

To fulfil these roles however, he has to have a degree of personal security in relationships with, and an understanding of, the firm and to possess the stakeholders, superiors, peers, subordinates and clients' confidence and to be able to know and understand what constitutes a 'profitable business'. The practice representative is essentially a planner, because he plans not only the individual contacts, but also his entire business relationship with his clients. The process of long-range profit planning is essential for practice development. It is through a planning partnership with his colleagues and clients that an integration can occur into commercial clients' business and into important aspects of the activities of private clients.

Finally, the practice developer is or should be an innovator. He will seek out needs for new services and new markets and actively preside over a combined client–professional approach to anticipating their needs and the means of satisfying them. He performs a long-term business or life management planning function; helps clients to identify their corporate and personal aspirations, maintains wide multi-function access inside commercial client companies, draws on the full complement of his firm's activities, resources, skills and services for his support.

The practice representative has the responsibility of closing the client–professional service firm communication loop substantially by developing strong, positive inter-personal links. He and his firm must recognize that the actual offering and purchasing of professional services is only one significant part of the total practice development.

# Appendix 5A   A check list for practice development planning[9]

1. What is current fee income and profitability?

   Is it identified according to work type, geographical location, etc.?
   Has it been analysed?
   How does current situation compare with objectives?

2. Does the firm have budgeting and management accounting procedures?

   In what form?
   Are overheads and marketing expenditure clearly identifiable?
   Is regular monthly monitoring undertaken?

3. Has a practice development plan been considered and a formal plan prepared?

   Is it up-to-date?
   Does it define agreed objectives?
   Are fee and profit targets defined?
   Do they allow for inflation?
   Which are the periods of consolidation and which of growth?
   Are individual objectives and tasks defined, allocated and monitored?
   Is the plan freely available to responsible staff?
   Is it generally understood, accepted and supported by all staff?
   If not, why not?
   Does the plan define priorities?
   Does it incorporate contingencies for failed objectives?

4. Does the firm need to develop new services and/or new markets?

   Why?
   Are there any current plans for such development?

   What is the basis of such plans? Are they justifiable?
   What are the gaps in resources needed for such development?
   Which are the targets—new clients, existing clients?

5. Do existing services satisfy objectives?

   Have all the opportunities for present services in existing markets been explored?
   Could increased productivity/efficiency improve situation and, if so, how?
   What do existing clients require that the firm cannot provide?
   Why have these requirements not been satisfied previously?

6. Are past and current work/clients systematically documented?

   Is the system easily accessible?
   Periodicity of repeat instructions or consultation?

7. Are all contacts with clients and potential clients recorded?

   Is there a system for automatic recall or follow up?
   Do staff use it?
   Is it simple and effective?

8. Is the capability, qualification and experience of each staff member recorded?

   By speciality or interest?
   By geographical location?
   Is the information updated regularly?
   Has it been assessed for strengths which might be developed?

9. Based on an approach developed by Christopher Ratcliffe 'Expanding an architect's practice'. A paper given at a joint conference sponsored by the Royal Institute of Architects and the Institute of Marketing (London, May 1982).

9. What particular categories of experience does the firm claim?

Are they defined in order of strength?
Which are truly justifiable?
Which are wishful thinking?
What action is needed to strengthen weaknesses?

10. Are clients satisfied with the services provided?

Are they ever asked?
Has any formal survey been carried out?
Is satisfaction monitored by an identified individual?
Is this individual independent of the fee earners involved?

11. What is current expenditure on practice development?

Is it identifiable according to categories?
Is the expenditure compatible with planned objectives?
What level of expenditure could be made available?
What level of fee income could this support?

12. Which members of staff could support practice development activities?

Have they ability to research markets?
Can they represent the firm at senior level?
Are they experienced in presenting and negotiating?
Are they technically able?
What portion of their time is available for practice development activities?
Is the total staff time available for practice development compatible with the planned objectives?
Are the selected members of staff free to support the practice development plan without bias?

13. Where does the firm think that its future markets exist?

By work type and by location?
What is the estimated growth of these markets?

What competition is expected and can it be matched?
Will these markets provide the target objectives?
Have the potential clients been identified?
How would the firm operate in these markets? Own local office? Association with local firm?

14. Are organization and communication procedures formally defined?

Who has overall responsibility for practice development?

15. Are memberships of professional and other organizations listed?

Is full use made of their facilities?

16. What publications, bulletins and market information documents are received?

Do they reflect current and future plans/services?
Are they regularly reviewed for effectiveness?
Who is responsible for monitoring them?
How is monitoring carried out?
Is circulation controlled to ensure prompt action on opportunities?

17. What brochures and leaflets does the firm produce?

Do they reflect current strategy?
Has specialist production assistance been sought?
Is attention paid to practice image?

18. Are referral sources traced?

What actions are taken to acknowledge referrals?
Is there any basis for reciprocation?
Is there a central register of inter- and intra-professional referrals? Are staff encouraged to use it?
Is there new business potential among staff of corporate clients?
Is there new business potential among employers or private clients?
Can these market segments be contacted within any mandatory rules of practice which exist?

# Appendix B. Example of information format

Examples of information which can be obtained from internal records and used for practice development planning. Column 1 gives the subject; 2, the reporting frequency; 3, the standard by which the data should be judged; 4, the variance indicators to be used; and 5, who receives the data and for what purpose. The model is only to illustrate the subject and should not be followed too closely, except where deemed applicable. (Adapted from *Marketing Audit Check Lists*, op. cit., pp. 205/206.)

| COLUMN 1 Performance Indicator | COLUMN 2 Reporting Frequency W = Weekly M = Monthly YTD = Year to Date | COLUMN 3 Standard | COLUMN 4 Variance Indicator (Value Number Per cent Weeks) | COLUMN 5 Performance Information Reported To: | Chief Executive | Senior Partner | Practice Administrator | Managing Partner | Professional Staff |
|---|---|---|---|---|---|---|---|---|---|
| | | | | C = Control Purposes    I = Information Purposes | | | | | |
| **Fee income by:** | | | | | | | | | |
| – type of service | W or M/YTD | Forecast | Actual & % | | | | | | |
| – geographical | W or M/YTD | Forecast | Actual & % | | | | | | |
| – type of client (size, activity, frequency of use, timing) | W or M/YTD | Forecast | Actual & % | | | | | | |
| – key clients | W or M/YTD | Forecast | Actual & % | | | | | | |
| **New business by:** | | | | | | | | | |
| – type of service | W or M/YTD | Forecast | Value & % | | | | | | |
| – geographical | W or M/YTD | Forecast | Value & % | | | | | | |
| – type of client | W or M/YTD | Forecast | Value & % | | | | | | |
| **Profitability by:** | | | | | | | | | |
| – whole practice | W or M/YTD | Forecast | Value & % | | | | | | |
| – type of service | M | Forecast | Value & % | | | | | | |
| – type of client | M | Forecast | Value & % | | | | | | |
| – individual professionals | M | Forecast | Value & % | | | | | | |
| – timing | M | Forecast | Value & % | | | | | | |
| – key clients | M | Forecast | Value & % | | | | | | |
| **Non-recoverable costs by:** | | | | | | | | | |
| – type of service | M or YTD | Budget | Value & % | | | | | | |
| – type of client | M or YTD | Budget | Value & % | | | | | | |
| – individual professionals | M or YTD | Budget | Value & % | | | | | | |
| – geographical (client location, branch, or other types of offices) | M or YTD | Budget | Value & % | | | | | | |
| – delayed account settlement | M or YTD | Budget | Value & % | | | | | | |
| **Client accounts gained (lost) by:** | | | | | | | | | |
| – region | W or M/YTD | Plan | No. or % | | | | | | |
| – services utilised | W or M/YTD | Plan | No. or % | | | | | | |
| – individual professionals | W or M/YTD | Plan | No. or % | | | | | | |
| **New Service development by:** | | | | | | | | | |
| – current status of project | M | Plan | No. of weeks | | | | | | |
| – new projects initiated | M | Plan | No. of weeks | | | | | | |
| – new services introduced | M | Plan | No. of weeks | | | | | | |
| – new projects abandoned | M | Plan | No. of weeks | | | | | | |
| **Personnel by:** | | | | | | | | | |
| – number engaged full time on practice development | M | Budget | No & % | | | | | | |
| – number engaged part time on practice development (days/hours) | M | Budget | No. & % | | | | | | |
| – unfilled vacancies | M | Budget | No. & % | | | | | | |
| – number exposed to practice development training | YTD | Plan | No. | | | | | | |
| – number to be exposed to practice development training | YTD | Plan | No. | | | | | | |

# Chapter 6.   Deciding the service offering of the practice

The range of services which a firm or individual practitioner offers to his clients and potential clients obviously has a pervasive effect on the overall performance of the practice in terms of the fees it generates and the profits which ensue as well as the opportunities the practice will provide for work satisfaction for the professionals it employs and their careers. For this reason the techniques for making the fundamental decisions concerning which services to adopt or adapt is dealt with in greater depth than the reference in the previous chapter permitted in the context of total practice development.

A fundamental part of the marketing activity is 'product development'. The characteristics which typify professional services do not in any way reduce the need for planning the services to be offered. Too often professional service firms and individual practitioners make the initial mistake in their strategy and planning of limiting their consideration to existing services. Because most professional service firms originated on the basis of the skills of their initiators, and because these skills are frequently viewed narrowly, the question of 'service' development is usually neglected. The existence and quality of services are the means of achieving the objectives of the practice. Thus study of service opportunities and alternatives and a constant search for improving existing services and identifying new service needs is manifest. Too parochial a view of a practice and its business mission can lead to an unnecessary limitation of its opportunities. Chapter 3, 'Creating a client-centred practice', page 25, emphasized the importance of identifying the role of the firm and this must correlate with the services it offers to its publics.   Most professional service firms are built around a core service (see Chapter 2, 'Understanding service businesses' (Figure 2-3). The decisions to be taken in creating a service policy for the firm are substantially those related to the satellite or add-on services. These questions to be answered can easily be listed:

- Which services shall be incorporated into the firm's total offering?
- What new services are required to augment the existing range or replace existing services?
- In what depth and with what variations will services be offered?[1]

In one respect at least the professional service firm has a great advantage over the product firm. Increasing services rarely creates new inventory costs, does not involve heavy capital expenditure and, if the personnel involved are not specialists, there are few problems of 'down time'. It is perfectly possible to offer a wide range of services, just so long as the skills are available. No costs or very few costs are involved until the service is invoked. Thus in adding

---

1. Range depth can be defined as a number of different options of services of the same genre, for example, technical research, application research, market research, image research. Range depth would be alternatives available within any one type, for example, application research into integrated circuits, head up displays, electronic displays, interface units.

or divesting themselves of services professional firms can be far more liberal in defining the supplementation or withdrawal criteria.

## Service range

The pressure for a greater variety can come from both within the firm seeking to exploit under-utilized resources and achieve growth and from the client looking for variations from the offered services which will better fit his total requirements.

Thus, professional service firms are faced with the need for, and the opportunity to offer, not a single service but a range of services. The decision as to the correct 'mix' is a difficult one. No formula has yet been devised for identifying the factors which will make a firm more profitable by either increasing or narrowing its width of services and the depth in which they are offered. How extensive should the variation in the range of services be and what effect will a wide range have on the image of the service firm? What is the spread of demand likely to be over the entire range? What is the optimum-minimum range? These are questions which have to be answered by the use of judgement, experience and knowledge of clients' needs and activities. For most practices, demand tends to be concentrated over a few of the available services.

So far only an empirical approach can provide indications to the answers to these questions and it is usually impossible to assess what would have happened had the opposite decision been taken. The essential nature of the problem is to determine what role each service in the 'mix' plays, even if it is only a poor performer. For example, in order to be seen by clients to be seriously in a business, the practice may have to offer a bigger 'package' than the viability of individual elements of the 'package' may justify. Nevertheless the image impact of a 'full line' is frequently an important decision-making factor which will improve the competitive position of one firm against another. Management trained in financial rather than in marketing disciplines find this concept difficult to accept, since the yield on a single service may not appear to justify its presence in the range yet its contribution to the acceptability of other services or of the practice itself may be immeasurable but considerable.

Thus, the basic sources of information on which service range decisions can be made are from the clients or would-be clients themselves, from within the practice and also from the competitive environment. The actions necessary to work outward from these three sources, but not necessarily in the order given, are:

- Identification of market targets.
- Study of lost business to determine how far it is attributable to lack of a required service or apparent lack of capability in the service area concerned.
- Evaluation of existing service 'packages' and relating them to client needs.
- Research into clients' present professional services, policies and methods of purchasing. (What do our clients buy from others that they could buy from us?)
- Study of internal capabilities for range extension.
- Study of competitive offerings.
- Examination of changes in content or coverage of existing services which would provide a new or improved facility for clients.
- Emerging technical, economic, social or governmental trends which may create demands for new services.

One major application for marketing research is to determine the needs of users and potential users of professional services in terms of the type, quality, and extent of services required. Research in this context, however, is not merely to quantify a likely demand and to probe any synergy or counter synergistic effect which will occur in varying standard services. A more impelling need is to examine the image aspects and implications of the adjusted range. Will the changed service make the practice more credible to existing or potential clients? Will it produce the opposite effect of a vacillating firm desperately in search of its true role?

The lack of any soundly based method for range optimization and the almost totally empiric nature of range decisions bedevils all aspects of strategy. There seems little indication that theorists are going to be able to provide practice developers with a formula for devising optimum ranges in the foreseeable future. Trial and error used with a wide information base will at least give reliable guidelines until a more scientific method can be devised.

## New services

Another dimension of service policy is the identification of new services to add to the existing range or to replace those which no longer meet client needs.

To begin with it is necessary to draw the definition for what comprises a 'new service' as widely as possible. A highly practical and useful grouping which avoids the hazard of an artificial dichotomy between new and old can be used.[2]

- Second and subsequent generation services.
- 'Services' new to the firm's range and mix, but in basic functional form already available on the market served.
- Services already available, but adapted for a new market.
- Totally new services.

In considering new services, there is a danger in treating them in isolation from the existing services and although this division is made here for the sake of clarity it is not a realistic one. Many of the techniques and approaches suggested for optimizing ranges by extensions and changes in the core services are also relevant for new 'service' development.

Totally new services can often evolve from clients' requests for higher performance standards or new additional features for an old service. Such requests will often derive from changes in the client's own position or environment. New technology and the advent of the electronic office have placed a stronger emphasis on re-training and induction techniques which is an obvious extension of the training and recruitment satellite services of accountancy and management consultancy firms.

However, just where the new services and ideas on which they are based are to come from is usually far from clear. There are, of course, within every firm 'stables' of ideas awaiting a winner to be drawn from them: there are personnel with their own particular propositions and there are formal, but usually unstructured, attempts to feed through new ideas by brainstorming, surveillance, or more exotic techniques such as synectics, morphological analysis, bionics or just waiting for that most ephemeral of all qualities, inspiration.

This mélange of idea generation is quite the most usual, even in firms which offer as their expertise 'creativity'. The creative problem-solver, irrespective of his area of expertise, is often incapable of being consistently creative on his own behalf.

Completely new services can, of course, emerge from attempts to adjust old services to provide new facilities. One way of achieving this is by a systems approach. Application

2. Mary Griffin. 'Generation of new product ideas'. In Aubrey Wilson (ed.), *The Marketing of Industrial Products*. Pan Books (London, 1972), p. 24.

engineering, value analysis and human engineering combined together could form such an approach which, at its simplest, is the creation of a new service by the technical and commercial study of processes, methods and other systems, to determine whether a new service or a new combination of existing services cannot improve the activity to which they are to be applied. The systems method differs only from the others in that it is an interdisciplinary and orderly technique, not a random 'architectural' technique, for dealing with complex problems of choice under conditions of uncertainty. The task of the analyst is to specify a closed operating network in which the components will work together so as to yield the optimum balance of economy, efficiency and risk minimization.

For a systems approach the following sequence is suggested:

- Definition of the problem.
- Testing the definition.
- Building a model.
- Setting precise objectives.
- Developing alternative solutions.
- Deciding criteria for tests of relative value.
- Quantification of some or all the factors or variables.
- Manipulation of the model.
- Verification of results.

The systems procedure to new service development from old services is a methodical operation within a frame of reference which includes all aspects of the problem to be considered. It enables the co-ordinated deployment of all appropriate tools of practice development to occur. Greater efficiency and economy can be achieved and the quicker recognition of impending problems is made possible by a better understanding of the complex interplay of many trends and forces to be perceived. Finally it is a stimulant to innovation and a means of quantitatively verifying results.[3]

Once the definition of what constitutes a new service has been formulated, consideration of the ways in which each type may evolve has value in that it enables the boundaries of searching to be set. 'Open minded' searching, lacking a focal point or confines, risks waste in the examination of search areas which have no relevance.

## Service/market matrix

It is possible to express the four situations which a professional must consider in devising a satisfactory range strategy. Figure 6-1 illustrates these and the resources involved.

Situations 1 and 2 predicate a fixed service range while 3 and 4 require new services. Situations 2 and 4 place the emphasis on acquiring new clients.

## Existing services and existing clients—resource-based development (Square 1)

A study of resources, as was recommended in Chapter 4, 'Preparing for practice development', should be the first task of the professional firm seeking to adjust or augment the range of services it offers.

3. Lee Adler. 'Systems approach to marketing'. *Harvard Business Review* (Cambridge, Mass., May/June 1967).

|  | Existing services | New services[4] |  |
|---|---|---|---|
| Existing clients | 1<br>Existing capabilities facilities and clients | 3<br>Client resource. No existing capability or facility resource | Resource used |
| New clients | 2<br>Existing capability and facilities. No client resource | 4<br>Nil | Resource used |

**Figure 6-1**  The service/market matrix

Many firms, even extremely well-organized and managed ones, fail to audit all the activities in which they have or could develop a capability. Whereas it is usual to maintain detailed inventories of equipment, managers of firms providing human skills will frequently not know that their personnel have actual and latent capabilities beyond those for which they were specifically employed. Clearly a census of capabilities and resources can, for many firms, be the first important step towards developing range variables of the type which will more fully exploit their resources.

Studying the opportunities from the client's end of the spectrum, may call into use marketing research which can be employed to determine the requirements both fulfilled and, more importantly, unfulfilled, of actual and potential clients. Of course an unfulfilled need may be unmet because the requirement is not practical, the cost to the client is too high, or for the particular practice it is not viable. A balance is required between the demands of the user of services and that which it is sensible for the service firm to supply. Ideally, the resources available or acquirable should be matched with the services the user wishes to purchase, and offered under the conditions which make them acceptable.

This two-dimensional view will provide a valuable input to identifying service possibilities which, combined with a study of the competitive climate, not just directly competitive but also indirectly competitive, will define the services for consideration.

## Old services for new clients (Square 2)

Existing services can always be considered for new clients since in these markets they may represent a new or improved facility. The possibilities of technological transfer are as great for services as for products. Computer applications, operational research, information technology, once the activities of specialists, are now adjunct to many core services in other types of professional organizations. At a less esoteric level services drawn from other professions are being adopted and adapted. Banks have moved into building society business;

---

4. 'New' in this context does not necessarily mean innovation but 'new' to the practice.

building societies are increasingly seeking to take over part of the legal profession's services; and trade and research associations are adding professional services from all disciplines. The PIRA (Paper Industry Research Association) offers its members training, consultancy, efficiency audits, arbitration and information services.

It is also true that services which have 'topped out'[5] for one type of client may be an innovation for another. The time lag in the acceptance of a service across the commercial or private client spectrum can span many years. Similarly the use of professional services in less well-developed overseas areas may also offer new opportunities.

Searches for new markets for services entail envisaging all the possible applications of a service, the techniques embodied in it, or those employed in its operation. These then have to be matched to a client need, otherwise only half the problem has been solved. The transfer of a service which is new to the recipients can only occur if there is an actual or latent demand for that service. Thus both a broad view and understanding of the service content and of the range of applications in which the service is not familiar is needed.

## New services for existing clients (Square 3)

This approach depends for its success on an understanding of the operations, activities, problems and requirements of clients and potential clients and the constant monitoring of their needs. These studies almost invariably produce, as a spin off, identification of requirements of peripheral markets.

The enquiry technique termed 'industries we serve' simply asks: 'What services do our clients buy which they do not buy from us but which we could provide?' It is basically an exploitation of a client resource rather than a 'production' resource. It may involve a much higher degree of diversification in comparison to the substantially linear mode of expansion so far discussed. New technical skills and, possibly, infrastructure may be needed as well as a new 'image' and substance for capability in the chosen field.

Perhaps no better or more successful example of developing a new service for existing markets has occurred than in some parts of the accountancy profession. The leading firms were in an unusually good vantage position to observe the problems of their commercial clients. By adding a management consultancy arm to their business, some accountancy practices were able to offer a new service in clearly identified areas of need, starting from a point of total credibility and in the position of an existing supplier with all the advantages which that confers (see Figure 8-7 in Chapter 8, 'Professional services and the commercial client').

Since these early ventures in management consultancy, accountancy practices have added many new services for commercial and private clients. A publication by the Institute of Chartered Accountants lists 13 activity areas where a qualified accountant can assist companies and individuals and within the 13 are many 'spin off' services such as insurance, retirement planning, wills, trusteeships, executive search and marketing consultancy.

## New services for new clients (Square 4)

This clearly is the most difficult situation from which to extract profitable new 'service' ideas or clients. It is very much in the 'blue skies' area of planning.

5. The term 'top out' refers to a position on the life cycle curve where it flattens and after which a continuous decline in demand begins until the service is finally withdrawn as no longer viable and has thus ended its life cycle.

It is improbable that professional staff will propose truly visionary or 'blue sky' services. Nevertheless, ideas that are capable of immediate translation into a viable service, and those which have probably only a far off future, have their place in a firm's planning and both warrant careful attention. Many professional service firms have what are termed 'lead products' that is services destined for introduction some years ahead. It is in a sense the R & D department of the firm.

While it is easy to call for creativity in developing a new service for existing and new markets, it is not possible to achieve it for the asking. So far, the creative process has obstinately resisted analysis and understanding. Its study has been hampered by the problem that it is in motion. Traditionally, the creative process has been considered after the fact—halted for observation which negates the very thing to be studied. The traditional emphasis on sequential logical thinking has certainly not changed, but new developments hold out high hopes for removing creativity from its conventional classification as a 'gift' to that of a skill. Approaches such as 'lateral thinking' and 'synectics' are opening up ways by which individuals can develop their creative thinking and thus their creative activity capacity.

In the development and use of structured approaches to creativity, particularly in relation to new services, the opportunity exists to shape the conditions of market leadership since most individuals and firms have barely considered the subject, leaving the issue of new services to be dealt with reactively. However, the danger of failing to distinguish between being creative in the abstract and the equally difficult process of being innovative in the concrete is always present. The need for a balance is paramount.

## Conditions for success

The success of any service strategy will be heavily dependent on both the attitudes of those within a practice to adaptation and innovation as well as their ability to be creative.

Whichever range optimization strategy is adopted in the final analysis the practice developer will have to evaluate the services considered against his own criteria which link the services to the objectives which the firm has set. Typical criteria might be:

- Extent of demand for the service(s).
- Existence of direct or indirect competition including the possibility of clients undertaking the service for themselves (e.g., do-it-yourself tax returns or conveyancing).
- Demand trends.
- Compatibility with the firm's skills, resources and aspirations.

Searches for new services should be a continuing process, as routine as paying salaries. If a systematic procedure is adopted, all the defined areas will be scanned regularly and the findings recorded. The new ideas should be classified in accordance with their basic characteristics in order to facilitate the rapid retrieval of those which offer most promise in the light of the special requirements of the firm at any time.

Whether the life cycle of a professional service is a long or short one, it must succumb to the erosion of environmental change and innovation. The need for unremitting search to identify threats to existing services and the way to avert them must be accompanied by the positive, rather than accidental or sporadic, generation of new service ideas and an open-minded approach in the consideration of their introduction.

# Chapter 7.  Professional services and client needs

A great deal of what has preceded this chapter is also applicable to services which are not necessarily regarded as 'professional'.

In 1966, a considerable advance was made in the understanding of the concepts underlying professional services—an advance which was necessary before it was to become possible to adapt and develop marketing tools specifically for the purpose of professional service marketing. The work of Warren Wittreich must therefore be acknowledged as the breakthrough which service marketers had been looking for.

Wittreich succeeded in identifying the dividing line between professional and all other services in that he defined three desiderata clients expect from a professional service. Unlike so many definitions, classifications and 'goods-versus-services' distinctions which describe rather than explain observed phenomena, these requirements have a practical unity and thus gives very considerable guidance as to the 'message' which the practice development strategy has to convey.[1]

In purchasing a professional service there will be for clients:

- A high degree of uncertainty.
- A need for the professional to demonstrate an understanding of the client's problem.
- A requirement for total and unwavering professionalism.

These three factors are now examined and their implication for practice development explored.

## Uncertainty

Every decision to purchase a professional service, retain a practice or consult a qualified practitioner, is surrounded with uncertainty. For a simple consumer service such as, say, dry cleaning or house decorations the extent of uncertainty is low since an objective assessment of success or completion is not difficult to establish. Moreover, most usually the consequence of failure while inconvenient is not of major significance. The client for professional services, no matter how skilled in purchasing such services and no matter how sophisticated he may be, is always subject to uncertainty varying from perhaps slight unease to virtual neurosis. With professional services a number of factors, not the least of which is the frequent inability of the user to understand the technique of the profession retained, increase the level of uncertainty to a point often of extreme tension.

1. Warren J. Wittreich. 'How to buy/sell professional services'. *Harvard Business Review* (Cambridge, Mass., March/April 1966).

If the major sources of uncertainty which exist in a decision to retain a professional service can be identified and understood, then it is possible to ensure that the information the individual or practice provides for clients and potential clients will at the very least mitigate uncertainties rather than, as is so frequently the case, intensify them.

Major sources of uncertainty in deciding on a professional service can easily be ascertained and understood.

## Is a professional, or indeed any, service needed?

It is by no means always clear to the potential client that he has a need for any service at all. While to the professional it may be obvious, to the client it can be a matter of extreme doubt. Does he need planning permission for a building extension? Is immunization really called for? Is it permissible to remit funds? Doubts about any given situation do not necessarily lead to the firm conviction that consultation with an expert is needed.

Some situations will provide a clear-cut answer. Businesses continuing above-average staff losses, brand forgery, product liability, low return on investment, and a high rate of new product failure, may well be indicators of a need for professional assistance. Foreshortened life cycles, a rising sales curve in a declining market, the rapid development of technically superior and different but competitive products may not point unequivocally to the need for assistance.

For the private client what might be a serious subsidence in his house might be seen as merely 'settling', a pet's loss of appetite as a passing upset or a redundancy notice not appreciated as 'unfair' dismissal. Thus, uncertainty is often piled upon uncertainty at the outset. Is there a problem at all?

It is easy to see, if looked at objectively, that in very many daily circumstances the need for a professional service of any type is neither so obvious nor so pressing as most professionals feel or indeed as the situation might warrant were the client better informed.

## New situation for the client

The retention of a professional service or practitioner may be a new experience for the individual or firm. Uncertainty as to what is involved in consulting a professional can be a dominant factor in the relationship. An anticipation of an intimidating atmosphere and, for some professions a history of detachment and arrogance, a failure to make conditions of consultancy clear and other factors all create a high degree of uncertainty as to what commitment is involved, how to act, what attitude to adopt, how to extricate themselves or terminate the relationship. All these are often unspoken but real causes of concern.

## Lack of confidence in the professional service concerned

Some professions do not have a good image or indeed reputation. Solicitors and insurance companies have particularly poor images and are only usually mentioned in the media when an act of wrongdoing or neglect occurs; architects are subject to the most virulent criticism both for aesthetic and technical reasons; a spate of well-publicized and massive errors of omission and commission by some leading accountancy practices reduced confidence not just in the ability of the profession but sometimes in their integrity too. All these factors add to the uncertainty element which firms and individuals suffer in choosing to consult or retain any profession or professional.

## Which practice or professional to choose?

The rules of practice of the qualifying professions have in the past made it virtually impossible for the client to choose one practice rather than another, using knowledge rather than guesswork. While some relaxation is taking place and certainly will increase in the future, it is still difficult to an extreme for a client to make his selection based on information and not on luck. In any one geographical location there may be a choice of hundreds of professionals in the same disciplines and little or no indication of the skills, experience, resources and interests of any of them. Thus even when a choice is made the visceral feeling may well remain that it may not have been the best one. Uncertainty again abounds.

## Ignorance of alternatives

Just as a client, even a highly literate one in a business sense, may not be certain a service is needed, he may be equally uncertain as to which service is appropriate. In any one situation it is possible to consider perhaps four or five viable alternatives all offering the same end result—a problem solution (see Figure 7-1).

The decision as to which service to choose is clearly of fundamental importance and yet each practitioner offers the client a different service with equal advocacy that it is the correct one for the particular client needs. There is little substance on which the client can make his decision as to which profession is the appropriate one for the circumstances.

While Figure 7-1 only considers competing services a totally different but potent form of competition already referred to can exist through products. Design module planning books for home or office renovation or decoration can replace the architect or designer; self-diagnostic medical equipment which is now available in retail outlets can lessen or remove the need for medical advisers; improved formulation toothpaste reduces the need for dentistry services; tax-planning software for calculating corporation tax liability can diminish requirement for accounting services.[2]

## Unspecified or open-ended cost commitment

Many professional firms and individual firms cannot provide a cost estimate for the matter in hand. Indeed some cannot even give an approximation. This is not necessarily a failing of the service but its very nature. How long will the treatment need to be continued? Will the opposition defend the case and even go to appeal? Are the tax authorities likely to accept the tax returns without question? The professions cannot necessarily be blamed for being obscure or even evasive on cost and commitment. Needless to say it does nothing to ease the client's nervousness to know that he is about to enter into an unspecified and indeed open-ended cost commitment which may well be out of all proportion to the advantages to be gained even assuming the problem is satisfactorily solved. There are few private or commercial transactions in which the buyer is expected to take the vendor totally on trust that he will deliver the service or goods as specified and at a fair price.

2. Theodore Levitt explored the products versus services concept a decade ago in two articles. 'Production line approach to services' and 'The industrialization of service'. *Harvard Business Review* (Cambridge, Mass., September/October 1971 and September/October 1976 respectively).

| Competition to: | Subject | Alternative service |
|---|---|---|
| Solicitors | Planning appeals | Architects<br>Surveyors<br>Town planning<br>Consultants<br>Do-it-yourself |
| | Probate | Banks<br>Advice centres<br>Do-it-yourself |
| | Taxation | Accountants<br>Tax consultants<br>Banks<br>Insurance company<br>Estate planners |
| Accountants | Corporate and<br>financial planning | Merchant banks<br>Consultants<br>Do-it-yourself |
| | Computer development | Consultants<br>Computer manufacturers<br>Software services<br>Do-it-yourself |
| | Taxation | Solicitors<br>Tax consultants<br>Banks<br>Insurance companies<br>Estate planning |
| Doctors | Healing | Acupuncturists<br>Osteopaths<br>Psychobiologists<br>Faith healers<br>Placebos and self-healing<br>Pharmacists |
| | Preventive medicine | Homoeopathics<br>Herbalists<br>Pharmacists<br>Diagnostic centres<br>Para-medicals |
| Surveyors | Town planning | Specialist consultants<br>Architects<br>Do-it-yourself |
| | Structural surveying | Architects<br>Specialist consultants<br>Structural engineers |
| | Marketing of property | Estate agents<br>Property shops<br>Computer services<br>Do-it-yourself |
| | Property management | Specialists<br>Developers<br>Local government<br>Do-it-yourself |

**Figure 7-1**  Service alternatives

## Lack of objectivity by the professional

While it is understood in the professions and by those closely associated with them that an essential part of professionalism, indeed substantially what the client purchases, is total objectivity and freedom from bias the client does not necessarily see the situation this way. It is anything but a *sine qua non* that the client believes in the absolute integrity of the professional. Because most commercial organizations and individuals who offer goods and services in exchange for the client's money are not by training or motivation objective, the view must exist that professionals are no more unbiased than a seller of double glazing. The client has no means of knowing if, in describing what a practice has to offer, the professional involved is being totally unbiased and would in fact not recommend the use of either the professional service in question or his own practice or service if it were not appropriate or suitable. While such a refusal is the essential part of professionalism, the client does not know this to be so and, thus, on top of the other uncertainties that exist, he faces the uncertainty of being subjected to 'sales talk'.

## Inability to assess value for money

Because there are no absolute standards and because so much in a client–professional relationship has to be taken on trust, value for money becomes difficult if not impossible for the client to assess. Even complex consumer products are capable of fairly tight comparison on a value for money basis. Although one video set may cost £50 more than another, its additional facilities can be evaluated by the potential buyer in terms of whether they are worth to him the incremental difference. It has already been suggested in Chapter 2, 'Understanding service businesses', because a large part of a service is 'invisible' to the client the cost of services always appears high in relation to the part of the service which is visible. The concomitant is that there is great unease about whether value for money will be or has been obtained and there is no really effective way of checking. While it is true a client of a legal practice can call upon the courts or The Law Society to assess just how fair fees are, even if a reduction is given the client does not necessarily consider he has received value for money. More likely his attitude is that the final sum is fractionally closer to value for money but that he has still overpaid for the service.

## Rejection of liability

Only barristers among all professions cannot be proceeded against either for breach of contract or for negligence. Other professionals are not immune from the risks of litigation. Nevertheless, there is a strong element of rejection of liability. Advice given in good faith, and based on the professional's use of his skills and experience no matter how disastrous the outcome for the client, does not lead to any automatic recompense. Hence, as was pointed out in Chapter 3, 'Creating a client-centred practice', guarantees and warranties are notably missing from the professional relationships. Unlike many non-professional services and all goods, there is no liability and thus responsibility is rejected and client uncertainty must result.

These nine sources of uncertainty by no means exhaust all the factors which create uncertainty for both the corporate and private client. It can be seen that the degree to which the professional can understand sources of uncertainty and convey the fact that he understands (and cares) to the client, the quicker will a satisfactory rapport be reached.

# Understanding problems

All professions have in common that they are designed to solve problems. While many such problems might have a pleasant connotation—for a private person the investment of an inheritance; for the manufacturer the decision to expand production—most problems are a source of worry and indeed might well be traumatic. Thus the professional often begins a relationship by facing a client already stressed, deeply troubled and anxious. The need to probe the problem and then to express an understanding of it, in a sympathetic and caring way, is that part of professional training that is most neglected even in medicine where such attitudes should be inherent in the service.

In an ideal world a purchaser of a professional service would approach the firm or individual with a clear brief. 'I have a problem. These are the facts of the situation. How do I resolve the problem?' This situation occurs infrequently.

Problems are not necessarily neatly packaged. They may well take several forms and in each case the role of the professional is somewhat different (see Figure 7-2).

| Client | Professional |
| --- | --- |
| Only parts of the problem are observable or understood | The task is to integrate the various parts of the problem into its substantive whole |
| An incorrect assessment has been made of the problem | A transfer must be achieved between the given and the real problem and client must agree the problem as re-stated is correct. Without this agreement any solution is unlikely to be considered satisfactory |
| The actuality is that the client does not have a problem at all | In these circumstances no true professional would offer his service nor accede to a request for the service |
| No problem is seen while in reality one exists | This might appear unreal in that the client will probably not consult the professional. Nevertheless, problems emerging for one type of client may well signal their existence for another. The professional must identify not only the problem but also show its relevance to an as yet unconvinced client. It is this situation that probably offers one of the best approaches for client retention planning (see Chapter 5, 'Devising a practice development strategy and plan', pages 58–9 |

Figure 7-2  Problem matrix

There are two approaches the professional service firms can adopt in their practice development activity relative to their problem-solving role. First, when the firm (or individual) has only a minimal understanding of a client's problem either because it lacks generalized experience in the field or because the client will not or cannot explain it, the emphasis by the professional service firm will be on extolling its own problem-solving abilities. This is done by describing a generalized approach to most problems (persuasion by method), describing the abilities, experience and qualifications of key personnel in the firm (persuasion by personnel), or giving successful case histories (persuasion by success story). This is the *extrinsic* approach.

Second, when the primary emphasis of the service organization is on coming to grips with a problem, it attempts to show its capability by concentrating on obtaining an understanding in depth of the problem. This is to enable it to generate both the confidence and interest of the client in having further discussions with the service firm. This is the *intrinsic* approach.[3]

3. The extrinsic approach is discussed in detail in Chapter 16. 'The use of personal contact', pages 191–2.

## Skills of problem identification

The skills of problem identification and formulation and the interviewing styles appropriate for this purpose, while obviously having a marked impact on client–professional relationships and thus practice development as a whole, are a subject better encompassed within the context of the professional training. Briefly, however, they have been admirably summed up for both the medical and legal professions.[4]

An overall organizing framework which can be adapted for the individual's style is as follows (see also Figure 7-3):

1. Greet and introduce.
2. Elicit reason for visiting with opening question, etc.
3. Listen carefully to basic outline or personalities and circumstances from client's own unhindered words.
4. Question on facts for gaps, depth, background, ambiguities and relevance.
5. Sum up and recount professional's view of facts, *and* check for client's agreement or amend.
6. State advice and/or plan of action and deal with question of costs.
7. Repeat advice/plan of action *and* check for client's agreement or amend.
8. Recount follow-up work to be done by client.
9. Recount follow-up work to be done by professional.
10. State next contact between professional and client.
11. Ask if any other business and deal with it.
12. Terminate, leave taking.

NOTE TAKING →

| Client centred | | Professional centred | |
| --- | --- | --- | --- |
| **Use of client's knowlege and experience** | | **Use of professional's special skill and knowledge** | |
| Silence listening reflecting | Clarifying and interpreting | Analysing and probing | Gathering information |
| Offering observation | Broad question | Direct question | Direct question |
| Encouraging | Clarifying | Correlational question | Closed question |
| Clarifying | Challenging | Placing events | Correlational question |
| Reflecting | Repeating for affirmation | Repeating for affirmation | Placing events |
| Using client ideas | Seeking client ideas | Suggesting | Summarizing to close off |
| Seeking client ideas | Offering observation | Offering feeling | Suggesting |
| Indicating understanding | Concealed question | Exploring | Self-answering questions |
| Using silence | Placing events | Broad questions | Reassuring |
| | Summarizing to open up | | Repeating for affirmation |
| | | | Justifying self |
| | | | Criticizing |

**Figure 7-3** Fact finding interview styles

4. Avrom Sherr. From a paper presented to a Law Society Conference 'Developing and improving your practice', The Law Society (Coventry, 1983) and P. S. Byrne and B. E. Long. *Doctors Talking to Patients*, Department of Health and Social Security (London, 1976).

## Requirement for total professionalism

Achieving this necessary goal is very largely contingent on the achievement of the first two—minimizing uncertainty and understanding problems. If this is accomplished then the practitioner has, by definition, established his role as that of a professional.

While it is true to say that clients buy or hope to buy results, their expectation of such results is based on what they see as professional skills and professionalism—not quite the same thing—of the individual or practice they select. The client consciously or unconsciously seeks three forms of professionalism. The first is that associated with the discipline practised. In many instances the client will take as his first guideline the existence of accepted qualifications awarded by examining bodies (the qualifying professions) or membership of a professional association (in the case of non-qualifying professions).

The second aspect of professionalism relates of course to the way the individual or practice is perceived in terms of the manner in which he or it gives the service and the physical environment of the practice. The highest qualifications will not necessarily counter-balance what is seen as an unprofessional manner, poor quality support staff or inadequate equipment and premises. Conversely, top quality equipment and premises, friendly support staff and the very best professional manner will not compensate for lack of qualification and demonstrable skill. The two are so closely inter-related that there is a degree of unreality in attempting to unravel the two elements, although this has in fact been attempted in Chapter 2, 'Understanding service businesses', in order to identify the components of a professional service.

There are however, as Wittreich pointed out, two critically important aspects of professionalism which the sentient client will be conscious of and the less informed client will perhaps feel viscerally:

- The professional must have and be able to demonstrate a knowledge and skill in his claimed area of competence.
- He must also be able to acknowledge the limits of his knowledge and skills, that is the ability to recognize the boundaries of his competence.[5]

The failure of many professionals to recognize that admitting a problem is beyond the skills or experience of the individual or firm or that a problem has unique, puzzling or unfamiliar aspects can paradoxically create a high degree of client confidence in the professional. By the same token, responding to such a situation by stating that there is a need to take the problem to others in the firm or outside it, not only might reduce confidence in the practitioner but could well project him as a 'seller' of the firm's service rather than a 'doer'.

There is however a third aspect which requires comment. Qualifications and professionalism in the rendering of the service, so far as practice development is concerned, have to be combined with professionalism in how the service is presented to clients and potential clients. In other words, because of the constraints and indeed taboos which surround what many professions call pejoratively 'touting' but which in reality is marketing,[6] there have been considerable inhibitions in most attempts to present a profession as a whole or anyone or firm operating within it to corporate and private publics. It must be repeated, as was emphasized in Chapter 1, 'Why practice development?', 'Marketing can be performed with grace and

5. Warren J. Wittreich, 'How to buy/sell professional services'. Op. cit.
6. The word 'touting' is actually written into the Law Society's Rule 1 as shown in Chapter 1, 'Why practice development?', and was used by F. A. R. Bennion, a leading commentator, as a title for one chapter of his book *Professional Ethics*, Charles Knight (London, 1969) and certainly expresses the disdain which many professionals feel and take no pains to disguise towards commercialism, most particularly marketing.

sophistication. Marketing approaches need not be loud, aggressive, crass or intrusive. The practice of marketing is itself a sophisticated art and discipline.'

The way that clients judge the professionalism of a practice will therefore be based on wholly objective and ascertainable factors: qualification, infrastructure, support staff and even clients' lists or track record and on totally judgemental, indeed emotional aspects; the manner, personality, appearance of the professional, his success in reducing uncertainty and understanding problems and the way which the practice and its relevance to the client is presented.

Favourable enhancement of the client and prospective client's perception of the practice will depend upon how closely the individual or firm conforms to the criteria by which professionalism is judged. This may be a trivial symbol, black jacket and trousers, or fundamental such as total familiarity with the latest complex, high technology diagnostic equipment. Either way understanding clients' perceptions of professionalism must be followed by a willingness to conform to those criteria or, if necessary, to attempt to change them.

In presenting a practice the true professional perceives himself first and foremost as wholly competent in and committed to his profession. His ability to identify and isolate key factors of a problem provide his main business, intellectual interest and job satisfaction. He seeks (sometimes to the detriment of the overall practice development activity) to become personally concerned in situations because he can do the actual work involved in the problem solving. He knows either by instinct or training that he must be capable of demonstrating a personal competence commensurate both with the competence of those whom he represents and those to whom he is offering the service.

If practice development is made the true professional's responsibility he will, both by training and personal imperatives, undertake the task by what is essentially an *intrinsic* approach.

In contradistinction, if the task of expanding a professional firm's business is assigned to marketing personnel, administrators or practice managers and practice secretaries, they will perceive their role as virtually that of 'selling' and the appropriate personal qualities will be those of the empathy, ego drive and charisma of the salesman. They may, of course, have professional qualifications, but they do not view these as major strengths. They typically fail to bring them to bear on the substantive problems, but call on the services of others to provide the technical skills. These types of practice development personnel can sell energetically and aggressively, but offer the practices' services on extrinsic considerations. When they are forced into an *intrinsic* selling situation, they tend to adopt the set approaches which are virtually sales clichés, and they depend on others in the marketing or professional team whom they identify as experts in the problem under review.


## Inter-connections

The implication of the Wittreich concepts for practice development are considerable since they affect fundamentally the way professions act, the way the practice is presented to its public and the 'message' that is to be communicated.

It is important that all practices convey to their actual and prospective clients that they make a direct contribution to the reduction of uncertainty in their personal lives and in their businesses. For clients to assess a service accurately they must take into account the impact of its performance on their lives or their businesses. The uncertainties inherent in deciding to use a professional practice combine with the uncertainties which lead a client to the practice so that the total situation, so far as the client is concerned, is one of very considerable misgivings.

Equally, a professional service must convince its clients and prospective clients that it will come directly to grips with the fundamental problems of the individual or business purchasing that service. The successful performance of a service, far more than the successful manufacture of a product, depends on understanding the client's personal situation or business. The fact that achieving this understanding is part of the professionalism of the firm must be conveyed.

Finally, it must be emphasized that there can be no departure from whatever standards are regarded as manifestations of professionalism, be they fundamental or trivial, objective and ascertainable, or perceptual and emotional. Moreover, the fact that a professional service can only be purchased meaningfully from someone who is capable of rendering the service, must influence the choice of presenter of the services. Selling ability and personality alone are without significance.

The pervasive nature of these three factors; uncertainty, the requirement for problem solutions, and the need for total professionalism in the client–professional relationship creates, for the client if not for the professional, a series of different roles any or indeed all of which both client and professional may find themselves fulfilling, albeit unconsciously. It has been suggested for example that a solicitor or barrister can be regarded and might well regard himself as 'mother or father', 'social worker', 'psychiatrist', 'psychologist', 'life manager', 'business manager', 'accountant', 'confidant', 'co-conspirator' (in trial preparation), 'employer', 'friend' and 'unattainable object' (client fantasy).[7] Just how wise it is for the professional to accept or reject any of these roles depends very much on the infinite variables involved in the manner, attitude and training of the professional as well as the discipline concerned, the personality and needs of the client and the type of problem situation. It is not possible to generalize, but it is important to understand that the professional's role will invariably involve more than his discipline and that essential qualities which might be termed 'humanistic' are as much part of developing and consolidating client relationships as the professional skills which are possessed.

No one would disagree that a doctor's 'manner' is as likely to influence a patient's progress as is his knowledge of medicine. (Indeed part of the major criticism of doctors working with the National Health Service stems from their lack of time to get to know their patients and their backgrounds.) This truism can be applied, if not so obviously, to private clients and within all their professional advisers as well as those individuals within a commercial client company who use the services of the professionals.

Two statements summarize the compatibility to be achieved between practice development and client needs:

- The representative of the practice must be capable of demonstrating a personal competence commensurate with the competence of others within the practice and those to whom he is offering their services.
- Users can only recognize professionalism when the professional can demonstrate he understands the sources of uncertainty which prevail and the users' problems.

From the foregoing it will be clear that the consistent, but almost invariably unspoken, need of clients and prospective clients is for an understanding and removal or mitigation of any uncertainties they may experience, empathy with the professional in terms of problem identification, formulations and solution and the reassurance of a totally professional approach. These requirements never vary.

7. Kathryn S. Marshall. 'The client interview—a marketing opportunity'. A paper given at a Law Society Conference (Leeds, February 1983).

## Benefits

A passing reference was made in Chapter 5, 'Devising a practice development strategy and plan' page 59, to the content of any message which it was said must convey clearly and with relevance and conviction the benefits which the client will receive from retaining or using a particular service. Although not necessarily verbalized, benefits are what the client ultimately purchases. In a very real sense the client does not pay fees for the qualifications of the professional staff, its experience, its expertise, interests, resources, facilities or any other features of the firm. The client buys the benefits he expects to receive as a result of the application of the service. In this respect the buyer of services, whether professional, commercial, private or governmental, does not differ from the buyer of goods. It must be quite clear to everyone involved in expanding a practice that all the elements which make up the practice—objective and perceptual—are, so far as the client is concerned, only the means by which the benefits will be obtained or else are the surrogates from which he will deduce he will receive the benefits.

The translation of the features of a practice and what it offers into precise benefits for the clients is perhaps the most important part of the message which must be conveyed. Not all features will necessarily imply the same benefits for every client. The speedy application of a service (a feature) for one client might provide (benefits) 'peace of mind', for another 'cost saving', while for a third 'convenience'.

What is an apparently simple service component in banking, the current account, can be 'decomposed' into a number of different features which all lead to the same benefits.[8] These are the facility for face-to-face transactions; for example, in a shop the ability to complete remote transactions such as payment by post; the receipt of and crediting of funds, cash dispensing and safety of financial assets. The benefit from all these features is convenience and security.

It is necessary therefore to make the transposition from feature to benefit related to the client type of segmentation (see Chapter 5, 'Devising a practice development strategy and plan'). For many professional firms it is perhaps easier to work the other way round by asking what benefit does the client want (or could be shown to need) and then see how the features of the practice's services could deliver it.

It is easy to generalize a transposition from features to benefits and such generalizations do illustrate a way of thinking in respect of meeting clients' requirements. It is true for example that what all types of insurance represents in benefits, apart from the obvious monetary value of any claim, is that it provides 'peace of mind' and the feeling that the insured is both prudent and responsible.

While it may be axiomatic, particularly to the practitioner, just what benefits emerge from the services provided, it is not always so obvious to the client. Even if it is, it should be an absolute rule not to make the client carry out the transposition but to do it for him, if only to ensure that the 'benefits' message has indeed been received. Furthermore, even when the benefit is obvious, clients may not necessarily be convinced that the benefit will indeed be obtained. Reverting to Figure 3-2 in Chapter 3, 'Creating a client-centred practice', it will be seen that the last stage in the progression from knowing of a practice (visibility) to the decision to appoint it is 'conviction' and benefits alone are not convincing. What is required is some proof, or if not proof a reliable indicator, that the benefit will be achieved. This in practice development terms is the purpose of the 'features'. They provide proof or surrogates of proof

8. L. L. Altick. *Success in the New Financial Services Industry.* Published privately by SRI International (Menlo Park, Calif., July 1983), p. 23.

90

that the benefit can and will be delivered. These features may be as intangible as the service itself and thus perceptual; they may also be tangible 'evidence'[9] but they will be used by clients—consciously or unconsciously—to reassure themselves that the benefits will be obtained.

Almost all professionals are proud of their own and the combined skills of their practice, the quality of the services they offer and their practice's resource and facilities. As a result they often unknowingly dilute the client-centred approach since these very attributes encourage the professional to concentrate on his own and his practice's needs, not those of the client. The professional must always ask himself 'do we offer what it is the client purchases?' The difference between the two is obvious from Figure 7.4.

| Features of a professional service | Benefits to the client |
| --- | --- |
| Expertise in tax law | Higher retained profit or income |
| Financial skills | Problem solution |
| Excellent relations with other practices (inter- and intra-professional) | Quick results |
| Interdisciplinary skills | Assumption of responsibility |
| Commercial knowledge and experience | More efficient business operations |
| Advanced diagnostic techniques | Reduction of stress |

**Figure 7-4**   Features converted to benefits

Interrogation of clients or an objective re-appraisal of past comparable experience can assist materially in identifying benefits which clients themselves may not be aware of consciously or cannot verbalize. The professional may question the clients as to why a particular situation exists or a function is carried out in a particular way; whether they have a preference for a change in situation or activities and why; improvements—quicker, safer, cleaner, cheaper, greater accuracy, increased flexibility, more certainty and, of course, again why such a change is wanted; would they prefer to avoid the situation or cease the activity altogether? This type of probing can frequently reveal the benefits sought and thus enable the professional to assess how far the features of his service and his skills can go in achieving the benefits.

A useful check list format, difficult to complete but extremely valuable in devising the 'message', is given in Figure 7-5. Columns 1 and 2 will create no problem. Column 3 is the very difficult transposition from columns 1 and 2. Column 4 provides the link between the feature and the benefit, that is the 'proof' factor or if not 'proof' then at least powerful indications that benefits are almost certain to emerge. The last column prepares the practice developer for the questions which arise and also those which may not be spoken but nevertheless must be dealt with.

A caution is needed here. It must not be assumed that even if all the benefits the client requires are given and received this implies the client is 'satisfied'. It is prudent to assume that the only statement the client is making in choosing a practice is that he prefers the selected service firm to any other and that this preference does not indicate satisfaction. There is almost invariably a gap between the perception of satisfaction and the performance of the chosen service and practice. To test the validity of this statement, any practitioner need only examine his own choice of other professional advisers, goods or non-professional services to see how frequently there is a gap between the 'ideal' and the 'available'. Few people would claim to

9. See Chapter 2, 'Understanding service businesses', page 11 and Chapter 10, 'How the individual practice is selected', pages 116–18.

COMPLETE FOR EACH SERVICE AVAILABLE _____

| Features       1 The facts about each service, the firm system, etc. | Functions      2 How they operate. Applicability to clients' problems. How it is used | Benefits       3 What does this mean to the client? Be specific | Proof          4 How can it be proved that the client will receive the benefit? | Questions      5 Does the client need the benefit? Does the client want it? |
|---|---|---|---|---|
|  |  |  |  |  |
|  |  |  |  |  |
|  |  |  |  |  |
|  |  |  |  |  |
|  |  |  |  |  |
|  |  |  |  |  |
|  |  |  |  |  |
|  |  |  |  |  |
|  |  |  |  |  |
|  |  |  |  |  |
|  |  |  |  |  |

**Figure 7-5**  Format for devising the benefit approach

have the car of their dreams or a doctor with superlative skills and an incomparable manner and approach.

Believing that the choice of a practice is a recognition of satisfaction can produce a dangerous complacency and in any event is totally untrue when the practice or the service the client receives has not been experienced previously. The only satisfaction involved is that the client is satisfied he has made the best choice under the circumstances which is a long way away from saying that he is satisfied with the service, the firm and the professional.

# Chapter 8.  Professional services and the commercial client

While needs, whether those of private individuals or commercial organizations, do not differ substantially, the methods by which professional services are located and appointed by commercial firms bear little comparison. Aside from the fact that in many instances the commercial client will have a greater knowledge and probably experience of different types of services, there are also organizational constraints and requirements which shape policies and circumscribe actions.

Thus it is necessary to distinguish the commercial clients from private clients because if the decision-making processes are different then the practice development strategies must also vary to meet the circumstances.

It is many years since the idea was disproved that corporate decision making was the responsibility of one individual, a single moment of truth choice based overwhelmingly on a solitary factor—price. It has however taken a considerable time for the fundamentally incorrect nature of this concept to penetrate into those firms supplying industry and commerce. This is largely because marketing is targeted at the individual with the title 'buyer'. Those occupying this job function deliberately project the impression that they have substantial if not total responsibility for decisions and that they arrive at these decisions based on the conformity of the offer to their requirements in which price is dominant.

Since 'buyers'' own job performance is assessed on commercial factors, i.e., in obtaining the best price, credit, discounts, delivery time, there is a very natural and human tendency to be observably and measurably efficient at achieving satisfactory offers that meet these criteria. Behind the buyer however are many other functions with quite different choice criteria. It is not surprising that the implications of the research[1] which disproved the long-held theory did not penetrate the service sector, if only because the appointment of professional practices is almost invariably a high-level decision and rarely, if ever, falls within the responsibility of 'buyers' or buying departments. Extraneous influences such as occur in industrial product purchasing, and which can easily emanate from the shop floor, gate house or typing pool, were not thought to be relevant, nor indeed are they, although as will be pointed out, it is always unwise to ignore the unofficial influence of relatively low-level personnel who have the access to decision makers.

If practice development is to be successful for those firms to whom the commercial client is important, then the corporate decision-making process must be understood. While there are relatively few firms with their own or retained medical advisers, a very substantial part, if not all fee income, of many accountancy, architects', surveyors' and veterinary practices and, of course, the different branches of financial services are derived from commercial clients.

1. J. Robinson, C. W. Faris and Y. Wind. *Industrial Buying and Creative Marketing*. Allyn & Bacon (Boston, Mass., 1967).

The three aspects of corporate purchasing activity which have to be understood are:

- Who are the decision makers—the decision-making unit (DMU)?
- How is the decision process undertaken—the incremental decisions leading to the final selection?
- The decision-forming factors considered—objective and subjective.

## The decision-making unit

The idea that one person acting alone makes the decision on appointing a professional adviser or practice is dangerously misleading. While it cannot be denied that because of the high managerial level of the decision makers involved in choosing a professional practice, perhaps the entrepreneur, an autocratic chairman or the majority shareholder could indeed be the sole decision maker. This however occurs in only an insignificant minority of cases and decreasingly so. The larger the organization the less likely is the decision to be one person's choice. The reality is that several people will be involved even though there is one apparent decision maker. The others, while not being in a position to issue the final instruction, will have had considerable influence in the decision and therefore must be regarded as part of the 'team' which decides.

Studies of corporate decision making in the USA, Canada, Germany, France, all Scandinavia and other countries have shown an astonishing similarity in the numbers involved in a decision. Overall in more than 80 per cent of cases two or more people take part in some way in all corporate purchasing and the number can extend beyond seven or eight, some of these individuals not even members of the firm, for example the consultant professions themselves, as well as bank managers, customers, government and other supply firms.

The decision-making unit can be broken down into functions which clarify their respective roles and likely influence.

The role of 'purchaser' in Figure 8-1 would only appear to occur in a very limited number of cases when appointing a professional service. 'Buyers' or 'negotiators' are not usually involved

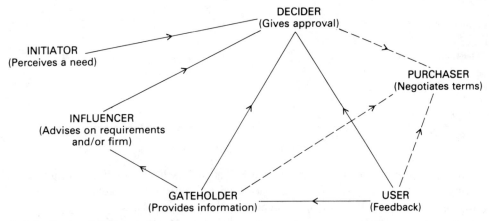

**Figure 8-1**   Buying influence centres[2]

2. Figure 8-1 is based on the work of Thomas V. Bonoma. 'Major sales—who really does the buying?' *Harvard Business Review* (Cambridge, Mass., May/June 1982) and adapted for professional services with his permission. Since relatively few practices have a negotiator or buyer the dotted lines represent a further possible participant in the decision process.

in the decision-making process for professional services. The separations have, of course, an element of unreality since one person can fulfil more than one role and, equally, in a large organization one role might be further divided. Thus the 'decider' and 'initiator' could be the same person as also could be the 'influencer' and 'gateholder'. In contradistinction the 'gateholder' role might be divided between those who provide technical and commercial information and those who report on other user experience. The situation can be illustrated relative to barristers' chambers. Here the senior clerk might well be the influencer, the gateholder, the decider and, even in his intermediary role, in a sense the purchaser, although of course the actual user is the solicitor and ultimately solicitor's client. The senior clerk's power can be such that it has been authoritatively commented 'just as a senior can make a barrister, so he can break him'.[3]

Bonoma[4] points out, rightly, that power does not necessarily go with organizational rank. While professional services might be chosen at a high managerial level, they may well be used at a middle or low level. The actual user of the service can feed back favourable or unfavourable comment. Moreover, in many situations top management will prefer to placate or satisfy by the appointment of one professional or practice rather than another even against its own preference. A comment from a secretary on the crude, brusque or arrogant behaviour of a professional or his staff can easily—all too easily—predispose decision makers against him.

Thus, although it may be possible to identify the key decision makers in the decision-making unit, it could be more difficult to locate others with influence. It is unwise to regard any personnel with whom the professional has contact as without the opportunity of making some contribution to a decision. This is saying no more than the normal courtesies and friendliness apply to everyone in a client firm, not just the decision makers.

Bonoma has attempted to identify the way power is *usually* exercised. Figure 8-2 must be viewed with the important corollary in mind that buying centres and individual managers usually display one dominant power base in decision making.

| | Advocate (positive influence) | Veto (negative influence) |
|---|:---:|:---:|
| Reward (can benefit others) | ● | |
| Coercive (can punish others) | ● | |
| Attraction (can persuade others) | ● | ● |
| Expert (can dominate others) | | ● |
| Status (can instruct others) | | ● |

**Figure 8-2**  How power is exercised

However interesting the model in Figure 8-2 is, it has little practical use unless those attempting to obtain business from corporate clients have some guidelines as to how to identify the individuals with strong influences in the decision. These it is suggested[5] are as shown in Figure 8-3 and the warning is repeated that while power and authority usually go

3. *Royal Commision on Legal Services Final Report Volume 1*. HMSO Cmnd 7648 (London, 1979), paras 34–36, p. 492.
4. Thomas V. Bonoma. Op. cit.
5. Ibid.

| | |
|---|---|
| • Observe communications in buying company | More powerful buyers are authoritative, less powerful use persuasion |
| • Note level of deference given to individual managers | Managers not subject to reward/punishment usually have substantial decision-making powers |
| • Assess which decision makers are disparaged or disliked | Powerful decision makers are resented by those with less power |
| • Identify if decision makers are one-way (recipient) information centres<br>• Establish if anyone is acting for another member of management | Powerful decision makers demand to be kept informed without involving themselves. Delegation without decision-making authority often occurs |

**Figure 8-3**  Identifying the powerful decision makers

together, although the link is far from perfect, there is nevertheless no correlation between a manager's or indeed anyone else's function and his power. Bonoma suggests the behavioural clues to be sought in every individual client and prospective client company.

It will have become obvious that in very many circumstances practice development personnel must be sensitive to the fact that no matter how authoritatively the person with whom they are discussing their services may speak and act, the overwhelming likelihood is that while he may be the screen through which they must penetrate, there will be others, visible and invisible, who will also be involved. These others will fulfil different roles and because they do so, their need for information and the benefits they seek will be different.

## The decision-making sequence

It has already been stated that the decision process is not a single moment of truth. It is in fact a 'creeping commitment' that narrows down choice at each stage. The original research sponsored by the Marketing Science Institute[6] and many more recent studies identified some eight stages of the decision making, most of which will be found to apply in the corporate purchase of professional services. As with the decision-making functions, where any individual might have a multi-role function, any decision stage may be combined, sub-divided or omitted.

Figure 8-4 is a simplistic model adapted from the work of Robinson, Faris and Wind.[7] A development based on this sequence takes account of a number of important aspects which were not included in the original concept (see Figure 8-5).

The differences between the two models are:

• The acceptance that the recognition of the need may well come from some external stimuli, for example, a change in the market, the environment, legislation or from a new awareness of what a particular profession has to offer the client.
• For many firms there is a choice whether to buy in a service, to appoint their own in-house professional or develop their own professionally staffed department, for example, a company solicitor, an architects' department, an in-house medical facility or patent department. The independent practices' major competition may come from their potential clients not from another professional or profession.

6. J. Robinson, C. W. Faris and Y. Wind. Op. cit.
7. Ibid., p. 14.

| | |
|---|---|
| 1. Anticipation or recognition of a need or a problem | This can emanate from any part of the client organization and be stimulated by a variety of factors |
| 2. Determination of the requirements the service must meet | At this stage all viable alternatives will be examined (see Figure 7-1, Chapter 7, 'Professional services and client needs'). Product alternatives to services may also be considered |
| 3. Specification or description of the service and the service firms | The actual type of service having been chosen a decision will be taken on the type and content of the service, e.g., international operations, specialized knowledge of a particular problem, size, location and profile of what would constitute a suitable practice or individual |
| 4. Search for and qualification of the individual or practice | Suitable professional firms or individuals will be considered to see how far they conform to the requirements now specified |
| 5. Obtaining offers and presentations and analysing them | Depending on the profession, this may be a very formal or totally informal contact between the client firm and the professional practice. Accountants might make a formal presentation; a stockbroker merely gives a description of his firm and services |
| 6. Examination, comparison and evaluation of the 'offers' or approaches of individuals or firms short-listed and selection of most suitable as perceived by the decision makers | Comparisons will not be exact as many subjective factors will prevail |
| 7. Designation of the methods for carrying out the service; liaison, internal contacts, billings, etc. | Although this is often agreed after the selection it can still be regarded as part of that process since failure to conform by either party may lead to termination of the arrangement |
| 8. Performance feedback and evaluation | The loop is closed by the feedback and the retention of the practice, unless for a finite period, is 'rolled' forward so long as its performance is seen as satisfactory |

**Figure 8-4**  Decision-making sequence

- The appreciation that in the search for a suitable practice, previous contacts, use and recommendations will always be influential and indeed may be the only method used to locate and evaluate a practice.
- Because of the element of uncertainty and intangibility, it is useful and usual for a client accepting the services of a firm or using a service for the first time to seek information concerning the experience of others who have used the practice and/or service.

The second model in Figure 8-5 illustrates:

- The value of a constant flow of appropriate information.
- The awareness and availability of the service may come from the practice development techniques and promotion.
- The risk of competition from a direction not usually expected, namely the clients themselves.
- Recommendations and past experience will always carry a strong if not decisive influence.
- The track record of the firm with existing clients will have a considerable bearing on any decision to appoint the practice.

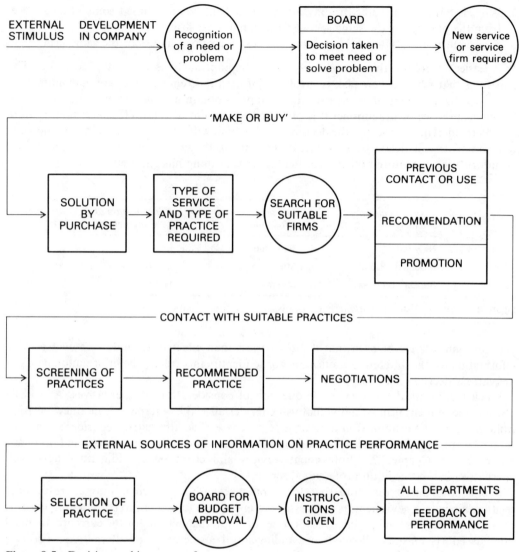

**Figure 8-5** Decision-making process[8]

## Decision-making classifications

While the decision making will always be conducted sequentially, it can be materially foreshortened if it is simply a repeat of some past transaction or arrangement. Thus the classification of the decision must impact on how it is reached. More importantly, two diametrically opposite strategies emerge depending on whether the professional firm is already established as a supplier of its services or not. Every decision to appoint a professional service (or indeed any service) falls into one of three classifications:

**1.** A first-time use for the client organization; that is it has never purchased that service before, or never from that particular firm.

8. Gordon T. Brand. *The Industrial Buying Decision.* Associated Business Programmes (London, 1972), p. 40. Adapted for professional services with the author's permission.

2. What is termed a 'modified re-buy'; that is the client has purchased some other services from the practice or the same service from some other firm.
3. A straight re-buy, which is a decision to re-use the same services of the same firm.

It is easier to follow this taxonomy with a diagram such as that of Figure 8-6. This illustrates that where a new task is involved, information requirements are maximum since every sensible commercial enterprise will attempt to obtain as much knowledge as possible about the practice or practitioner it is proposed to appoint or retain. It is also important to note that different members of the decision-making unit will require different information and thus selectivity will always be desirable. In returning to the same practice for the same service no information is required other than the fact that nothing has changed.

| Type of decision situation | Requirements information | Consideration of new alternatives |
|---|---|---|
| New task | Maximum | Important |
| Modified repurchase | Moderate | Limited |
| Repeat purchase | Minimal | None |

**Figure 8-6**  Distinguishing characteristics of decision-making situations

It can immediately be seen that it must be less than effective to under- or over-provide information for the different classifications or to identify incorrectly the information needs of the various decision makers.

Much more critical however is the question of consideration of alternatives. As will be obvious the sentient firm or individual will consider all viable alternatives in a new decision while none will be examined in a straight re-purchase. The alternatives considered will not simply be other professional firms or individuals but also competing professions and products. Figure 7-1 in Chapter 7, 'Professional services and client needs', illustrates how such alternatives can occur in all professional services.

It can be deduced therefore that for a practice wishing to enter into a professional relationship with a new client, it is necessary to encourage that client to consider alternatives of which the professional practice itself is one. In contradistinction, for the currently retained firm, its efforts must be directed to avoiding any consideration of alternatives. The two strategies to accomplish these different objectives are at opposite polarities. The strategic implications of the classifications of decision-making situations for the professional service firm in its relationships with existing clients and its attempts to acquire new clients and the relevant actions they imply can be summarized (see Figure 8-7).

Methods for stimulating an examination of options will depend on the prospective client knowing that alternatives do exist and thus once again the task of achieving 'visibility' as described in Chapter 3, 'Creating a client-centred practice', and illustrated in Figure 3-2 in that chapter, is a pre-condition. To encourage an examination of alternatives there has to be some innovative aspect to the offer because, as has been demonstrated, when all things are equal the existing provider of professional services will always succeed in holding that position.

Innovation can take many forms; a new service, a change in an existing service, the acquisition of personnel with special skills, a unique way of dealing with a particular problem, the possession of novel equipment, reduction of fee scales, speed in completing the service. The list is a long one and these items by no means complete it. What is essential is that the innovative aspect is so different and beneficial to the client that he will consider the appointment of the firm or individual. Moreover, the greater the innovation the less the influence of price or fee and the higher the propensity for senior management to be involved and, where such a function exists, the most senior negotiator will participate. While a single innovative element within the offer may force a re-consideration of the situation, it is more likely it will be a combination of factors. The client will, nevertheless, balance the value of the innovation against the advantages held by an existing professional adviser and also the uncertainties which are endemic in not just a change of firms but also in a totally new service. The result of a conscious or unconscious trade-off between the innovative content of the offer, the other aspects of the firm and its services, will be key to the decision.[9]

## Decision-forming factors

It has already been stated in Chapter 7, 'Professional services and client needs', that the client is essentially, consciously or not, seeking 'benefits'. A whole range of such benefits will be equally applicable to and desired by the commercial client as by the private client.

While the commercial client might be thought to be concerned only with the furtherance of organizational rather than personal goals, this is not wholly or even largely true. The members of the decision-making unit are not immune to the influence of personal considerations in performing their organizational tasks. The duality of their motivations in purchasing must be understood if successful new client acquisition and old client retention is to occur. Decision makers in commercial firms are no less human when involved in their business activities than when acting in their private capacity. They have the same psychological drives, desires, ambitions, urges and physiological needs whether purchasing for themselves or their firms. The idea of the commercial market for professional services comprising decision makers who are rational, expert and possessing complete knowledge of values and substitute services is totally incorrect. The private client or buyer has been characterized as irrational, prone to impulse, inexpert and imperfectly knowledgeable regarding values, services and products available. It cannot be ignored that the designated organizational buyer may be very little different and, while he is constrained by organization policy, is subject also to personal goals and aspirations in executing his organizational role.

The differences that do exist between consumer and commercial decision making are largely, but not wholly, in the organization of the buying function. In terms of motives there are many similarities. It is the impact of the commercial purchaser's milieu which conditions him to express his needs and desires in a certain, but perhaps more restrained, way because of his vocation and training.

A conditioned response of decision makers of Pavlovian characteristics is to demand twice the service at half the fees with immediate results. This is a purchasing decision cliché since they would not want to pay a price premium for a quality of service input which is over-designed for their purpose. Timing is relevant to each situation and indeed a quick answer or solution might often in itself be suspect and could imply the firm has not given the problem due consideration. Price has strong psychological implications (see Chapter 14, 'The role of fees in practice development') and a service which can never be accurately evaluated in advance of its performance will often be pre-judged by the fee or fee scale. While high price does not necessarily imply high quality, low price might well suggest corner cutting or unqualified or low-level staffing. The cliché of commercial decision makers' criteria is invalid.

9. The concept of the innovation content of an offer was first enunciated by David Rowe and Ivan Alexander. *Industrial Selling.* Hutchinson (London, 1967), pp. 42–47.

| Existing clients | Comment | New client | Comment |
|---|---|---|---|
| **Advantages of the professional service firm**<br>Knowledge exists of client organization and needs<br>Cost to the client of changing service firm or service<br>Client uncertainties regarding unknown or untried new service firm or service favour existing practice<br>Inertia<br><br>Client desire for risk minimization<br>Client's lack of time to identify, select and appoint new service firm or evaluate new service | A change of supplier will always involve the client in some expense. This may be trivial—merely an entry in the bought ledger; or considerable—change in internal organization and systems, increase or decrease in staff, time involved in briefing new service suppliers, etc. | **Advantage of the professional service firm**<br>None | |
| **Strategy**<br>Keep the buying situation as a simple repeat purchase | | **Strategy**<br>Seek to force a consideration of alternative suppliers or services so that the decision becomes either a modified re-purchase or new purchase | |

**Tactics**

Maintain regular and adequate communication

Maintain and improve performance

Monitor direct and indirect competition

Monitor changes in client organization and in personnel and adjust to their changing needs

**Tactics**

Identify why present professional advisers hold that position

Equal and surpass any advantages the existing service firm possesses

Obtain familiarization of the internal organization of the clients and of their needs

Identify and familiarize with the decision-making unit and power centres

Identify benefits clients seek from service features

Seek and/or develop within the service firm some unique aspect or grouping of aspects which are unique to the practice and of benefit to the client

Obtain immediate and unprompted visibility (recall) of the firm and its personnel and services

Demonstrate, where possible, cost effectiveness of the firm or its services

Where all things are equal no client firm changes its professional advisers. In such situations the *status quo* always wins

Benefits, features and unique selling aspects are dealt with in Chapter 7, 'Professional services and client needs' earlier in this chapter and specifically in Chapter 11 'Identifying potential clients'

Only if the professional service firm is 'visible' when consideration of a new appointment or an additional appointment is made will it be possible for it to be selected. This hurdle must always be cleared effectively

**Figure 8-7**  Strategic framework

What the client wants even when he does not verbalize it himself is 'benefits' which may be interpreted in the form of cost-effective problem solutions or results.

Every feature of a professional firm's service purchased has some client benefit otherwise it can be safely assumed it would not be sought. No one, private or commercial, buys any products or any services where there is not a conscious or unconscious assessment that they will yield a benefit greater than that which the same money could achieve used in some other way.

As has already been pointed out in Chapter 7, 'Professional services and client needs', features of a service do not produce the same benefits for each purchaser of that service. A diagnostic medical service for a company's personnel can as easily be bought for 'peace of mind', 'actuarial advantage for pensions or insurance', the benefits of 'proof of fitness for specific work', 'confirmation or refutation of previous diagnosis' or even 'stakeholder confidence', these all stemming from the same diagnostic service.

It is important in identifying decision-forming factors in business to make the same translation from the features of a service to the benefits the client will obtain as has been suggested is applicable to private clients. It is again emphasized that in essence the features, e.g., speed, high skill level, inter-professional contacts or links, location, play no part in the decision. What the client wants are the benefits which derive from these features.

Figure 7-4 in Chapter 7, 'Professional services and client needs', illustrated that the transposition from service features into client benefits is not simple but must be accomplished and for the corporate purchaser there are mixed and often conflicting benefits as between the purchaser's corporate role and private interest. Figure 8-8 shows how such conformities and contradictions can arise in any one decision.

The whole emphasis must be on explaining to the client and convincing him of the benefits to be obtained. The features, as already shown, do however have an important role to fulfil. They are the means by which an intangible can be made less ephemeral since they offer deducible proof factors. A qualification which is accepted as proof of skill will also contribute

| Financial (for the decision-maker's firm) | The service (for the decision-maker's firm) | Social or political (for self) | Personal |
|---|---|---|---|
| Absolute lowest fees | Pre- and post-service around the central service | Enhancement of decision maker's standing with own management | Internal liking and respect as a result of the decision |
| Greatest cost effectiveness | | | |
| | Specific features to be introduced into the service | | Compatibility of decision with decision maker's self-perceptions |
| Operating or administrative cost reductions | | Creation of personal leverage with professional service firm | |
| Long credit | Speed of completion | | |
| | | Prestige derived from reputation of retained firm | |
| Contingency payment pricing (fee based on acts to be performed or accomplished) | Allocation of specific personnel | | |
| | Acceptance of responsibility and liability | | |
| | Compatibility between service firm and own staff | | |

**Figure 8-8** Examples of benefits corporate decision makers seek[10]

10. This figure as Figure 8-1 is adapted from the work of Thomas V. Bonoma. Op. cit.

to the conviction that the application of that skill will produce a satisfactory solution to the problem or 'peace of mind' if that is the benefit sought.

A commercial client will seek for the firm the most advantageous financial deal he can obtain, operating cost reductions, back-up services, punctuality in delivering and completing the service, compatibility between his own and the professional service firm's staff. At the same time he will also be aware and will be negotiating on the basis of whether the decision will enhance his own standing within his company, whether it will give him personal leverage with the practice chosen, whether as a result of the decisions he will be the subject of greater respect and liking and, not unimportant, if the choice of firm and service is compatible with his self-perceptions. He will be looking for the best 'mix' between his business and personal needs.

Just as with private clients it cannot be assumed that converting features into benefits will convince clients they will actually receive those benefits. Clients will search for objective evidence and subjective indicators of proof as was emphasized in Chapter 2, 'Understanding service businesses', page 11, and in Chapter 7, 'Professional services and client needs'. Reference back to pages 90–3 and Figures 7-4 and 7-5 will show the link between features, benefits and proof as well as a simple format to assist the process of identifying these issues.

It is a practical and useful exercise for all personnel involved, however remotely, with practice development to identify the issues given in Figure 8-9 and translate them as appropriate to the needs of their individual clients. The information in columns 3, 4 and 5 will have already been established if the check list in Chapter 7, 'Professional services and client needs', Figure 7-5, has been completed.


## Consolidation

The decision-making process can be summarized in a single matrix as shown in Figure 8.10.

The example given is a decision to change a bank. Heading the columns are the job titles of those within the decision-making unit who are responsible for the decision functions shown earlier in Figure 8-1. Across the bottom are numbered factors each member of the decision-making unit would consider as being relevant to his activities and interests. Along the left-hand side are the steps in the decision process given in Figure 8-4. Every number on the matrix represents the factors considered by the person in the job function listed at the decision stage shown in the left-hand column. Thus the Financial Director along with the General Manager see the need for a new banker based on a requirement for 'administrative efficiency' (No. 7). At the next stage 'Determination of the characteristics of the needed service' some seven different departments and individuals are involved. Now the 'asset base' (No. 1), 'interest rates' (No. 3), 'charges' (No. 2), 'speed in decision making' (No. 6), are all factors the Financial Director is taking into account while additionally the General Manager is now also concerned with 'range of services' (No. 4) and 'geographical coverage' (No. 5). This illustrates how the different factors become significant at different stages of the buying process and for different personnel involved.

The value of attempting to re-construct either a successful acquisition of a new client or an unsuccessful contact is that it sensitizes those responsible for improving their commercial client business to the three key factors which must be understood and appreciated for the critical importance they hold:

- Identifying the decision-making unit and power centres.
- Understanding the buying sequence and classifications.
- Determining the factors which will create favourable decisions.

| 1 | 2 | 3 | 4 | 5 | 6 | 7 |
|---|---|---|---|---|---|---|
| Which individuals are in the decision making centre and what is the basis of their power? | Who are the powerful decision makers and what are their priorities? | What specific benefits does each important decision maker want? | What are the features of our services and how do they meet benefit requirements? | How can we prove the features will yield the benefits? | How do important decision makers see us? | What practice development strategy and tactics do the answers imply? |

**Figure 8-9**  Encapsulation format for major issues

106

## Decision to change a bank

| DECISION PROCESS | Collective Decisions: Board | Collective Decisions: Inter-department Management Committee | Individual (Non-Departmental): Financial Director | Individual (Non-Departmental): General Manager | Departmental Decision: Chief Accountant | Departmental Decision: Export Manager | Departmental Decision: Personnel Manager | Departmental Decision: Credit Manager | Departmental Decision: Share Registrar | Departmental Decision: Buying | External: Others Outside Company |
|---|---|---|---|---|---|---|---|---|---|---|---|
| | Decision factors considered | | Decision factors considered | | Decision factors considered | | | | | | |
| 1. Anticipation or recognition of a problem or need | | | 7 | 7 | | | | | | | |
| 2. Determination of the requirements the needed service must meet | | 2, 4, 6 | 1, 3, 2, 6 | 4, 5, 6, 7 | | | | | 7 | 4, 5 | 9 |
| 3. Specification or description of the service and the service firm | | 2, 4, 5, 6 | 7, 1, 2 | 7, 8, 4 | 1, 7, 9 | 5, 4 | | 2, 3 | 7 | 4, 5 | 9 |
| 4. Search for and qualification of the individual or practice | | | 2, 3, 4 | 4, 5, 7, 8 | 2, 3, 7 | 5, 2 | 5, 4 | 2, 7 | 7 | 2, 4, 8 | 7, 9 |
| 5. Obtaining offers, presentations and proposals and analysing them | | | ALL | | ALL | | | | | | |
| 6. Evaluation, comparison and selection of the most suitable firm and individual | 1, 2, 3, 8 | | 2, 3, 7, 8 | | 1, 2, 3, 8 | 5, 6 | 5, 7, 4 | 2, 3, 6, 8 | 7, 8 | | 1, 7, 8 |
| 7. Designation of the methods for conducting the service, liaison and contacts | | | 7, 9 | | 7, 9 | | | | | | 7, 8 |
| 8. Performance feedback and evaluation | 1, 2, 7, 8 | 1, 7 | 7, 2, 1, 8 | 1, 2, 7 | 7, 2, 1, 8 | 1, 2, 7 | 7 | 7, 2, 1 | 7 | 7 | |

### How to use the Matrix

Below are a number of typical decision-forming factors which will be considered by different managers at various stages of the decision-making process. Others can be added. To use the matrix indicate in each management function and at each stage of the decision-making process at which they are likely to be involved, those factors they will take into account in arriving at a decision. Check that the managers concerned have the appropriate information on your service and that the method of communicating this information to the managers involved is effective.

### Factors for Consideration

1 = Asset base
2 = Charges
3 = Interest rates
4 = Range of services
5 = Geographical coverage
6 = Speed in decision making
7 = Administrative efficiency
8 = Other user experience
9 = Security of information

**Figure 8-10** Purchasing matrix

# Chapter 9.  How a professional service is selected

The previous chapter has shown the complexity of the buying decision so far as corporate clients are concerned. But before a client can make any decision on the individual practice or practitioner to be appointed, a selection process must occur which decides between competing services, competing products (which can often substitute a service as was shown in Chapter 2, 'Understanding service businesses') and competing practices offering similar services. Formally or informally, consciously or unconsciously an elimination process will occur. At one extreme the prospective client will consider every option narrowing it down to the final selection; at the other extreme it will be simply a return to the original supplier of professional services. It is however necessary to distinguish between the selection process adopted by private individuals and those used by corporate clients.

It may appear illogical to describe the selection process after the decision-making process which in effect is the last stage of selection. The order has been deliberately reversed because the concept of the three level decision-making process (decision-making unit, decision-making sequence and classification and decision-forming factors) has to be understood if the explanation of selection process itself is to carry its full meaning.

Both in this chapter on selection and in the next one on how the individual practice is chosen, the emphasis is on the commercial client although the private client is by no means ignored. Selection and choice by private clients tend to be far more simplistic and direct than those of commercial organizations. Such little research as has been undertaken into methods of selection and choice used by individuals in identifying, appraising and appointing their professional advisers indicates that there is very little consideration of alternatives as between different services and between different practices. The power of recommendations, most particularly when the referral source is respected, is dominant. Thus individuals, even knowledgeable ones, in the majority of cases make decisions as to the appropriate service either by themselves or as a result of informal discussions with friends, associates and other professional advisers and then approach either known practitioners or firms or those suggested by others. Possible minor exceptions could be those services which are either permitted to advertise or where retail outlet merchandising occurs (e.g., banks, opticians). The test of the validity of these statements is for every reader to consider how he reached and decided on his own professional advisers, whether they be accountants, stockbrokers, dentists, doctors, architects, surveyors, insurance brokers or others.

In examining the processes which narrow down the choice to the final decision, both types of clients' thinking, perceptions and activities need to be understood if practice development is to succeed with either or both groups of users. One of the absolutes in marketing as will be seen from Figure 3-2 in Chapter 3, 'Creating a client-centred practice', is that unless a profession or a practice is known when the selection process is under way it cannot possibly be chosen. This is a pre-condition for success for acquiring additional clients of either category.

If the answers can be found or at least reasonably deduced to the following questions, then the practice development activity can be sharply focused in terms of timing, the methods to be used to convey information and the content of the message itself:

1. Is a professional service needed?
2. Why is a service needed?
3. What professional service is needed?
4. Who (within a commercial client company) needs the service?
5. What information does the prospective client require to aid his decision as to the correct service?

These questions, in essence, are inherent in the various stages of the decision-making process as shown in Figure 8-4 in the previous chapter. In particular Questions 1, 2, 3 and 5 above link closely to the same numbered stages in Figure 8-4.

## Is a professional service needed?

Chapter 7, 'Professional services and client needs', emphasized that a major source of client uncertainty might well be a doubt if a service of any description is needed at all. The first stage of the selection process for the client has to be a belief that a service is indeed required. In terms of practice development and 'messages' this implies a requirement for a constant, easily available and understood flow of information concerning the specific type of service and its relevance to client situations where the need for a service is not necessarily obvious to the client. Examples were given in Chapter 7, 'Professional services and client needs', but at its simplest and one to which almost everyone can relate is the vacillation which often occurs in a decision to call out a doctor during the night.

A vague feeling that some sort of advice, assistance or support is required does not necessarily imply that there is a case for consulting a professional service. The doubt as to whether a service is needed may be fully justified and the true professional would not under any circumstance seek to offer his service or suggest any other if there was no fundamental need for one.

In contradistinction, however, the unease or doubt which may lead a private client or firm to speculate on the advisability of calling in professional help may indicate a real requirement, in which case the role of the professional is to remove the doubts and demonstrate the alternatives to not using professional help.

The implication of understanding a client situation where the use of any service at all is unclear is the opportunity it provides for ensuring that the client is fully informed as to the relevance and value of a particular professional service. Doubts concerning the need for a service or the possibility of using a 'do-it-yourself' approach have to be eliminated if the next stage of the screening and selection process clients adopt is to include the profession and the practice likely to be involved.

## Why is a service needed?

For the practice development personnel it is of considerable value to know why it is thought a service is needed. Reasons can range from the obvious—expert advice—to the obscure—an assumption of responsibility by the professional, and can be an amalgam of a number of motives.

Some of the reasons an individual or company seeks professional help can be exampled but, as Figure 7-1 in Chapter 7, 'Professional services and client needs' illustrated the reason for seeking a service does not necessarily indicate which one is most appropriate. If the reason is known however, it will at least enable emphasis to be given to the relevant features of that service (see Figure 9-1).

| Reason | Private client | Examples Professional | Corporate client | Professional |
|---|---|---|---|---|
| Need for special skills for a specific reason or circumstance | Threatened prosecution | Solicitor | Staff losses caused by poor induction techniques | Industrial psychologist |
| Intermittently recurring requirement or need for temporary extra capacity | Investment advice | Banker or Stockbroker | Acquisition of a property portfolio requiring structural surveying | Chartered surveyor |
| Nature of problem—one off, sporadic recurrence, long term | Invention protection | Patent agent | Building extension | Architect |
| Need for total objectivity and/or freedom from internal pressures | — | — | Pension fund management | Investment counsellor |
| Lack of physical resource | Polluted water supply | Chemist (and laboratory equipment) | New product development | Contract R & D |
| Cross-industry fertilization | Employment change | Career consultant | Diversification | Management consultant |
| Anonymity or confidentiality | Illness | Doctor | Company acquisition | Financial analyst |
| Emergency requirement | Injury to animal | Veterinary surgeon | Threat to computer system | Security specialist |
| Legal requirement | Conveyance | Solicitor | Audit | Accountant |

**Figure 9-1** Need for a service

## What professional service is needed?

Because recognition of a need for some form of assistance will not necessarily lead to a given profession, there will be many circumstances when the results required could be achieved with varying degrees of satisfaction from totally unrelated services or from products. Figure 7-1 in Chapter 7, 'Professional services and client needs', listed a number of problems which could be resolved by completely different services; solicitors competing directly with accountants, surveyors with architects; accountants with computer software services; estate planners with merchant banks and, of course, products can also substitute for services. It can already be seen that with the rapidly growing population of home computers and software programmes, the private client may well be able to dispense with some of the services of accountants and other financial services.

The examples of varying interpretations of a service need, as applied to a single issue, raise a particular problem for the professional. It is expecting too much of human beings to assume that any provider of a professional service will not, in the first instance at least, attempt to see a need in terms of his own disciplines. However, an ethical and professional approach will ensure that if the best 'fit' is not one which the practitioner can give, he will say so and even recommend alternatives. No matter how much professional service firms may know and practise this, is not necessarily apparent to the prospective client. Thus, a primary objective in practice development is to ensure that the potential client has faith that he will be advised objectively on the correct service to meet his needs.

Those who offer their professional services in situations where the need for a specific type of service is not unequivocal, must make their initial appraisal of the client's problem on a totally open-minded basis. In these circumstances it is important to be sure the appropriate service is offered, not only in terms of the firm's professional expertise, but also within the full range of other services (or indeed products) which may be available to meet the particular need even if the firm itself cannot provide what is required.

Relative to the choice of services, certain important implications for practice development personnel are raised. The successful projection of an image of competence in one field may eliminate the service firm in another. This is how it should be if the choice were, for example, between a firm with expertise in marine insurance to the exclusion of all else, and another whose areas of activity were limited to life insurance. However, a practice with an image and a substance of capability in mathematical modelling, linear programme, and computing sciences may not be considered in a situation in which a transportation and supply problem is involved because management cannot always make the transition necessary to relate mathematical modelling to its particular problem. The answer is as always communication, but on an individual level.

## Who needs the service?

Because a service must be perceived as appropriate to clients' requirements in terms of both the skills involved and their availability, for practice development purposes it is necessary to ensure the potential recipient of the service can indeed connect the discipline to the problem. Unless this can be achieved there is every chance that what would be a totally appropriate service may be overlooked or rejected because the link between problem or situation and the profession is not wholly clear or convincing to the client. Again the screening process will eliminate some professions and practices within them, perhaps unfairly, because of poor understanding and communication.

The private client is most usually the user of the services he purchases although there are circumstances where an outside influence might require his retaining and using a service. A bank manager could be insistent that a client in personal financial difficulties consult an accountant, a dentist might demand medical treatment prior to undertaking major conservation or cosmetic work, an architect could require structural or geological surveys. However, in none of these cases are the prime professionals likely to insist on the use of a particular accountant, doctor or surveyor, even though they will jointly be the recipients and users of the other professional's advice.

Substantially however, in seeking to save the corporate client there is a need to identify the actual users of the service who may not be decision makers in the choice of service or practice.

The distinction must be made between those within a firm who actually experience and are involved in the service and those who decide on which service and which firm (the decision-making unit). In the Bonoma model given in Figure 8-1 in Chapter 8, 'Professional services and the commercial client', the user is shown as part of the decision-making unit but this is not necessarily always the case. In the appointment of a company medical adviser the majority of users will have had no say whatsoever in the appointment.

With exceptions such as these in mind, it is safe to conclude that so far as corporate clients are concerned the users will frequently have decision influence in either a positive or negative way, as is illustrated in Figure 8-2 in Chapter 8, 'Professional services and the commercial client'.

Nevertheless, the problem of identifying who in the firm actually needs the service has its own complications and its own unsureness: falling sales might imply that it is the sales department and the sales manager who need help, but this decline in sales might well stem from product inadequacies which might call for the services of a consultant engineer to reorganize production and quality control and to assist the production manager; it might be a final price acceptability problem requiring the work of a cost accountant; it might stem from bad logistics which would require an expert in operational research to aid the merchandise or transport manager; it could be the result of badly apportioned sales territories which need to be reorganized by a marketing expert called in to guide the marketing director; or the effect registered may be outside the firm's control, some aspect of environmental change which a sociologist or economist might probe and analyse and suggest to the board how the threats posed could be avoided and the opportunities exploited.

Moreover, although the client's objective may be the same, there can easily be a need for different professional services at different managerial levels, and thus different personnel, different activities and at different times. Given the expansion of manufacturing activity was the objective, an econometrician, statistician or marketing researcher may be required to validate market size and growth hypotheses upon which the extent of expansion will be based. Another decision might well be whether any expansion should be based on present plant or should new plant be built? This may be the province of consulting and production engineers as well as accountants and other financial experts. If new plant is decided on, then where should it be located for optimum results? Here the logistic, operational research and infrastructure experts may be needed. What type of structure will be needed and at what cost will be questions for architects, quantity surveyors and structural engineers to consider. Will new plant and systems create labour problems which may call for the special expertise in industrial relations? The questions form a decision tree along which, at various points, different professional services may be needed to take the firm to the next critical point.

Decisions are arrived at in a variety of ways, but the question which is posed in the situation exampled is: 'If management has been familiar with the professional services available for reducing the areas of uncertainty and resolving problems, would it have used such services?' The answer almost certainly is 'yes' which again underlines the need for continuing communications between service providers and the clients they seek to service.

It can be seen that just where in a business organization a professional service may be needed and which individuals or group of individuals would be the actual beneficiaries of the service is not necessarily self-indicative. If in any circumstances the answer is not obvious, as it may not be, then the professionals involved must probe the situation and ensure that the benefits to the actual user are not submerged in seeking to promote the more general benefits to the firm. Figure 8-8 in Chapter 8, 'Professional services and the commercial client', illustrates this situation.

Failure to identify the actual users can easily lead to the communication of inappropriate benefits and to the loss of what might be powerful advocacy on behalf of the profession and the individual practice. Thus the risk of elimination at this stage of the selection procedure is as great as at any other, even though the need for a service has been accepted, the reasons for seeking a service are understood and the service required is accurately identified.

## What information does the prospective client need?

The information requirements of prospective clients must be viewed at two levels. First, that which is needed in the selection process which will tend to be general and which gradually narrows choice. Second, the specific information on the individual profession related to the client's situation. Thus information needs will vary not only at the different stages of selection but also between the different individuals involved in decision making and the users who will receive the services. The position of the prospective client and professional service firms can be summarized.

| Client | Professional service |
|--------|---------------------|
| 1. Uncertainty as to whether a need for a service exists | Analyse situation and assist client to a decision by objective questioning and comment |
| 2. Why the service is needed | Probe the reasons and relate service skills, experience and availability to the reasons |
| 3. Which service is needed | Identify and bring client to agree the substantive problem. Demonstrate relevance of the generic service to the problem or recommend an alternative appropriate service |
| 4. Who within the firm will actually use the service | Link the specific benefits of the individual job responsibilities and the criteria which are used to assess the service user's own performance |
| 5. What knowledge is required to make a sound decision | Ensure that the correct category of information is communicated to all personnel in the client firm involved and that it is comprehensible in their terms and is convincing |

**Figure 9-2**   Client–profession interface in selection process

The client will have passed uncertainly through the different stages of selection, whether this is done consciously or not. Therefore, the professional who is presenting his discipline must be sure not to omit the sequences which parallel the decision process for the client as he moves towards his final choice.

# Chapter 10.   How the individual practice is selected

The previous chapter attempted to show the development of the screening process by which the choice is narrowed down to a manageable number of practices, perhaps not all of the same discipline. It also sought to align the practice development task with the progress of the screening. Now it is necessary to turn to the presentation of the individual practice in a way that will encourage a favourable decision to use that practice.

The answers to the questions posed on page 109 will give the guidelines the practice developer must use to influence a favourable decision. The actual procedures which are adopted finally to select an individual professional service firm, while being extremely varied, can at least be summarized in a usable way.

## Client criteria

The prospective client is likely to have established a number of decision-forming factors; among them the degree of specialization or the availability of a 'full line' offering, types of services available or work undertaken, appropriateness of facilities for the problem under consideration, professional recognition, numbers, types, qualification of staff, location, overseas or inter-professional links. The existence or lack of any of these or other relevant factors may be the decision-forming factor as to whether the professional service firm or the individual will reach the short list.

Because, as yet, the service company can have little or no knowledge of the nature of the work to be undertaken, contact is on a generalized level. For the would-be buyer of a service, this has the inestimable advantage of making it possible to obtain factual data on the service firm not coloured, deliberately or accidentally, by a claimed bias towards the problem area. The service firm, faced with the dilemma already referred to, of being asked to demonstrate its suitability for a project of which it has little knowledge, is forced to adopt the *extrinsic* approach referred to on page 85 that is, in presenting the practice concentrating on its resources, skills, experience, rather than addressing these to the substantive problem the client has presented. Exaggeration and bias, even if not discounted at this stage, will not be particularly harmful to the client since the enquiry is to obtain a short list, not actively to select the service company.

In Figure 8-5 in Chapter 8, 'Professional services and the commercial client', it was shown that the need for a service can be stimulated by external factors among which would be the practice development activities of the service firm. If this should be the source of potential business, then although the selection process will still occur, the professional service firm which has stimulated the enquiry will be in a dominant position as initiator. Thus what is described next might well be short circuited.

If then the need for a service has been identified and generated by the individual company requiring it, rather than by a service firm, the first steps in the process of deciding who is to provide the service will be to obtain information on firms or practitioners which can, or which claim to be able to, satisfy the requirement for the service.

The actions of prospective clients with previous experience of the firm and those to whom it is a new experience will vary greatly at this point in the process of selection.

While both types of clients may construct a list of 'possibles' from which the service oganizations they consider unsuitable will be eliminated, it is highly likely that previous users of services will return to the firms which have satisfied them on other occasions. The very least they will do is to include a previous and successful practice on the list they intended to select from.

Each stage of the selection procedure, which can be likened to an inverted triangle, will eliminate firms. The inverted base of the triangle may be large or small, depending on: the total number of firms which could be included; the extent of knowledge of the enquirer both relating to suppliers of the services and to his own needs; and the time available for the selection procedure.

## Identifying the individual practice

Given that the 'prospect' has no previous contact or experience in the service area concerned, he will tend to seek and consider information on all possible suppliers of the service.

An old and limited study[1] of 250 commercial concerns and 250 individuals, and for which no statistical accuracy is claimed, but according to most professions contacted appears to conform to their own experience, shows the overwhelming importance of the referral system or inter-personal network. It would seem that given the very limited use of other marketing tools and methods the referral system is overwhelmingly the most important method by which a client reaches a professional adviser.

The study referred to revealed the details displayed in Figure 10-1.

| Private clients | Commercial clients |
| --- | --- |
| Listed in order of number of mentions | |
| Friends and business associates | Friends and business associates |
| Directories[2] | Directories[2] |
| Retail outlet merchandizing[3] | Professional associations |
| Advertisements and editorial comment | Advisers in other professions[4] |
| Professional advisers[4] | Social or business groups |
| Social groups | Advertisements and editorial comment |
| Exhibitions | |
| Outdoor advertising (site boards) | |
| (Other mentions included universities, government departments, foreign chambers of commerce, trade and professional journals) | |

**Figure 10-1**   Sources of information

1. Industrial Market Research Limited (London, 1977).
2. Substantially the directories referred to were local classified directories.
3. These appear to be largely insurance broking and financial services, estate agencies and building societies.
4. Bank managers dominate.

It is not unknown, however, for seekers of services to examine a bibliography of the subject and then locate authors of books, articles and learned papers, in order to commission their authors' services either directly or through their firms. An examination of 'leads' of professional service firms confirms that a small but useful proportion of initial contacts which were client originated came through the publication of material related to the subject area, or to lectures and papers.

This method of preparing a first screening list, although likely to be laborious and in some respects haphazard, has the advantage to the enquirer of giving a first impression of the capability of the individual and his firm and his interest and experience in the professional area under consideration.

The implication for individuals and firms of these sources of information are obvious in that they are important 'third party' referral targets. Chapter 13, 'The referral (recommendations) system', Chapter 16, 'The use of personal contact', and Chapter 17, 'Non-personal methods of practice development', all contain information on the creation of third party referrals and the utilization of this invaluable method of practice development.

One circumstance which may particularly favour a practice is if it is mentioned favourably or listed in a number of different sources. A firm appearing in separate lists provided by authoritative institutes, knowledgeable groups and perhaps a university and a trade paper, may prove to be a natural candidate for inclusion in the short list.

However, the more usual process, at least in respect of those firms which have not been eliminated on totally subjective grounds, is for information or the literature of the service firm to be requested or for an initial correspondence or a telephone conversation to take place to establish the scale, scope, and extent of the services and resources of the firm. At this point, the prospective client is likely to be watching for the degree of specialization, client and assignment listings, the appropriateness of the facilities for the problem under review, professional recognition and how closely these aspects of the firm's services, resources and skills conform to the original criteria devised.

Again, reference to Figure 8-5 in Chapter 8, 'Professional services and the commercial client', will show that it is usual for commercial purchasers of professional services to seek external opinions and information on experience concerning the reputation and performance of any practice under consideration. Depending on the sources themselves and the extent of their experience or exposure, the views expressed can have a very significant influence in the final choice of a professional practice.

If at the end of this information-gathering process, which of course can be and usually is highly informal and unstructured, the prospective client still has too many names a further elimination will take place on what are largely subjective grounds: 'inconveniently located', 'address looks like a private house', 'must be a one man firm', 'too big to be interested in the volume or type of work we require' and so on.


## The importance of evidence

Those firms which have survived the elimination process will then be most likely subjected to more detailed scrutiny.

A skilled purchaser of professional services will never omit the opportunity of visiting a prospective supplier while the less skilled will regard it as a matter of status that the professional, being the vendor, will visit him, the purchaser. For some professional services, but by no means all, the firm may well be expected to permit the prospective client to tour its offices and to meet members of the professional staff. The objection that a breach of confidence may ensue if this is allowed is not likely to carry very much weight and, in fact, may destroy confidence in the service firm's claims at the very outset. While it is obvious that no proprietary information can be given in such conversations, a general discussion can provide important insights into the service firm's skills and resources, and can be to its advantage.

Buyers of services, both the skilled and the inexperienced, will usually use the detailed screening process to ask questions about the professional company's organization, background and performance. How, for example, does a service firm staffed by economists deal with the need for expert scientific guidance in a particular subject area? If from internal staff, then the qualifications and experience of these experts will be requested; if external help is sought, from whom? What is to be the nature of the relationship between the service firm and its own external suppliers of services?

It is at this point in the selection procedure that the importance of 'evidence' already referred to in Chapter 2, 'Understanding service businesses', becomes obvious.[5] 'Evidence' makes a considerable contribution to the assessment of suitability of a practice. Evidence which was previously divided into only two categories—peripheral and essential—can now be further subdivided into **human**, **environmental** and **collateral** evidence. In the selection process all three types of evidence will be used consciously or unconsciously to assess the suitability of the practice or individual under consideration.

## Human evidence

Extreme as the example may be, it is easy to exemplify the importance of human evidence. A surgeon in Hari Krishna attire or an accountant dressed as the Lone Ranger are both likely to generate discomfort because of the dissonance between the expected and archetypal appearance of professionals. Conversely and less extreme, but nevertheless in the same category in using human evidence to achieve acceptability, is the decision of a government department training senior and older counsellors in management techniques, to use mature lecturers and trainers rather than young and (to the counsellors) relatively inexperienced personnel.

Information will also be sought on the qualifications and the experience of staff, for which supporting evidence may be required.

It cannot be overlooked at this point that part of the human evidence will relate to the extent to which the prospective client judges the professional staff to be sympathetic, understanding, involved or simply compatible with his own personality, needs or those of his firm or his personnel. Human evidence is not just technical, but 'human' in the widest sense of that word.

## Environmental evidence

Examples of environmental evidence are the firm's premises and equipment in use. Because of the intangibility factor in services the prospective client is searching constantly for material evidence of a firm's suitability. Although it may be trivial the physical (environmental) evidence of the firm's material possessions, if not in itself critical, cumulatively and in combination with other assessable evidence, can have an important influence in the ultimate decision.

5. Lynn G. Shostack. 'The importance of evidence'. *The American Banker* (New York, 25 March 1981).

It takes little imagination to deduce the effect on a private patient of ancient apparatus, a less than hygienic surgery and uncomfortable examination equipment in the premises of any practitioner concerned with personal care. The effect can be just as negative in other types of professional services where equipment and premises play no part, or a very minor part, in the delivery of the service. Lack of telex, facsimile, word processors, photocopying or a host of other office aids may well say something about the success of the practice or the attitude of the practitioners. Thus, claims regarding the possession of some physical resources such as laboratories, audio-visual equipment, computers, information retrieval systems, and special purpose premises, may be covertly checked.

## Collateral evidence

Collateral evidence comprises such items as stationery, graphics, reports and practice identity logos and symbols. While human evidence can have an immediate and pervasive effect in eliminating a firm from consideration or can even terminate a relationship, environmental and collateral evidence is not as potent but inconsistencies can and do have a cumulative effect. Practice development, particularly in attempting to influence the selection process, must include a definition of the desired effect of all three forms of evidence on the potential client and activities and evidence must be adjusted and manipulated to achieve compatibility.[6]

Because the purchasing of professional services for most commercial concerns lacks any formalized technique or methodology, the opportunity to observe 'evidence' is often lost by the refusal, already mentioned, of the would-be client to visit the practitioners. There is still as already indicated an element of status involved in which the purchaser adopts a superior role to the vendor. This buyer–seller relationship, redolent as it is of the Victorian pejorative of 'trade', persists more to the disadvantage of client than the service firm. A visit to the professional service organization apart from the evaluation of 'evidence' can also give a 'feel' for the firm, its ambience and indeed the reality of some of its claims. For example an organization claiming to employ 30 architects might be expected to occupy more than two or three small rooms. Professional status symbols are not necessarily indicative of top-quality work, but then neither is the use of very old equipment and furniture likely to invoke in any prospective purchaser of the firm's services the feeling of a successful organization.

## The independence factor

Another aspect of the screening process narrowing down to the final choice of professional adviser relates to the degree of independence of the firm—a factor of considerable importance in some professional services but totally inapplicable or irrelevant in others. Some professions such as architects, accountants and solicitors, are permitted to hold directorships in limited companies. The question of cross-directorships may be important. Professional service firms may not consider that because one of the partners or its professional staff sits on the boards of companies their professional independence is compromised or that client confidences are at risk. It does not follow *pari passu* that the client shares this view and that he will not feel exposed and vulnerable. Accountancy firms with their own management consultancy divisions could be in an invidious position when their auditors find that performance of the client has

6. Once again the author is indebted to Lynn G. Shostack for permission to quote from and to adapt her work on evidence in service marketing. 'How to design a service'. *European Journal of Marketing*, **16** (1) (Bradford, 1982). Also 'The importance of evidence'. *The American Banker* (New York, 25 March 1981).

been adversely affected by the advice given by another part of the practice. Professional institutions and associations have continued, if somewhat weakly, to insist on declarations of divided interest. The Architects' Code of Practice concerning 'concurrent practice'—that is acting as an independent consultant and as a director of a property development, contracting or manufacturing company—imposes an obligation to declare and resolve any conflicts of interest but only in the 'traditional professional manner' and a requirement exists to provide the Professional Conduct Committee details although prior approval of concurrent practice is not needed.[7] Clients may well, and increasingly do, demand that their putative professional advisers clarify the degree of their independence and almost certainly this requirement should be met by far stronger statements than are at present commonly used or else remain unspoken.

## Other screening factors

A number of other aspects may be used to screen and eliminate firms in specific circumstances depending on the client, the problem and the discipline involved.

## Extent of repeat and on-going business

The incidence of repeat or on-going business is another measure of a professional service firm's satisfactory performance and is one which the client may link with the client list by checking on repeat business claims.

There is no standard ratio of new to repeat business which indicates the firm satisfies its clients. The newer the practice the more likely that first time clients will dominate; the smaller the catchment area from which work is obtained the higher will be the repeat business. The buyer of services in asking the question must judge for himself what he would regard as a satisfactory division. Just asking the question will indicate to the practice that the prospective client is attempting to assess performance as well as the other factors involved in the decision.

## Reason for seeking a service

Understanding the client's reasoning concerning the need for a professional service has obvious value in assisting the selection of the individual practice. The very reason for seeking a service will eliminate any firms which cannot meet the reason. Thus from the examples in Figure 9-1 in the previous chapter, if in the case of animal injury or a threat to computer security the emergency service is not immediately available, then that particular practice or individual will be removed from further consideration.

## Clients' information needs

At the choice decision as between competing practices, information needs become very specific indeed. Although it may not be simple to identify them, it is possible to make some very accurate assumptions even with limited briefing and client information.

To revert to the model in Figure 8-10 in Chapter 8, 'Professional services and the

7. Annual Report of the Royal Institute of British Architects (1982).

commercial client', which concerns a financial service, it can be seen that different members of the decision-making unit's interests covered a wide span of information. The chief accountant was concerned at various times during the decision-making continuum with the bank's asset base, administrative efficiency and security of information. The export manager's interests were confined to geographical coverage, range of services available and speed in decision making. With this information the content of the message addressed to each individual becomes clear.

In contradistinction, emphasizing an international network of offices when the basic requirement is for high-level governmental contacts within the individual countries is either to emphasize the wrong facility or else to hope the client will be able to deduce that the network of overseas offices implies that the types of contacts needed exist. Either way the approach is ineffective.

In Chapter 4, 'Preparing for practice development', considerable emphasis was placed on the value of the information resource within a firm. Just how valuable this is can be seen from the importance it can be made to play in the screening process which is part of the selection of a professional practice.

In their attempt to eliminate any form of what the consultant professions prefer to call 'touting' rather than marketing, the rules have been so oppressive and all embracing until very recently it has been virtually impossible for a professional firm to provide information to prospective clients except at their own request even when such information is totally factual and without any persuasive or laudatory content whatsoever. The confusion of persuasive with factual material has the effect of constraining many ethical attempts at practice development with all the advantages that this may bring. At the same time it has opened doors to unqualified and often uncontrolled competition. The limits of absurdity have surely been reached when an optician is prevented from using a bold type entry in a classified directory!

The considerable relaxation or at least interpretation of the 'touting' rules which is now occurring will enable professional firms to convey to prospective clients information they need to assist them to make sensible and profitable decisions. Quite unlike the Bar Association's view given to the Monopolies Commission 'If barristers were to advertise, the advantages would go not to the best qualified, but to the barristers with the longest purse and least scruples', the opposite would be true. The barrister able to state unequivocally his experience and interest would receive appropriate briefs and in all likelihood increase his depth of knowledge. Perhaps it might also go some way to protect clients from the results of a situation Carr-Saunders described: 'The greater part of a barrister's experience and probably much of his experience of chamber work, is acquired at the risk and expense of his clients after he has begun to practice.'[8]

Information and persuasive advertising are not one and the same thing and moreover advertising as any marketing man knows rarely, if ever, convinces the public to purchase what they do not want. A graveyard of heavily advertised products and companies which no longer exist testify to this truism.

## Allocation of professional staff

With the larger service firms another problem, which arises for the prospective client and which may need to be cleared at the detailed screening, is precisely who in the organization will undertake the work. It is a common and an all too often justified criticism that a partner deals

8. Carr-Saunders and P. A. Wilson. *The Professions*. Cass (London, 1964), p. 10.

with the client at the outset but a legal assistant, audit clerk or others actually do the work. Such a transfer of responsibility might be thoroughly justified in terms of lower fees in that the work is not conducted by someone with a higher level of skill or qualification than is justified, but it does not stop the client who discovers such a situation feeling if not cheated, then at least, misled.

The problem of the professional service company in designating which staff will be assigned to projects when the details and timing are not yet fixed is very considerable, but the advantages to the clients of knowing with whom they will deal are also considerable. This information removes the faceless aspect of the service organization and indicates where responsibility for the work will lie. Moreover it ensures that if the service is successful and further work is required, the same practitioner can be asked to undertake the assignment. Professional service firms may have a continuous corporate life, but the individuals they employ change and there is no guarantee of consistently high standards merely because the same firm carries out the work. The skilled selector of professional services, and often the less skilled, will seek satisfaction on all these points before getting down to a discussion of the problem with the service firm.

## Detailed discussions

Assuming the would-be buyer is satisfied on all the issues, the nature of the enquiry may now be discussed, or a further meeting may be called specifically for this purpose. It may have been delayed until this stage is reached because, unless the prospective client is reasonably certain a service firm is going to be asked to undertake the assignment, he may not wish to reveal details. To do so will often mean that confidential or sensitive information must be presented. The client will not want to talk in confidence with more individuals or practices than is necessary to enable a decision to be made as to which one will be appointed.

It is when the subject of the enquiry is revealed that the professional service firm can begin to exhibit its expertise. While it is unreasonable to expect an immediate understanding in depth of a problem as soon as it is presented, if the subject is within the area of the firm's capability, it is possible for it to demonstrate a familiarity, at least with the terminology of the subject if not with the problem itself. It is here that appropriate analogies are most useful, but the client firm may be more impressed by the quality of the questioning than by instant answers, potted assumptions and glib solutions.

## The offer

For the private client the offer of service will usually be nothing more formal than an explicit or implicit statement that the practitioner or practice can indeed help and is willing to do so. It may include a statement on timing and on actual or indicative fees. It will also suggest the initiation process, the client's role and information required from him.

For the corporate client the offer may be far more formal. Indeed it may take the form of a full presentation with all the appropriate personnel involved and contributing, complete with audio-visual aids. Because many professional services are complex and perhaps esoteric, it would be usual for the offer to be in writing and to be most detailed even if this document is only a confirmation of a verbal presentation. Today few commercial firms will enter into a commitment of financial or consequential significance where the content, timing, cost and yield of the proposed activity has not been outlined or detailed.

Thus, whether weeks of work have gone into the preparation of the offer or whether it is a simple confirmation of a conversation, the proposal still has to convey to the prospective client everything on which the buyer requires information or seeks assurance. In other words the client must clearly see in the offer the benefits he will obtain from the service. It has to meet the three basic concepts of minimizing uncertainty, conveying an understanding of the substantive problem and being totally professional. Additionally, it must project the image which the practice wishes to convey. Unless there is a clear image objective then the offer presentation and documentation is unlikely to lend support to the substance and the image of the practice.[9]

Although the decision is not taken in a single moment of truth but rather as a series of incremental choices, the stage has now arrived when there must be a determination made whether to appoint the practice or not. The prospective client will now appraise if the practice or individual has really grasped the problem, and if the solution or the route to its solution appears to be practical, to have a high possibility of succeeding and will be cost effective. The offer will be the most tangible thing the individual or company will have until the final results are available, and thus it becomes a measure or a symbol of whether value for money has been and is being obtained. The offer whether verbal or documented fulfils several purposes for the buyer:

- It is an insurance policy which enables him to check that he finally receives that for which he has contracted for.
- It defines the services, facilities and information to be supplied by the client and thus, his non-financial commitments.
- It makes a considerable contribution to the reduction of uncertainty in the choice decision, both as regards the service chosen and the firm selected to provide the service.
- It provides a first measure of the professionalism of the practice by indicating how it has identified and come to grips with the problem, and how it rates its own capability in resolving the problem.
- It forms the legal basis for the contract.

Where a formal proposal is made it will usually contain some of the following elements:

- Appreciation of the client situation.
- Statement of problem.
- Objectives of the assignment or consultancy.
- Approach and methodology to be used.
- Definitions adopted.
- Scope of the project with, if necessary, detailed check lists of items to be included, or drawings and plans.
- Expected yield and its application in relation to the problem to be resolved.
- Time.
- Cost.
- Staffing.
- Conditions of contract.

Unless the proposal, if it is documented, is precise, unambiguous, detailed and relatively unqualified there is every likelihood that it will be rejected or else heavily amended and qualified in some way. Just as a professional who is capable of making an excellent personal presentation will convey confidence in the approach suggested, so the offer must speak for the

9. Images and perceptions play a vital role in the selection and choice of a professional service firm. The whole subject is discussed in Chapter 12, 'The importance of images and perceptions'.

practice with equal confidence. This is conveyed in its coverage, style and presentation including design and typography. 'Packaging', rarely important in professional services, has a special role at this stage of the proceedings with the final hurdle just ahead.

Not all offers whether presented personally or in writing are accepted without modification. In fact in many instances and for many professional services the offer becomes more a 'position paper'. The clients may require more details in one section, a facet of the service may be eliminated or divided between the client or his own staff and service company. Whatever changes are introduced must be agreeable to both parties, otherwise the likelihood of disagreement and disappointment at the end is very high.

Any revision introduced and accepted at this stage will require incorporating into the final offer which will remain as a fixed reference throughout. Because of the intangibility of services, the need for this is vital, although it is not usually invoked until there is a dispute as to what is supposed to be achieved or how long it is to take or how much it is to cost.

The buyer of professional services will want to ensure that as many of these points as possible are covered by the terms of the offer and that it is as unequivocal as it can be made.

## Rendering the service

The rendering of a service for both private and corporate clients can create its own problem and an important influence on the final selection will be both the manner of the rendering of the services and of the people involved. The 'how' and the 'who' of services are closely interlinked. One will, to some extent, depend upon the other. But generalizations are useful at this stage. Clearly, in deciding how the service will be rendered, the client is concerned not only with timing and with place, but also with the way in which the service will affect day-to-day operations or his way of life and, where applicable, how service personnel will impact on the commercial client's staff. The long-term gains of the effect of the service could be easily nullified by the immediate adverse conditions created by the use of the professional service firm. A new product search commencing with a corporate audit of strengths and weaknesses which, through tactlessness, ineptitude, or inexperience of the service firm staff, may well be interpreted by senior management as a threat to their personal positions, may result in heavy loss of staff or non-co-operation with disastrous results. Thus, the client sees the 'fit' of the service firm and personnel to the purchasing company to be important.

During the execution of the service there must be constant feedback of information on progress and results to the individual or the management of the purchasing company. This provides a stable operating arrangement. Service projects will sometimes change during their execution. Without good communication and feedback the areas of uncertainty can widen and become more intense. Trying to effect an insurance policy entirely by the use of self-completed forms without personal consultation or where it is insisted that meeting occur at the broker's offices rather than the client's location choice could well abort the enquiry.

Finding a 'fit' within the context of screening can be summarized as the achievement of *compatibility* (or 'chemistry' between the professional and his client), *convenience* (in location of the service, reporting points in time, methods and completion dates) and an assurance of *competence* (in all professional staff involved). The three C's may well have to be assumed until experience is gained, but if the prospective clients have doubts on any one, despite circumventing all previous hurdles, the professional or the practice may still be eliminated at this last stage.

This description of the screening system and the elimination criteria is of course a very general one and like all check lists it is only intended to summarize the majority of factors and not to suggest that each and every one will apply in all circumstances. Ranging from a situation where no screening occurs because the referral is so persuasive to one in which every step is incorporated, the professional concerned with practice development must use judgement as to which activities and considerations any given client might adopt.

Acting on the assumption that all steps described will be accomplished it is far less likely to lead to errors than assuming that few if any will be adopted. A fail-safe approach is to conduct practice development on the basis that most of the screening procedures will be used.

## Finding a fit

For the corporate client the submission and agreement of the offer is not, however, the final act in the selection process. The client still has to decide if the service firm will be able to work successfully with him or his staff (this appraisal may well be made before the offer is in fact submitted). Personal contact is the only way to assure the rapport develops which is so essential for a satisfactory relationship. Thus, at this stage in the process, the client, if he has not already done so, will wish to meet the professional personnel of the service company who are to be assigned to the project. These meetings will now be less concerned with the service firm's capability than with the **human evidence**, that is with assessing its ability to work with the client or his staff, its understanding of the problem, belief in its own offer, and to obtain reassurance on the internal and external empathy of the service company.

The prospective client may also want to know how much of the practice's directors', partners' or senior executives' time will be devoted to him, each individual's responsibilities and what contingency arrangements exist for substitution in the event of professional staff leaving, falling ill, or otherwise becoming unavailable during the project.

When the client is satisfied as to the ethics, competence and empathy of the service firm, there remains the final task of ensuring that the scheduling is satisfactory and that everyone involved is perfectly clear about what is to be done by whom and when. The commercial client may want the service firm to devise a detailed plan or provide a critical path analysis, so that the process and progress of the work are clearly defined and meet the requirements stipulated.

The client will need to know the type, frequency and quality of the liaison which will be developed. This is particularly true where activity on the client's premises is either inappropriate, as in external training programmes, or intermittent, as in financial consultancy.

The client may also designate key dates for progress reports to be made. Generally he is less interested in the contents of these preliminary reports than in obtaining reassurance that work for which he is probably making progress payments is, in fact, proceeding. He, unlike the developer who has commissioned a contractor to erect a building, has no monthly certificates of progress nor the sight of the bricks, mortar, girders and concrete rising above the ground as evidence of activity.

## On-going contact

Just as the delivery of a product is not necessarily the end of the supplier's involvement and responsibility neither is the completion of a service assignment the end of the service firm's involvement. The providers of professional services often have an open door through which to watch the developments stemming from the completion of their work. They do not always take advantage of this. The continued interest shown in the client's performance or activities after the completion of an assignment clearly indicates the service firm's confidence in its own work and demonstrates its commitment and sense of responsibility. It is one manifestation of its professionalism. It also provides opportunities for appraising new needs. The 'hit and run' service provider is a menace to himself and his profession.

Once again, the purchaser of services needs to feel in advance that the service will be taken through to successful completion and beyond and the professionals' interest will not end on receiving the last cheque.

No profession, however rigidly controlled, prevents its members from showing an on-going interest in its clients or patients. Too many professional services do not know when a client is inactive or lost. Regular creative contact ensures that this situation does not occur. The opportunity for expansion this presents is of extreme value and indeed is referred to in Chapter 4, 'Preparing for practice development', as the 'client and referral resource' (pages 37–8).

The selection process, as described in this and the previous chapter, has been over-elaborated if it is viewed as a pre-requisite for the purchase of all professional services by either private client or corporations in all circumstances. It is in fact in a sense only a check list of what steps the clients might take to ensure that they obtain precisely the services they need from individuals or practices they are confident in and can work happily with on a fee basis which is regarded as fair and cost effective.

# Chapter 11. Identifying potential clients

'A wise man will make more opportunities than he finds.'

Francis Bacon

Successful practice development depends not just on satisfying needs but also on identifying them whether or not the prospective client recognizes a requirement or that a need can be satisfied by any particular service.

The two previous chapters examined the processes by which a prospective client might locate and appoint a professional service. This chapter reverses the process and sets out methods by which the individual practitioner or professional service firm can identify prospective clients. Once identified how they can be approached or informed about the service will depend to a considerable extent on the mandatory or accepted rules of conduct of the particular profession. In Chapter 16, 'The use of personal contacts', and Chapter 17, 'Non-personal methods of practice development', a range of techniques whose acceptance will vary from one profession to another is offered for consideration.

## Market knowledge

For most professional services the size of a national or local market is of no great significance, certainly not enough to justify heavy market research expenditure as might be the case with an industrial or consumer service. For most firms, as has already been indicated, it is sufficient to say the demand is 'big enough' and to concentrate on identifying the form the demand takes or, where appropriate, to influence the demand towards the correct service and the practice which can meet it satisfactorily or stimulate it. For example, it is both desirable and ethical to dissuade sick people from using spurious or untested medical therapies administered by unqualified or unrecognized practitioners, to persuade people to seek medical advice early and to have medical checks. These circumstances typify where practice development and public good are aligned. The only area of contention is if it is desirable and ethical for individual professionals to inform prospective clients of their services. The polemics are fascinating but do not advance practice development techniques or motivations. The decision must be that of the individual practitioner or firm, within the constraints of the profession.

While marketing research may be superfluous for the individual firm, there is certainly a case for the professional associations to undertake this for their members since there are many aspects of the markets which remain unknown or where perceptions are based on folklore. Suggestions that the associations and institutions controlling the senior professions fund a totally non-competitive (between themselves) study of precisely how the inter-personal network or referral system operates has been resolutely resisted despite the fact that it is probable that 'recommendations' account for more than 80 per cent of the average professional practice's business. But if major research by individual firms is not required or possible there is much information the individual practice can gather at low cost or no cost from its own resources.

Chapter 4, 'Preparing for practice development', and Chapter 3, 'Creating a client-centred practice', referred respectively to information as an important resource and to the need to understand clients. In seeking new clients and new business these two factors come together. A better knowledge of clients, for example, might well reveal needs that could be met. Similarly, as any marketing researcher knows, careful perusal of national, local, trade and professional publications gives many clues as to actual and emerging demand for specific services. However, such a perusal can be time consuming and unrewarding unless it is structured and unless the person charged with monitoring has a clear idea of what he is looking for. Actual or proposed changes in the law can initiate demand for more than legal services; such a change may carry in its wake demand for additional or new accountancy, architectural, surveying, insurance, pensions and other financial services affecting different segments of a market in different ways.

It has been recommended in Chapter 5, 'Devising a practice development strategy and plan', that the technique of segmentation be adopted. If this is done then the field for surveillance will have been considerably narrowed down. Thus if one target was, for example, companies involved in mineral exploitation, the coverage is relatively narrow and easily encompassed.

Even if the activity area is far wider, say, a socio-economic target—married couples in white collar middle-income groups, on a local basis at least, and through normal information and communication channels, business and social—a great deal of information can be obtained which if properly edited, ordered and easily retrievable will make a considerable contribution to identifying opportunities, for example, the ACORN system of classification (A Classification of Residential Neighbourhoods).

It is useful however to apply some screening questions to the call for information, most particularly if it is claimed that the strategy and actions inherent in it cannot be undertaken without information. These questions are listed in Chapter 17, 'Non-personal methods of practice development', page 214.

Objective answers will reveal very quickly if the cost of research is likely to be commensurate with its value. At its simplest the practice developer must ask 'What will we do with the information when we have it?' or 'How will our strategy and activities vary if we do not have the information?' Unless there is a clear application for the data obtained there is no case for information gathering or research. Care is therefore needed in selecting research projects to be sure that any results are actionable rather than just interesting; profitable rather than just useful.[1]

## Identifying the individual prospect

It is one thing to identify an opportunity to develop the practice in a particular way, but it is quite another to pinpoint the organization or individuals within it who could use the service. To say there is a market opportunity to provide some form of protection services for victims of intellectual property piracy is to describe a situation. This description makes no contribution to locating authors, publishers, producers and artists affected.

1. A check list of research objectives will be found in Aubrey Wilson's *Assessment of Industrial Markets*. Associated Business Programmes (London, 1973), pp. 357–377. Updated and reprinted as a separate brochure by the British Overseas Trade Board (London, 1982) and available free.

Thus the move from the generic to the specific is now required. The identification of the individual prospect will be a key requirement for the practice developer. The method of achieving this is a combination of two related approaches. First, it is necessary to structure the particular advantages or, as they would be described in marketing terminology, 'plusses' of the firm and to relate them to the market segments most likely to respond to them and to be able to use them; this is the area of unique competence or resource every firm possesses and which distinguishes an individual or practice from all others.[2]

Second, a profile should be drawn of the prospective clients to assist in recognizing them and their location in the geographical or activity area selected for the segment.

## Developing a unique competence or resource

The professional service firm has the initial task of identifying for itself a unique combination of skills, experience, qualifications, facilities and other resources which makes it most suitable, more than other firms, to meet client needs.[3] Reference to the importance of a unique offering has already been made in Figure 8-7 in Chapter 8, 'Professional services and the commercial client'. However, it is not usually the possession of one particular competence or resource which represents the distinction in the sense that a patented product is unique to its manufacturer. Much more typically it will be a mixture of a number of components of the firm's operation which will produce that unique aspect.

The simplest situation may be one in which a firm has no particular skills or resources other than capacity to meet a demand at a particular moment. A solicitor able to handle an urgent criminal case immediately offers a unique advantage to the accused over any solicitor who cannot attend court that day. In fact, capacity or 'lead-time' is the most common advantage firms can offer in a given situation where all else tends to be equal. However, it is not a 'plus' which can be built on since its very existence tends to destroy it.

The usual situation will be more complex. The examples given in Figures 11-1 and 11-2 illustrate how each additional 'plus' narrows down the competition, but they also illustrate how each additional 'plus' narrows down the potential market.

Clearly the combination in Figure 11-1, which is anything but unique at any one level, is an attractive grouping for an organization seeking to appoint an architectural firm for a new opera house if the award was not to be by competition. Possibly the same practice could re-package its 'plusses' if the proposed building was an industrial structure (see Figure 11-2).

An insurance company might 'package' its offerings in the way shown in Figure 11-3.

## Inventory of strengths and weaknesses

The advantages and dangers of this particular approach are obvious. Any system of opportunity identification by the relation of skills or resources to the market must be modular. That is, the skills and resources should be capable of being rearranged to open up a number of market possibilities, not just the single market at the end of a sequence.

The service company must be capable not only of identifying its own strengths and weaknesses objectively, but also of appreciating how they compare to the need as perceived by the client.

2. See Chapter 3, 'Creating a client-centred practice', page 26.
3. Ibid.

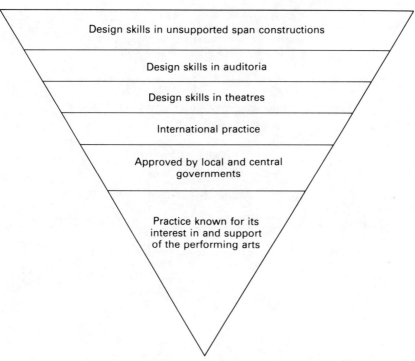

**Figure 11-1** Package of unique competences for an architectural practice market segment—municipal authorities

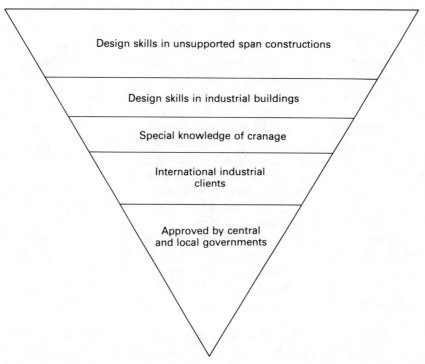

**Figure 11-2** Package of unique competences for an architectural practice market segment—industrial firms

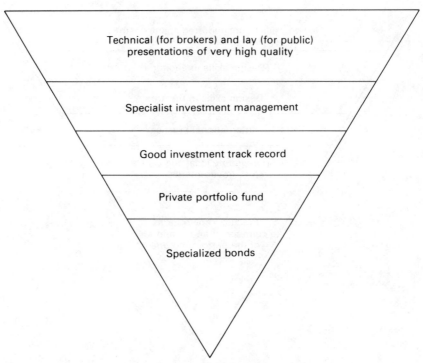

Figure 11-3 Package of unique competences for an insurance company market segment—brokers and wealthy individuals

The SOFT analysis approach described in Chapter 5, 'Devising a practice development strategy and plan', Figure 5-1, is one useful and very quick way of identifying the components of a 'package' of benefits which will be unique. Another method is the client interrogation technique described in Chapter 7, 'Professional services and client needs', page 86, and Figure 7-4. It is important to appreciate that an area of unique competence does not have to be unique in real terms. It is sufficient for practice development purposes for it *to be seen* as unique. Thus, more than one financial institution has promoted its services by listing out its numerous facilities as a combination which is unique. The reality is that other financial institutions, while being perfectly capable of providing any or all of the services, have not offered themselves publicly in this way or in this combination.

The skill needed is to be able to isolate those features of a service provided by a firm or individual—but most particularly the appropriate combination of them—which apply to a given situation and then to communicate and promote these to the prospective clients.

The whole purpose of identifying unique aspects of an offer as a criterion for segmentation,[4] is to reduce a total market into more homogeneous sub-sections. Such an approach is inherent in any professional service with claims to an area of specialization. The lawyer's practice with a known reputation for criminal work has segmented a total market for legal services to a narrow sector perhaps offering a unique competence by virtue of extensive experience in this activity exceeding that of other practices.

The accountancy firm with special knowledge, experience and staff familiar with taxation and business law and practice as between clients' countries and tax havens has segmented its

4. See Chapter 5, 'Devising a practice development strategy and plan', pages 55–7.

130

market by a particular type of client and geographically. These segmentations may be obvious and they may be intentional yet still not spring from a deliberate attempt to isolate the sector of the market most likely to respond to the firm's unique offering.

For most professional services, it is necessary to divide a market positively in order to concentrate resources on the segment offering the best potential opportunities compatible with the service company's corporate objectives and aspirations. Only when the segments are defined can the problem of identifying the prospect by name be attempted on a systematic basis.

Because the offering is unique it must bring the client to the firm if the skill, resource or facility need outweighs other factors which might make an alternative profession or professional preferable.

One well-documented example of a unique competence is worth quoting at length[5] as it provides an excellent example of how such a competence can be developed from a client need. It relates to professional services associated with the construction industry.

Traditionally, estimates of building costs are based on historical data obtained from other products.

> This is the limit of the cost information made available to many management boards when deciding to proceed with building projects. They tend to accept the cost estimates for the building as presented by the professional team at face value. At this stage they wish to minimise fee expenditure should they decide to cancel the project, and frequently begin by requesting an outline sketch plan from the architect together with cost information. The onus is then on the architect to produce the information required with minimal help from the specialists in costing and engineering.
>
> The client wants to minimise expense in the preparation . . . and the professional team at feasibility stage has the same attitude and for the same reason. The end result is often a set of cost estimate figures for the project based on a poorly drawn out brief and too little technical input. The consequences are that management may decide to proceed with the project on the basis of the questionable figures presented. Frequently, it is found that these original cost estimates are incorrect for various reasons. The obvious ones are neglect on the side of management in having their requirements thought through to any great extent and misunderstanding on the side of the professional team as to what the management really requires.
>
> Computer programs were developed to help form more correct estimates. The object was to use the concept of cost effectiveness analysis to set up as many alternatives of building type as would be helpful to examine. The programs would then work out every possible combination of structural shape and material of construction. Drawing on a file of costs, this would then produce very rapidly the cost of each design alternative for inspection by the design team and management. This meant that the consequences of a change in any dimension of the building, or material of construction could be examined and compared with costs for all other alternatives. In addition, the 'what-if'? type of query put by the client could be dealt with immediately. For instance, the typical industrialist would usually ask the question of the financial consequences following the removal of all internal supporting columns so as to give him clear production space. The programs in question dealt with these problems with ease.

The method produced helpful results and was successful in introducing more certainty at the feasibility stage of projects.

None of the foregoing implies that creating a unique competence for a service guarantees it will remain so. As Chapter 3, 'Creating a client-centred practice', stated, it is not possible to patent a service or to protect it. The unique advantage or as it is known in commercial terms 'unique selling proposition' is most usually applied to products which are patentable or protectable (brand name or registered design) in some way. Thus having found or devised a unique aspect to the service it can be copied by others but with varying degrees of difficulty.

5. John V. O'Conner. 'A discrete approach to selling the professions'. *Industrial Marketing Management* (New York, 1978), Vol. 7, p. 308.

For example, expertise might be matched by acquiring personnel with similar skills or experience, by opening offices or surgeries near competitors, increasing the range of services available. These are relatively easy, if not always cheap, to replicate. More difficult to follow and surpass are the image advantages which can be very valuable qualities when attached to any 'lead' service. The firm is then perceived as 'innovative', 'creative', 'professional leaders' as well as unique.

Thus, having created a differential advantage the practice development personnel must remain aware of competitive matchings and must constantly review their offering to develop new inputs and new combinations. Like most marketing activities it is a dynamic on-going activity.

## Profiling prospective clients

The professional responsible for practice development tasks will certainly require to know how to identify and focus on prospective clients most likely to enable the firm (or individual) to achieve its (his) objectives in whatever terms these are expressed. A technique known as 'profiling', which is simple and quick to adopt, will in most cases identify with a good degree of certainty the types of individuals and commercial clients who will respond most readily to the messages concerning the practice. The technique was developed by SRI as a method of improving its marketing to clients of a number of its economic, sociological and technical services.

The service firm can start the individual prospect identification process either from its own history of successes and failures or, if it is a new activity or practice, from an examination of the characteristics of clients in the market segment.

The problem of identifying the individual firm will vary in complexity from service to service. In the case illustrated in Figure 11-1 the total number of organizations likely to want, and to be capable of commissioning, a new theatre is limited in number and relatively little effort is required to locate them. Figure 11-2 illustrates a more complex situation. A much larger number of organizations may require the skills identified—individual industrial companies, speculative developers, local and central government, co-operative enterprises, para-statal bodies and others.

In these circumstances the total list of potential clients can be coarse-screened quickly to remove misfits and low possibilities of business. Small firms are unlikely to require large span buildings, speculative developers tend to concentrate on one type of use structures, e.g., housing, commercial buildings, service industries, do not for the most part require cranage, only few para-statal bodies are involved in commissioning structures and so on. A sensible consideration of the values to clients of different elements in the offer will enable the list to be narrowed down quickly.

From there on, the service company can fine screen by using its own experiences or by examining the characteristics of the firms in the segment concerned. Based on its own experiences the service company can identify the salient characteristics:

- Regular clients.
- Sporadic or inactive clients.
- Discontinued or lost clients.
- Non-clients (failed offers).
- Non-clients (no invitation to be considered).

**132**

Further self-questioning is required:

1. What reasons underlie our being invited to present our service for any particular enquiry?
2. What reasons underlie our successes?
3. What reasons do we, and does the client, ascribe to our failure to obtain their business? How far do the reasons accord?
4. What are the reasons for sporadic rather than regular business or periods of inactivity?
5. What is the history of each discontinued or lost client in the category under consideration?
6. What searches do we know have been made for our type of services in which we have not been considered and what reasons do we and the prospective client attribute to explain this situation?
7. How many individuals or organizations exist which use a similar service to that which we offer, but with which we have no contact?

An examination of the characteristics of clients for a contract or an assignment successfully obtained and fulfilled will provide an identification profile. But even without previous experience it is still possible to devise indicators of the existence of potential clients. Precisely which indicators are relevant is, of course, impossible to suggest without knowledge of the profession and the specific segments, but they will certainly be widespread and perhaps as many as 50 variables will be needed.

Appendix A of this chapter lists a number of profiling factors for consideration but it is not suggested that all should be used or indeed would be obtainable. They have been found to have a significant effect alone or in combination on the susceptibility of a firm or an individual to the offer of services by an organization.

## Matching by profiling

If the characteristics of known, satisfied, regular clients can be identified and then a match sought with non-clients with similar profiles, the high possibility potential will be revealed.

The original experiment with this technique conducted by SRI is worthy of explanation. Like most organizations marketing professional services SRI quickly realized that client interests tend to be very diverse and numerous, and that categorization is extremely difficult. However, it proved possible to reduce the categorization problem to manageable proportions. Seventy-eight companies, whose membership status (client or non-client) was known, were used for 'training' a pattern recognition system by in-putting information on a number of key profiling factors such as size, location, activity, form of oraganization, degree of specialization and so on. After 30 iterations through the data, the system became stable, forming two large groups of 'likely' and two smaller groups of 'unlikely' client companies. Then, an additional 59 companies were classified through the system. Of these, the client/non-client status of 30 was known. The system correctly classified 20 of these companies. Two of the companies selected by the system as being 'unlikely' but which were actually clients when the data were collected several months earlier, had subsequently ceased to be clients. In addition, four unknown companies were selected as being likely prospects.

The situation can be illustrated as follows. Without placing any values on the axis, it has been found that the weighting of activity by the average practice developer will produce a preponderance of effort at the lower end of the scale of business possibilities. The above average performer with perhaps a higher empathy, motivation, knowledge, entrepreneurial flair and a more knowledgeable approach to his task shows a greater contact rate in the middle reaches of the possibilities of success. The profile method would seem to move both the average and the above average into the sectors where their concentration through better 'targeting' is heavily on high prospects for business (see Figure 11-4).

Clearly, few firms will have the resources to indulge in long computer-based exercises, but the fundamental ideas underlying the prospect identification have clear implications for all professional service firms. The difficulties of correctly selecting the key criteria are no less than obtaining the criteria data both on client and non-client companies, but, even with inadequate data, much can be done along these lines.

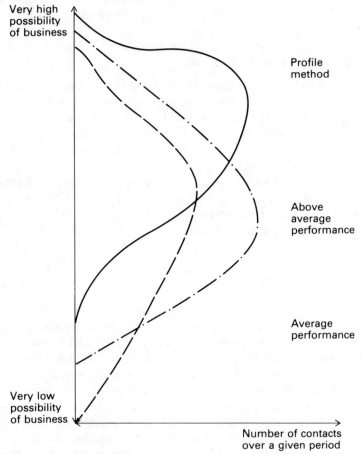

**Figure 11-4** 'Profile' performance contact rate

The value of the 'profiling' technique does not end with the identification of high potential clients. It can also reveal a patterning which can illuminate the other client categories.

Sporadic or inactive clients may well be in this group for reasons which can be identified. For example, a sporadic client may use the service irregularly because of shortage of capacity of the regular supplier of that particular professional service and thus an 'emergency reserve' situation exists. If a practice is sufficiently well regarded to be used in such circumstances, then there is a basis to move the sporadic client into a regular client category.

Similarly, questions can be asked to see if there is a patttern of discontinuances which can be eliminated by some change in activity or indeed personnel. Does one particular service, one particular professional, create lost client situations? Perhaps a record of unpunctuality or poor

**134**

communication may be the cause. These and other factors if identified are capable of correction and thus of improving client retentions.

The next category is that of non-clients but with whom contact has been maintained. They too may well yield to similar questioning. What were the reasons for rejections of offers made—cost, perceived lack of expertise or experience, over-specialization, no empathy between professionals and clients? Again a patterning might emerge which will give guidelines to corrective action.

Finally, the non-clients who have never considered the professional firm. Is it lack of 'visibility'? Was there a failure to understand the 'message'? Was the message irrelevant or unconvincing? Information of this type if it can be obtained (and it can be, given the resources are made available) gives an invaluable guide to practice development techniques and activities.

Following the SRI early experiment, subsequent use of the system by other types of services—professional and non-professional—as well as for industrial products produced an improving level of accuracy and more than justified the earlier optimism for this type of market analysis. Prediction scores are constantly improving.

It must be said, however, that the system will not work for all firms and in all circumstances but even at a lower success level there will be an improvement in the concentration of practice development resources which must result in both lower costs and a higher rate of success. In any event the system used in a fairly simple form will involve very little in the way of time and money investment even if it fails to produce spectacular results. Thus it is well worthy of examination and possible use by all professional service firms.

In identifying the prospective private client the professional firm has then, in the vast majority of cases, also identified the decision maker. The position is different with the commercial client. Identification of a company does not of course lead to the active decision makers in the company (see Chapter 8, 'Professional services and the commercial client'). The decision-making unit (DMU) can vary from purchase to purchase, from time to time and, most importantly, as a result of the situation which occasioned the purchase. Thus, it is quite impossible to designate in specific terms how a DMU may be composed at any particular moment. However, it is possible to build up a dossier over a period on DMU compositions by job title or definition under varying circumstances, so that a pattern emerges. This patterning may be by the activity or industry of the user of services, by size of company, by type or extent of service under consideration, or by using any of the criteria listed in Appendix A to this chapter.

The information is extremely useful as a profile guide to the correct people to contact in a would-be purchasing company and it is always relatively easy to identify the individual by name once the job title or function is known.[6]

However, it is necessary to keep prospect identification, once obtained, in perspective because it is unreal to examine it outside the context of the total and continuing practice development. It is part and parcel of a two-way communication process since informative and persuasive communications can materially assist in locating individuals and organizations which offer opportunities for business to the professional service firm. Thus, identifying applications for a service and the individuals both private and within the company with whom the decision-making authority lies is one part, albeit an early one, of the practice development activity, but it is one which will govern the strength, direction and content of the whole effort.

6. See Figure 8-1, Chapter 8, 'Professional services and the commercial client'.

# Appendix 11A. Master list of possible factors for inclusion in a profiling exercise to identify non-clients with similar characteristics to those of existing regular profitable clients

This list is based on commercial client characteristics but many of the factors for consideration can be applied either unadjusted or slightly adjusted for private clients.

1. Size of client by any or all of the following:
   - turnover
   - profit
   - assets employed
   - numbers employed
   - number of establishments
   - size of establishments
   - ROI
   - other

2. Form of organizations:
   - owner managed
   - limited company
   - international/multi-national/local/regional/national
   - extent of verticalization
   - co-operative
   - voluntary purchasing group
   - franchise
   - other

3. Extent of specialization (distributors):
   - full line
   - associated products
   - complementary products
   - general suppliers

4. Type of outlet (distributors):
   - retailer
   - wholesaler
   - cash-and-carry
   - merchants
   - stockholder
   - agent
   - dealer (franchised and others)
   - rack jobber
   - voluntary group
   - discount
   - mail order

5. Activity (see also 'type of outlet'):
   - construction
   - manufacture (by SIC including energy)
   - transportation
   - importers
   - exporters
   - consultancy
   - professional services
   - education/training
   - defence
   - research
   - institutional
   - industrial/commercial services
   - commission packer
   - jobbing

6. Psychographic factors:
   - ultra-modern
   - contemporary
   - old fashioned
   - receptivity to new services
   - sensitivity to aesthetic factors
   - changing requirements
   - static requirements
   - transitional

7. Reasons for selection of the specific professional service:
   - improved performance
   - insurance/security
   - full line service available or specialization
   - compatibility with existing operations, staff, location, facilities, systems, etc.
   - delegation of responsibility
   - legal requirement
   - lack of appropriate skills or capacity

8. Contact method:
   - personal
   - media advertising
   - editorial (public relations)
   - direct mail
   - telephone
   - referral
   - newsletter
   - exhibitions
   - other

9. Seasonality or cycle of demand:
   - nil
   - moderate
   - complete

10. Extent of usage:
    - heavy
    - medium
    - light
    - sporadic
    - one-off

11. Application for the service (see also 'reasons for selection'):
    - R & D assistance
    - production problems
    - storage problems
    - new product requirements
    - adaptation advice
    - testing
    - new material appraisal
    - legal requirement
    - insurance
    - emergency
    - other

12. Reasons for choice of the individual practice:
    - size
    - reputation
    - special capabilities
    - location
    - speed of initiation and completion
    - client list
    - recommendations
    - other

13. Location:
    - geographic
    - climate
    - urban, suburban, rural
    - capital, provincial

14. Demographic (private clients):
    - socio-economic
    - marital status
    - age
    - sex
    - occupation
    - education
    - ethnic/religion/nationality
    - life style
    - family composition
    - family life cycle state
    - home ownership

# Chapter 12. The importance of images and perceptions

'O wad some pow'r the giftie to gie us
To see oursels as others see us.'

Robert Burns

Because, far more than in the selection and purchase of tangible products, the user of a service buys an expectation, his image and perception of the professional, or of the practice and of the individuals with whom he deals are frequently the deciding factor in the final choice. Every person and every firm projects a series of images and perceptions. Images are created by the personnel of the practice with whom clients have any form of contact whatsoever, by the physical appearance of offices and equipment, by even apparently trivial things such as paper heading, quality of correspondence, vehicles and indeed all the essential and peripheral evidence referred to in Chapter 2, 'Understanding service businesses', and Chapter 10, 'How the individual practice is selected', pages 116–18.

The components which individually and collectively create the image of any professional activity, product or even an ideology are very numerous when related to the professions. The client rarely makes a conscious separation of these components. What the client receives is an overall impression of the practice and its personnel which is the 'image profile'. No individual, no service and no product can avoid creating images and being assessed and evaluated on them. It cannot be emphasized too strongly it is not just consumers responding to the weight and sophistication of the professional image makers who are influenced. Professional service clients are equally affected.

The validity of the statement is easily verified. Asked, for example, to name stores selling luxury goods or a *marque* of vehicles known for their superlative engineering most people would have little hesitation in identifying without any assistance to which company or manufacturer the descriptions apply. Thus it can be seen that these organizations or brands have succeeded in projecting an image of 'luxury' or 'quality'.

Similarly, professional practices whether they are aware of it or not project images to their clients; 'competence', 'well connected', 'friendly', 'involved', 'reliable', 'specialists' or perhaps less complimentary, 'cold', 'difficult to deal with', 'expensive', 'pompous', 'uninterested in small clients'.

There can be little doubt that successful practice development must to a large measure depend upon projecting an image which is attractive to the client types served and sought.

## The firm's public

In considering images it is necessary also to consider to whom the image is to be projected.

Most studies of image development concentrate heavily, and often to the exclusion of all else, on the firm's clients or customers. In fact there are many publics which have to be considered and which give momentum to the image development programme, positively and negatively. The firm's public can comprise, for example, apart from its clients:

- Referral sources (inter- and intra-professional and others).
- Professional bodies (own and other professions).
- Community.
- Professional and support staff.
- Financial institutions.
- Central and local government and institutions (e.g., hospital authorities, courts of law, tax authorities, etc.).
- Re-sellers (but rarely involved in professional services other than financial).
- News media.
- Opinion formers.
- Special interest groups.
- Educational bodies.
- Business, social organizations and trade unions.
- Suppliers.

In most circumstances it is not necessary to be concerned with all these or with any particular grouping of them at the same moment. The practice development plan must however decide which of these publics and perhaps others are of significance and which could contribute to or inhibit the practice's expansion because of the image the various publics have of the firm or of the individual.

There will clearly be hierarchy of importance probably starting with existing clients and potential clients with whom contact already exists, moving on to referral sources and perhaps ending with 'suppliers' as the least important group.

From the foregoing it will be seen that images will develop irrespective of anything the individual or firm may do or not do. What is important is that firms should consciously seek to shape the image in a way which will help them achieve the practice development objectives. Images are not an aspect of practice development from which a firm can contract out. Their existence is as pervasive and as real as any tangible possession of the practice.


## Image reference of the profession

One of the problems of image development and projection however is that the individual or the firm cannot easily become detached from the perception of the profession as a whole and indeed frequently has to work from a totally unfavourable base in that the publics—commercial and private—often have a jaundiced view of the entire discipline. Both the recognized professions and those who seek to emulate them have in the past been, and continue to be, almost totally insensitive to their image and to the important role that it plays in shaping choice. As a whole the professions have garnered an image of arrogance, detachment, self-protection, lack of commitment and indeed in some cases lack of responsibility, above criticism and perhaps the most heinous sin of all, high cost.

In truth this profile of the professions is no more applicable to an entire profession than is any ethnic, sexual, religious or age libel but it is nevertheless one that most professionals have to live with and which can only be altered by the profession as a whole. It can and does have the effect of moving the publics served either to alternative non-professional and non-qualified practitioners, do-it-yourself activity or substitution of products for services.

The gap between this generalization and the professionals' idea of how they are seen is very wide. Practitioners appear to think that the public's view of them is largely one in which they are held in the highest esteem as dedicated, skilled, altruistic, learned, with high moral probity, their status being achieved by virtue of long and arduous training, examination and qualification. 'The professions as a whole have traditionally been accorded a privileged position in society which transcends nationality, political, social or economic backgrounds. This position of privilege has been based on real and generally well founded respect for the qualities of integrity, expertise and independent judgement expected from professional people.'[1] But the corporate client and the general public have become more questioning, more cynical and more knowledgeable so that aided by inflammatory media any mistakes or misconduct within the professions has become instant public knowledge. Well-publicized errors by major accounting firms in which millions of pounds or dollars have been involved has cast doubt on the skill, care or probity of both the practices involved and the profession as a whole. Departure from the strict morality required by medical practitioners is instant news along with any claims for professional negligence. Architects have to face a barrage of criticism on both aesthetic and technical grounds. There is little wonder that the images of professions are tarnished, often quite unfairly, but unfortunately the official rejoinders are either weak or there is a lofty disregard for public opinion.

Practice development for every profession, at least so far as competition from outside the profession is concerned, will be constrained by the overall image of the profession which the individual can do little to alter for the good but a great deal to debase further. Certainly the image of a profession must be the concern, the constant concern, of its association or collegial organization to work towards achieving the reality on which satisfactory images can be built. There is however a great deal an individual or firm can do to ensure that its own image is a satisfactory one.

## The multiple image concept

While it is proposed in this chapter to offer suggestions for image development for practices, these suggestions, if adopted, will be applied with greater effect if there is an understanding of the theory of multiple images.

The perceptual conflict between the way a firm (or an individual) is seen and the way it thinks it is seen is only part of a wider dissonance.

- The *current* image—the way the image object is seen by its different publics.
- The *mirror* image—the way it thinks it is seen by its different publics.
- The *wish* image—the way it would like to be seen by its different publics.

The conflict between the *current* and *mirror* images has been illustrated in a generalized way in the profile given above of the public perceptions of the professions and the professions' self-image. Not quite so obvious, however, is the conflict between the *wish* image, whether translated into action or not, and the image which will produce the most favourable impact on the environment into which it is projected; in other words, the distinction between how the firm *wishes* to be seen and how it *ought* to be seen to improve its operations.

1. Sir Geoffrey Howe. Nigel Colley Memorial Lecture. Nottingham Law Society, May 1975.

This leads to the fourth image:

- The *optimum* image—the perception which will ensure the image subject achieves its objectives.

There is little wonder, therefore, that with conflicting objectives and conflicting perceptions, image building is a highly inexact and unpredictable activity. Only if practice development tactics take account of the multiple image concept is there any possibility of a suitable image being built. It is useful to point out that the multiple image concept precludes dishonesty or inaccuracy if only because if the *mirror* image deviates from the *current* image, it creates damaging internal attitudes of cynicism, self-deprecation and demoralization and externally disbelief and distrust. For example, if a service firm projects an image of reliability but professional and support staff are well aware that it is in fact inferior or unreliable, the internal attitudes which are engendered and cannot be wholly distinguished can only be corrected by an improvement of the service up to at least the level of the way it is projected and perceived. Thus reality and the *current* and *mirror* image must all be aligned, while at the same time both the practice and the way it is projected should be moved towards the *wish* image which in itself may not accord with the *optimum* image. It is a very frequent occurrence that within a practice the *wish* image, apart from varying between practitioners and often between partners and their qualified and support staff, is more likely to satisfy the self-esteem, social or emotional requirements of the participants than the public they service. Indeed in Chapter 1, 'Why practice development?', the self-image clash with the whole concept of practice development and its association with commercialism, marketing or selling, was referred to as a major obstacle.

An image that is 'all things to all men' is, of course, most desirable but since this is unlikely to be achieved, the objective is an image that is most attractive to most users and potential users of the firm's services. To establish the *optimum* image, tactics must be based on the image requirements for the services and co-ordinated with the firm's overall image desideratum and, of course, the reality of the practice and its achievements.

The development of the *optimum* image depends on inter-relationships and cross-influences. For example, the *current* image may perhaps be too strongly linked to a particular service, technique or problem some of which may carry the seeds of obsolescence, declining or changed requirements. In legal services one scenario might be simple registration of divorces and no-fault liability which would reduce demand for both types of legal services. The *optimum* image under these circumstances should at least assert the firm's capability in other legal problems and perhaps an expertise in a rapidly developing aspect of law such as time sharing.[2]

No matter how well image objectives are identified and tactics devised, or how sensitive the firm may be to environmental and internal changes, all will be of no avail if the practice as a whole is not aware of the need for and agreed on image objectives. It is not sufficient to identify incompatible images if no steps are to be taken to bring them in line with overall policy. It is here that image building so often falls short. The three tasks to be accomplished are, first to bring the *current* and *mirror* images into accord so that they can be superimposed and the firm perceives itself as it is really seen. The second, which is where the persuasion comes in, is to bring the *wish* and *optimum* images into focus, again so that they can be superimposed and that the firm, being an aggregation of all its personnel, services and resources moves together towards the *optimum* image. Thus there are now two benchmarks. The agreed point where the firm is currently placed (the superimposed *current* and *mirror*

2. Graham Lee. 'Future shock—a midsummer night's dream'. *The Law Society Gazette* (London, 28 October 1981).

images) and the agreed point towards which it must work (the superimposed *wish* and *optimum* images). The third task, having established the benchmarks, is to ensure that they are as close to each other as possible and that the 'image internal' that is the gap between the two is not allowed to widen.

This can be illustrated. A *wish* image for an architect's practice might be to be seen as a tight cohesive team of highly creative personnel with particular interests and skills in large-span buildings. In fact the clients may be more exercised with aesthetics, have a preference for working with an individual rather than a team and be concerned that the architect has some knowledge of the type of activities which will occur in the structure. While the *wish* image will always contain some element of the *optimum* image ('value for money', 'skill', 'independence') there will also be components that do more to satisfy the practitioners than their publics.[3]

After identifying the key 'publics' the practice has to establish just how the practice is seen, the *current* image, and this can be done by questioning of both clients, non-client contacts and even lost clients. The questionnaire technique referred to in Chapter 17, 'Non-personal methods of practice development', page 214, will make a considerable contribution to obtaining this knowledge, but where it is affordable there is a strong case for independent market research which need not be excessively expensive.

Establishing the *mirror* image is no more than gathering by internal interview information on how the individuals in the firm think it is seen and producing a consensus in the form of an encapsulated consensus profile bearing in mind that different services and different types of clients will have different perceptions.

The *wish* image can be established at the same time as the *mirror* image by again using the consensus approach. It is beneficial in arriving at the consensus if a Delphi technique is adopted. Opinions and the information on which they are based should be re-cycled to all participants. Each person can then re-consider his stated views against a background of the arguments and information provided by others to see if he should change them in the light of other comments.

The next step is to decide just what image will help achieve the firm's practice development objectives—the *optimum* image. This profile must be based on the reality of the firm as present constituted, any changes which are feasible, and client needs aligned with the personal and professional requirements of those in the practice.

Having decided the *optimum* image the last vital step before any image development work is undertaken is to ensure that the reality matches the images to be projected. As has been indicated to project and promote an image which is not based on reality is dangerous, destructive, costly, time consuming and difficult to correct.

To assist the practice developer in the complex but always interesting task a list of image factors for consideration is given in Appendix A of this chapter.

## Images and third parties

The inter-personal network is dealt with fully in the next chapter, but whatever images third parties have obtained can always be traced back to their own or other individuals or firms' contacts with the practice. Therefore, third parties' roles in image development are, in every sense, derived from the same sources. With third parties, however, incorrect images are much more difficult to correct as is the projection of new images because there is no direct contact.

---

3. The concept of the multiple image is explained fully in Aubrey Wilson's *The Art and Practice of Marketing*. Hutchinson (London, 1971), Chapter 8.

Thus referrers who report critically on a firm, and whose image of the firm must be changed because of their influence, have to be seen as remote but legitimate image targets. Their perceptions must be re-aligned and re-formed by those clients and prospective clients who have received and accepted the correct and more favourable image and by other means at the disposal of the practice.

The schematic is simple for the direct image formation (see Figure 12-1). For the indirect image formation the system reverses between client and referrer.

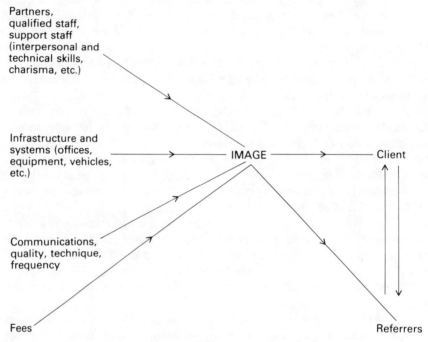

**Figure 12-1**  Image formation

## Images and the invisible part of the organization

In Chapter 2, 'Understanding service businesses', attention was drawn to the fact that within every organization there is a 'visible' and 'invisible' element. It would be an error to assume that it is only the 'visible' part of a firm which can create perceptions. The submerged section of the practice accounts for a considerable part of costs which in turn impact heavily on fees and fee structures which themselves are vital image components. Because fees are not broken down to reveal professional and support staff salaries and overheads, the global figure will be interpreted as an indication of quality, high or low, 'value for money', 'over-charging', 'fair', 'bargain' and a host of other image perceptions. The 'visible' and 'invisible' are not separated out by the client in his assessment.

Fees are just one aspect of the outcome of the 'invisible' part of the firm with a particular importance at the end of a professional assignment. There are of course others. It cannot be assumed that even if all the activities and resources the client sees and experiences are acceptable, a negative image will still not emerge because of the things client neither sees nor experiences. Thus any failure in the concealed section of the organization which cannot be, or more likely is not, explained to the client and even if it is, cannot be excused will work against the firm and in many ways more adversely than such problems occurring in the visible parts of the firm. In any event as was commented on in Chapter 2, 'Understanding service businesses', breakdowns in the visible parts of the organization are usually quicker to be noticed and therefore quicker in being remedied.

These points are made to ensure a sensitivity in practice development to both those aspects of the firm and services which are seen by the client and those which are not.

So far as the 'visible' part of any practice is concerned, much of it is accidentally or deliberately rendered invisible when its prominence would make a considerable positive contribution to the firm's image. Clients, private or corporate, want effort as well as results. Effort is part of the evidence clients seek and observe in evaluating the practice, the professional and the quality of the service referred to in Chapter 2, 'Understanding service businesses', page 17. This is not to say effort without results will be highly regarded, but results without apparent effort may well not equate in the clients' views with skills, utilized time involvement or fees charged. Thus in developing satisfactory images, it is necessary to project, not conceal, effort. Effort comprises both apparently trivial and major activities. A check list for a legal practice in the USA contains some important suggestions for all practices anywhere in the world.[4]

- Send your client a copy of *every* document you produce, including correspondence, pleadings, briefs, etc., as you produce it.
- Send your client a copy of all incoming documents as they are received, including pleadings, correspondence, etc.
- Return your client's calls immediately, or have someone else return them. Remember the slogan:
  - I needed a lawyer
  - I couldn't get in touch with you
  - I got another lawyer
  - I don't need you any more. . . .
- If you work on your client's case in the evening or on a weekend, call him at his home and ask him some questions, so that he knows you are devoting your 'personal' time to his matters.
- Bill monthly.
- Make 'house calls'.
- One of the most effective techniques is to visit clients at their place of business:
  - Visit your client's place of business to understand his business. Don't charge for the time you spend going through the factory, but do charge for the conference at the place of business to the same extent as you would have charged for the same conference in your office.
  - Go with your client to the scene of the accident in personal injury and workmen's compensation cases. This will impress your client as to your effort.
  - Go to the medical examination with the client when the defence doctor makes an examination.
- Inform clients of new cases or statutes which come to your attention which affect their affairs. They will appreciate your concern. They will feel you care about them and are putting forth efforts for them.

4. Jay G. Foonberg. *How to Start and Build a Law Practice.* Law Students Division of the American Bar Association (Chicago, 1976), pp. 39–41.

## First impressions of the practice

Needless to say, as in many other aspects of life, first contacts can mould into an unbreakable pattern the impression which is gained of a practice or individual. While these perceptions are often incorrect, in services which a client is expected to pay for, unless the first impressions are satisfactory, then the likelihood of a relationship developing which will give the opportunity for new and more accurate views to be formed will not occur. Thus it might be said that, in a sense, the first impressions are the initial image hurdle for the practice to cross. If it is not crossed nothing else the practice does, or is likely to do, will be effective.

First views are formed in five ways:

- Published material on the practice.
- The inter-personal network, that is from the views of people who have had direct or indirect contact with the practice.
- Telephone contact.
- Correspondence.
- Visits.

Because most methods of communication are not currently permitted for many professions, for example media advertising, exhibitions, sponsorship, direct mail, images are unlikely to develop from any source other than those bulleted items. In this respect at least one task of creating an *optimum* image is made easier since it is possible to ensure that the different ways in which images are formed are concentrated on the five routes listed.

## Published material

All printed material should be of a quality and design compatible with the image it is wished to convey. Whether lavish or simple there is never any excuse for poor design or graphics. If the talents within a practice do not include aesthetics it is always better to leave printed matter to experts.

Published material of course includes items which have been printed by others, perhaps news media. Here there can be no control over appearance but this is of less importance than the standing of the medium itself. Obviously there is greater recognition in being published in a respected source so far as the profession is concerned where readership encompasses a number of target clients than in an unrelated medium or one where the circulation is of little interest to the practice.

## Inter-personal network

First impressions created by third party comment can be the most powerful inducement or discouragement to seek the services of a practice. The inter-personal network being of dominant importance as a practice development method is dealt with on its own in Chapter 13, 'The referral (recommendations) system'. Within the context of images it has already been stated that images of a practice to third parties are of almost equal importance as the images which are held by actual or direct users of a practice's services.

## The telephone

There is no organization of any type where the switchboard or telephonist is not important. It is a statement made with regrettable frequency and certainly with a substantial element of truth that more business is lost at switchboards than by any other activity. In building images the switchboard is both the initial and the easiest place to start.

The first question to be asked is how frequently incoming calls are frustrated by engaged lines or failure to respond reasonably quickly or at all. All are unforgivable in image-building terms. If telephone lines are frequently engaged (and it is possible to monitor unconnected incoming calls) then more exchange lines are needed. Insufficient exchange lines is a false economy of some magnitude.

However, calls are not just frustrated because of lack of external lines, but also because internal extensions are engaged. Once more monitoring is required and a system developed whereby clients are not made to wait. There are several ways of dealing with this problem.

1. Separate telephones for inward and outward calls reduce the pressure on available lines. The person receiving an inward call can decide if it is more important than his outward or inter-office call and act accordingly.
2. The offer, if an extension is engaged, to call back as soon as the person becomes free. This however can easily end in considerable frustration if the return call is not made. Failure to return a call in these circumstances must rank among the top 'image-spoiling' factors.
3. If the client must or prefers to hold, then frequent reassurance from the operator that the call continues to be held and that the wanted extension is still engaged does much to reduce irritation. Long silences are destructive to good relationships.

The second important step so far as telephone contact is concerned, if it is to play a constructive role in building satisfactory images, is to assess the qualities of telephone call handling. A check should be made on how good those who take telephone calls are in projecting a cheerful, welcoming, efficient impression. While 'cheerful' is not perhaps an adjective that might be appropriate for funeral services there can be few professional services where 'cheerfulness' is not an advantage. The key characteristics of a good telephonist are efficiency, friendliness, interest and helpfulness.

The telephone is an instrument which is taken for granted in most offices. It is a powerful tool in image creation and destruction. A check list for establishing telephone efficiency follows. Someone not familiar to the operators can be used to test how well they perform or alternatively clients as well as new enquirers could be asked to comment on the telephone response. Additional guidelines for the effective use of the telephone are included in Chapter 16, 'The use of personal contact', pages 197–200.

### Evaluation questions for telephone response quality

- Did the caller get through first attempt?
- How long was it before the telephone was answered?
- What was the manner of the person answering?
- Was the caller asked his name/telephone number?
- Was he questioned on his enquiry?
- Was he connected directly to the correct person?
- If there was a delay, was he kept informed of progress?
- Did he speak to a secretary or an assistant first?
- Did he have to give his name again and re-explain his enquiry?
- What was his first impression of the professional or person dealing with the query?
- Did the professional or his assistant give his name?
- Was he asked by the professional for his name and address and telephone number again?

- If he gave it to the telephonist, did he say so or did he have to repeat it?
- Was he questioned for further details?
- Was he asked to make an appointment?
- Was there any need or any offer to call back?
- If so, was he and after how long?
- What was the final impression of the professional, his assistant and the telephonist?

## Correspondence

The quality of correspondence—appearance and content—projects a very definite image of a firm which is enhanced or reduced by the speed of response. Within a practice there will be varying correspondence styles and while superficially establishing a 'house style' has much to recommend it, it can reduce the quality of correspondence to a mechanistic and boring level. There should always be some room for personnel to use or adopt their own style provided it does not clash with the image objective of the firm. There is little doubt that a strong and lasting impression is generated by correspondence and is difficult subsequently to change. Thus there ought to be at least a loose surveillance by practice developers so that the firm is projected in a suitable manner by all who write on its behalf.

The design of the heading itself is also of importance and again should be compatible with the optimum image and should contain all the information a correspondent may require including a clear identification of the writer and his position, as well as any references which will assist the recipient in identifying the appropriate papers and other materials relevant to the matter which is the subject of the letter.

The art of letter writing has been dealt with in numerous texts but it remains true that there are some professionals who will never master it. At least they should attempt to avoid the more aggravating aspects which can induce impatience and irritation in clients and lead to errors, inefficiencies and ultimately client losses.

## The premises

Premises, their location, decor, condition, configuration, comfort, cleanliness, tidiness and privacy can all make a considerable contribution to the image required and, equally, can together be a toxic combination creating a totally negative impression.

- **Location**  Location often endows and conveys its own image. In London Harley Street and Lincoln's Inn immediately convey an image of firms, practices or individuals certainly high up if not at the top of their professions. While such an intense caste system does not exist in most provincial towns there are nevertheless areas of many cities wherein the professions tend to concentrate and which are perceived as prestigious. Practices with substantial interests in commercial business are not likely to enhance their image if they are located in the middle of a municipal housing estate. Conversely, this may be the most appropriate location for a legal practice devoted to servicing legally aided clients in minor civil and criminal matters.
- **Decor**  Without becoming involved in aesthetics which are anyway very personal, firms can convey an immediate specific image by virtue of their appearance. Modern decor, unusual materials and designs, project an image of modern, sophisticated, successful firms responsive to change. For some professions, however, heavy mahogany furniture, traditional wall coverings and carpets give a preferred image of longevity, stability, tradition,

148

experience and unchanging values. Either image can be appropriate for different types of clients and professions.

Clients respond positively to life styles they perceive as equivalent to their own and can feel uncomfortable or even intimidated by a different psychographic ambience as projected by the decor and equipment.

In reality of course firms have all types of clients and the decor cannot be made to fit each one's perceptions. The decision as to how the premises are to appear must be judgemental but based on client types not on personal preferences.

- **Condition**   It goes without saying that offices and buildings in poor condition immediately imply a firm which either cannot afford better or is so insensitive that it does not appreciate the value of good physical conditions for clients and staff. Peeling ceiling paper, chipped paintwork, torn upholstery and broken linoleum are not likely to give confidence to many clients. Come what may, clients prefer to work with successful practices rather than unsuccessful ones and those which appear to be in the last stages of terminal illness. Even the best decor in the best buildings will not overcome impressions created by poor maintenance, a symbol of neglect as well as shortage of resources.

- **Configuration**   Many professional practices are in old buildings which are highly inefficient as offices but must nevertheless be utilized. Obviously purpose-built offices or open space that can be divided to give maximum efficiency is one ideal but again it may create image conflicts. Given, however, the constraint of an existing configuration such apparently trivial aspects as having clients accompanied to the office they are visiting rather than allowing them to get lost in a maze of corridors, staircases and anonymous closed doors creates a caring image.

- **Comfort**   Ideally no client ought to have to wait but the ideal is also an impossibility. Waiting areas should be welcoming and comfortable and large enough to accommodate what might be maximum requirements or at the least alternatives must be available for visitors who cannot be accommodated. Reading matter should be recent (old, tattered, well-fingered free colour supplements or indeed even journals that have been purchased give an impression of not caring and indeed meanness). If the practice has its own and related literature this should be prominently displayed. The waiting area ought to be tidied up at frequent intervals during the day. In today's ethos the question of prohibiting smoking should be considered.

- **Cleanliness**   This ought to be a *sine qua non* but often is not. The entire offices including those parts the client never enters ought always to be immaculate. Filled ashtrays, unemptied waste paper bins, dusty chairs and tables, unpleasant washrooms, dirty windows in particular, soiled curtains and upholstery can make what is basically a good appearance into something squalid. While there may indeed be clients who feel happier in unhygienic scruffiness, it cannot apply to the majority of the population.

- **Tidiness**   Tidiness is not necessarily a symbol of efficiency but untidiness is more likely to have a negative effect on clients and give the impression that the professional is sloppy, overworked, or badly supported by his staff. Untidiness in reception and other offices inevitably projects an image of an insensitive staff and management. The desk piled high with papers and heaps of books and files on the floor, intended as it often is, to impress both clients and other personnel of just how busy and important the occupant of the office is, in fact proably has the opposite effect, namely that the work load is the result of bad personal organization and poor time and staff management. The fear that a tidy office means the firm is without work is nonsense.

- **Privacy**   Privacy is obviously important in many professions. If the client or patient can hear the conversation in the next room, then his conversation too can be heard and this will strongly inhibit the development of a relationship with the professional who might be the recipient of guilty knowledge on disease, crime or some moral issue. The question of privacy comes back strongly to that of configuration. Off-the-street clients or patients are frequently asked by the receptionist or person receiving them why they wish to see the professional. With a waiting area full of visitors or with practice staff within hearing, the casual prospective client may well not be inclined to reveal the reason for his visit. The image is created of a firm where discretion is not rated highly.

In contradistinction, closed rooms can leave a client feeling he is forgotten or abandoned. Just as with the enquirer having to hold on the telephone, when visitors are placed in rooms away from the mainstream of office activity, there should be frequent reassurance that they have not been forgotten. Indeed, if it is possible, the offer of tea or coffee goes a long way to make the person waiting feel both remembered and of interest and concern to the practice. Nothing could better sum up the way of handling the waiting clients than the words of an American attorney. Her staff are instructed to 'flutter around the client'.[5]

One final but important and indeed often intractable problem relates to premises. In some practices with a wide client and service spread, particularly solicitors, totally incompatible clients, in manner, appearance, habits, needs and importance may have to be kept in close proximity. The petty criminal on bail awaiting trial might not be regarded as creating the image desired to another waiting client, perhaps a wealthy individual visiting to give instructions for a trust. Where it is possible to anticipate incompatible clients in the waiting area and where the problem cannot be solved by appointment timing and punctuality, then arrangements would be made for separate waiting areas if possible even if it means temporary use of an ordinary office.

## Atmospherics

Atmospherics are closely but not wholly related to premises. In many products and services the atmosphere of the place where the transaction occurs contributes at least as much to the image and thus the purchasing decision as the product or service itself.[6] Restaurants, personal care establishments, centres of entertainment, are obvious examples where atmospheres are engineered and are deliberate image supports. Even away from the commercial arena it can be seen how 'atmospherics' contribute to the acceptance, non-acceptance or effective functioning of the facility involved—places of worship, recreational areas, social clubs, courts of law, are examples.

It is only in a limited number of activities where atmospherics are treated consciously although only the most insensitive clients are unaware of their existence. The main elements of atmosphere have been suggested as: visual—colour, brightness, size, shapes; aural—volume, pitch; olfactory—scent, freshness; tactile—softness, smoothness, temperature.

In developing a practice image, atmospherics ought not to be ignored since they can have a considerable influence on client behaviour and client acceptance. Too great a dissonance with expectation can produce a negative reaction but too great a compliance may have a similar effect. The client well versed in his *Pickwick Papers* may well expect to find his lawyer's office like Serjeant Snubbin's where 'books of practice, heaps of papers and opened letters were scattered over the table without any attempt at order or arrangement, the furniture of the room was old and rickety; the doors of the book-case were rotting on their hinges; the dust

5. Kathryn S. Marshall. 'The client interview—a marketing opportunity'. Developing and improving your practice. Law Society Seminar (Leeds and Bristol, 1983).
6. Philip Kotler. *Marketing for Non-Profit Organizations*. Prentice-Hall (Englewood Cliffs, NJ, 1975), pp. 219–221.

flew out of the carpet in little clouds at every step; the blinds were yellow with age and dirt', but he would not necessarily regard such a condition as appropriate for his needs.

A balance can be achieved only by a return to the segmentation principle. Where a professional service is directed to distinct business types, social classes or life style buyer groups, it is obviously easier to create an acceptable and positive atmosphere.

The following sequence of questions is suggested in attempting to create suitable atmospherics:

- Who are the clients sought?
- What are the clients seeking from the decision (buying) experience?
- What atmospheric variables can fortify the perceptions, beliefs and emotional reactions of clients?
- Will the resulting atmosphere compete effectively with alternative atmospheres available in other professions and other practices?

Atmospheres are a factor present in every decision situation, but in most activities they have tended to develop casually or organically. Atmospherics are the conscious planning of atmospheres to encourage favourable decision making. They are, incidentally, one more way of obtaining that differential advantage referred to in Chapter 3, 'Creating a client-centred practice', page 26.

## Support personnel

Early contacts within a practice will usually be the support staff unless the original impetus came from social or some other direct meeting with the professional concerned. Thus the support staff will be among the first and most powerful influences in creating the image. The desiderata for support staff who have client contact must be intelligence, businesslike manner and appearance, knowledge of the practice and personnel and an ability to demonstrate an interest in the enquirer.

Those who receive visitors should be able to do so without keeping them waiting or if they have to be kept waiting to at least acknowledge their presence. Where the receptionist has a dual role which includes handling the switchboard, and because the telephone always takes precedence over the person in the room, it is particularly important that the visitor is indeed acknowledged even if the words are only 'mouthed' in dumb show. It is also important that where the telephone delays interrupt reception procedures that it is obvious to the visitor that the receptionist/telephonist is engaged on a business not a personal call. It is discourteous to delay visitors while personal discussions are held. Equally, since the visitor can hear one end of the conversation nothing which will breach a confidence or might be considered as indiscreet must be said in the presence of the visitor. For this reason alone it could be important to separate the telephone from the visitors.

In the present relaxed social ethos it is not easy to stipulate just how support staff should dress. Nevertheless dress creates its own image. Strapless sun suits have their place but not generally in professional practices. Extremes in dress, hair styles and cosmetics can disconcert many clients who may feel that such appearances are more appropriate in a disco or boutique rather than where they have come to be advised on (to them) very important and serious matters which are perhaps causing personal stress.

The 'uncertainty' factor referred to in Chapter 7, 'Professional services and client needs', is heightened by any difference between what is expected in image terms from a profession or a practice and the appearance given.

The efficiency of a practice becomes apparent at an early stage when the support staff can demonstrate an understanding of the client's needs and how it relates to the practice and its professional personnel. That is, for off-the-street business, support staff knowing which member of the qualified staff would be most suitable for the circumstances and needs of the visitor, who is available or when he is available. For secretaries and assistants in particular, to be able to arrange appointments that suit both client and practitioner can be an important image component. The client will be aware of both how difficult or easy it was to arrange an appointment and how concerned the personnel were to meet the enquirer's date and time needs or preferences.

Support staff form a vital, on-going link between the professional personnel and the client. They can, alone and in combination, materially assist the development of an acceptable image. Conversely they can create one which is quite out of keeping with the reality of the quality and behaviour of practitioners.

## Professional staff

These are the personnel whose skills and experience comprise what is ultimately offered to the client but since these skills are intangible and untried at the outset, the client bases his expectations entirely on perceptions—those that were formed along the continuum until he reaches the practitioner and those projected by the practitioner himself.

### Pre-meeting image

The very first impressions may have been created before the first meeting in that the professional may seem difficult to reach, too closely guarded by other personnel or unpunctual. This fault, once identified, is very easy to eliminate.

Much more difficult is the face-to-face impression given by the practitioner. Again, appearance in the form of dress, tidiness, cosmetics, posture, age, physical characteristics will all have had their impact very early in the meeting perhaps even before a word is spoken. While it is true that clients do tend to think in archetypal 'uniforms', i.e., professional men should wear dark suits and professional women dress in dark two-pieces with white blouses, there is certainly no mandatory requirement, except perhaps in courts of law, nor good practice development reason why something a little less sombre could not be acceptable. It would be absurd to suggest what is and what is not acceptable in regard to dress and appearance. It is useful however to apply the tests of 'appropriateness', 'discretion' and 'expectation'. These are excellent guides to which aspects of dress and appearance will contribute or detract from images.

### Meeting image

These preliminaries can create or remove barriers which enhance or inhibit satisfactory relationships but the crucial aspect of the first impressions is ultimately the overall manner and technique of the professional. The way in which he expresses himself both in words and by non-verbal communication will create very sharply focused images both of the practitioner and, by association, the practice as a whole. Non-verbal communications are the 'messages' which facial expression, gesture, posture, body movement and tone of voice project. No matter what words are spoken individually and together non-verbal communication can totally alter the meaning and the feeling which they can convey.[7]

7. Kathryn S. Marshall. 'The client interview—a marketing opportunity'. Op. cit.

The relationship of the practitioner and client and the way this is developed and consolidated is clearly contributing in an all pervasive way to the total image. It is however a subject which requires far more detailed coverage than can be given within the subject area of 'images' and in any event such detail would be inappropriate. Nevertheless, a summary of behavioural styles which help to create images is a useful guide. The listing in Figure 12-2 will assist in identifying communication styles and selecting the correct one for any particular type of client or service or, as is more likely to be necessary, attempting to develop a particular style since few people will be capable of adopting all the styles at will.

*Punctuality*

Punctuality is perhaps one of the most frequent causes of poor images. While doctors may have a ready-made excuse for their constant, and it would seem, almost habitual bad time keeping which can always be explained by their life-saving or, at the very least, distress-removing activities which demand instant changes in priorities, other professions lack such an acceptable alibi. Punctuality it has been rightly said is the courtesy of princes. Punctuality projects efficiency, punctuality implies a valuing of the client's time as at least equal to the value of the practitioner's time, punctuality demonstrates caring and courtesy, punctuality reveals effective time management. Each one of these is a substantial contributor to the total image.

However, occasions must occur when punctuality cannot be maintained. It is important and not difficult to placate an irate visitor. It should be assumed every client who is delayed in his meeting will develop some sense of irritation or anger, even if it is not shown, and to act accordingly. A recognition of and apology for the delay with an explanation as to its cause is the first step. The visitor should then be kept informed of the position right up to the moment the appointment is fulfilled.

As any traveller by any mode of transport knows understanding the cause of a delay and being kept informed does more for good customer public relations than claims of comfort, speed or convenience. Similarly in professional practices any waste of client's time caused by delays which create irritation or worse, can be partially, if not wholly, mitigated by explanations and apologies and by hospitality in the form of the offer of refreshments. A small thing but one that clients note consciously or unconsciously.

The question of punctuality extends to the total practice. The office should be open the stated hours. If it has to close for lunch and if arrangements cannot be made to keep the switchboard open, at the very least a telephone answering machine should be available to give callers the option of leaving a message and being called back or telephoning again.

## Other image components

There are many other seemingly trivial but cumulatively important aspects of operations that contribute or detract from images. Routing and response to messages, payments with firm but friendly control, flexibility in timing to meet client's requirements, willingness to meet clients at places that are convenient to them and never suggesting in all these matters that it is the convenience of the practitioner that counts more than that of the client or patient.

## Last impressions

There has been a concentration on first impressions because if these are not favourable either the relationship does not emerge or it is an uncomfortable one. However, just as important,

| Style characteristic | Intuitor | Thinker | Feeler | Sensor |
|---|---|---|---|---|
| Emphasis | Ideas, concepts, theory, innovation, long-range thinking | Logic, organization, analysis, systematic enquiry | Human interaction, feelings, emotions | Action, getting things done, wants to see results of efforts quickly |
| Time orientation | Future | Past, present, future | Past | Present |
| Sources of satisfaction | Derived from world of possibilities, problem-solving oriented, but not terribly interested in implementing solutions | Enjoys seeing a problem through to implementing solution; enjoys anything well organized or methodically thought out | Enjoys 'reading between the lines', social interpersonal contact is sought out | Likes quick results, enjoys making things happen, likes feedback on efforts, likes to be in charge |
| Strengths | Original, imaginative, creative, idealistic, intellectually tenacious, ideological | Effective communicator, deliberate, prudent, weighs alternatives, stabilizing, objective, rational, analytical | Spontaneous, persuasive, empathic, grasps traditional values, probing, introspective, draws out feelings of others, loyal | Pragmatic, assertive, directional, results oriented, objective, bases opinions on what he actually sees, competitive, confident |
| Weaknesses (if style is over-extended) | Unrealistic, 'far out', fantasy-bound, scattered, devious, out of touch, dogmatic, impractical | Verbose, indecisive, overly cautious, over-analyses, unemotional, non-dynamic, controlled and controlling, overly serious, rigid | Impulsive, manipulative, over-personalizes, sentimental, postponing, guilt-ridden, stirs up conflict, subjective | Doesn't see long-range, status seeking, acts first then thinks, lacks trust in others, domineering, arrogant |
| On the telephone | Wordy, but aloof, impersonal | Ordered, measured, businesslike | Warm and friendly, sometimes seemingly too much so | Abrupt, to the point |
| In letter and writing | Writes as he speaks, intellectual and often abstract terms | Well-organized, structured, specific | Short and highly personalized | Very brief, action-oriented, urgent |
| In clothing | Erratic and hard to predict | Conservative, unassuming, understated, colour co-ordinated | Colourful, informal, mood-oriented | Informal, simple, functional, neat, but not fancy |
| In surroundings | Futuristic, modern, creative | Correct, non-distracting, tasteful, but conventional, organized | Informal, warm, personalized | Hard-charging, clutter |
| Opposite style | Sensor | Feeler | Thinker | Intuitor |
| Typical occupations | Scientists, researchers, artists, professors, writers, corporate planners, 'idea' people | Lawyers, engineers, teachers, computer programmers, accounts | Entertainers, salesmen, writers, teachers, public relations specialists, nurses, social workers, psychiatrists, psychologists, secretaries, retail business people | Entrepreneurs, construction workers, pilots, bankers, investors, professional athletes, sales, models, physicians, land developers |

**Figure 12-2**  Communication styles[8]

8. Reproduced by permission of John L. Bledsoe. Vice President, Paul Mok and Associates, Dallas, Texas and first published in *Legal Economics*, May/June 1981

and most particularly if the referral system is working for the practices, are last impressions. There is an obvious need to ensure that these are favourable if the client is to return to the firm and if he is to recommend it to others.

The closing image is the resultant of all the experiences of the client during the relationship with the practice and encompasses the various aspects described. However, at the end a new and critical image feature arises which can on its own totally cancel out or enormously enhance the image which has been built up. This is related to the fees charged. Whether the client knows what these will be in advance or whether they can only be calculated at the time, they will nevertheless carry with them an indelible impression.

As in any exchange of values, which is what occurs in a professional relationship, the client will always assess at the end if he feels the exchange favoured him or the vendor or both parties received equal value. Since barter is rarely involved what in fact the client perceives is 'value for money'. This perception is based not just on cost effectiveness, where such an analysis can be made, but on the sum total of the way the client has been received and nurtured and the benefits which he has or thinks he has received, the extent of effort observed (see page 145) as well as a range of satisfactions ranging from the purely emotional to the technical and intellectual.

Complaints of high fees are substantially complaints that the quality of the service received is not at a level which justifies the charges. In reality the quality could have been totally compatible with the fee but the client's dissatisfaction stems from factors other than the skill of the professional or the result achieved. His judgement is usually subjective and emotional and moreover he often does not have the background to judge 'value for money'. Thus, while it is never less than crucial to ensure that the client understands how the fee has been arrived at and any doubts are brought into the open, it is equally important for the professional to appreciate that the client may not be able to or wish to express this source of his dissatisfaction. Thus the practitioner must be sensitive to the fact that not all uncertainties in the client's mind can or will be verbalized by him.

It is worth while commenting here that the perception of high cost can often stem from the inclusion of disbursements in the final account. This is particularly true for legal practices and to a lesser extent medicine. While the client or patient may be aware that the disbursement forms no part of the fee and that the professional does not benefit from it, there is nevertheless a very real and human tendency to see only the 'bottom line' as the sum total of cost of the consultancy or work. Disbursements and fees in practice development should, for image purposes, be separated not just in the actual invoice but also in time. Fees and disbursements are better presented apart.

Of all business activities services are the most unforgiving and most services never get a second opportunity to demonstrate their effectiveness or to correct a poor image, rightly or wrongly garnered. There is no second chance so that the end of a transaction is either the end of the line or the introduction, however distant, to the next transaction. The professional will certainly avoid the worst mistakes and have a far greater opportunity of leaving clients at the end of an assignment, case or consultancy, with a favourable image if he remembers that clients' needs are not satisfied only by the results obtained. There are other very real, but usually unstated, needs which concern the client as a human being and not a file number.

## Optimum image described

In detail the optimum image will vary by profession, by practice and by client type but there are certain verities which will apply to all practices. It can be best summed up in the simple phrase 'Nice people to deal with' or 'A nice firm to do business with'. This desideratum can never be achieved unless all the relationships which comprise a professional practice are the subject of constant and careful attention; professional and client, client and support staff, professional and support staff.

Poor images and declining performance are often due to over-reliance on analysis, techniques, strategies, systems and structures with little heed taken of the human network of style, skills and staff. It is the absence of the latter that causes weak performance both of the discipline and of practice development.

Motivation for developing and maintaining a good image invariably starts from the top of the firm and partners, most certainly the principal partner's behaviour and attitudes will be critical. Indeed these attitudes and behaviours, given they provide guidance and encouragement to others, are as much part of the firm's resources as those listed in Chapter 4, 'Preparing for practice development'.

A practice in which internal human relations are good has far more satisfied clients than a practice where such relationships are only fair. Motivated staff themselves create a good image and it is their desire to want to offer a better and superior client-centred service which improves the individual and total image.

Because, as will be shown in the next chapter, the greatest part of a professional firm's business comes through the referral system being 'a nice firm to do business with' will be the motivation for many referrals. An image of caring and being human rather than mechanistic with both clients and colleagues is an attractive image all firms can strive for.[9] The creation and maintenance of an image is a continuous operation reflecting the pulse beat of the firm. Image tactics require constant supervision and *current* image testing because the image itself changes in response to changes in the environment into which it is projected. Developments within the environment, obsolescence, sophistication, deterioration, demand, innovation in techniques, systems and hardware are forces always at work to erode or exchange a carefully built image just as much as changes in the political, economic or social climate in which a firm operates.

Thus every practice should constantly review its multiple images and the factors which shape these ranging from the trivial to the fundamental. If practice development strategies are plotted along a critical path then agreement on an optimum image and the creation of a realistic ascertainable basis for this image must be accomplished before later tasks or 'events' can be satisfactorily completed. The image objective is one critical early 'event' upon which later activities will depend heavily for their success.

Individuals and firms select images and perceptions just as much as they select products and suppliers, but while the latter are relatively easy to assess, describe and even adjust to the demand, images are one more intangible superimposed on the basic intangible of the service. The difficulty of obtaining accurate image information and of identifying image objectives and making the reality match up to the image is not a reason for not attempting it.

9. Lynda King Taylor. 'A nice firm to do business with'. *The Law Society Gazette* (London, 23 June 1982).

# Appendix 12A.  Image profile factors[10]

1. Do we have a formal image objective and development policy?

2. What is it?

3. Is it relevant in the light of today's business conditions?

4. Assess the degree of image sensitivity both throughout the firm and particularly among those members of the firm and that part of the firm (e.g., premises, vehicles, stationery, etc.) that inter-face with the clients.

5. Who in the firm is responsible for image development?

6. How substantial a part of the job activity does this represent?

7. Should the time devoted to image development be increased/decreased?

8. What are the images of our competitors?

9. What is the image of our profession?

10. Does it represent the profession's own view of how it is seen, or is it an independent assessment?

11. How far does the profession's image impact on our own and on competitors' images favourably/unfavourably?

12. Does the profession's image affect competitors differently from ourselves?

13. If so, why and in what way?

14. What part of the image perceptions is based on direct experience of the firm?

15. What part of the image perceptions is based on hearsay?

16. How has the information on the previous questions been obtained?

17. What evidence exists to support the answers?

    The next six questions should be applied to the following key client and potential client groups:

    • regular clients
    • sporadic clients
    • one-off clients
    • potential clients where offers have been made but not accepted
    • potential clients we have contact with

10. These profile issues are adapted from Aubrey Wilson's *Marketing Audit Check Lists—a guide to effective marketing resource realization*. List 21 'Images'. McGraw-Hill (London, 1982).

18. How do we think we are perceived by our various 'publics' (mirror image)?

19. How are we actually perceived by our various publics (current image)?

20. How would we wish to be perceived by our various publics (wish image)?

21. What image is likely to assist most in achieving our objectives (optimum image)?

22. What reasons can be ascribed to any variation between the images?

23. What actions are required to achieve the optimum image?

24. How far does reality of our activities match up with our image and the optimum image?

25. What actions must be taken to close any gap between the image and the reality?

26. What is the image of the different aspects of the firm's services, facilities and resources?
    - availability
    - quality of services
    - fees
    - range of services
    - professional capability
    - performance history
    - size of organization
    - atmospherics
    - financial position
    - attitude towards clients
    - communication methods
    - management and organization
    - independence
    - geographical location
    - professional and other links
    - reputation
    - premises
    - client list

27. Are the communication methods we are using compatible with the image we seek to create?

28. How do the total and individual perceptions vary among the different members of commercial DMU's and private clients?

29. What is the image of the firm, services and operations as perceived by:
    - equity partners
    - other partners
    - professional staff
    - support staff
    - competitors
    - our profession
    - non-active stakeholders
    - news media
    - local community
    - opinion formers
    - educational bodies
    - trade unions
    - referral sources
    - suppliers
    - professional body

30. How frequently will image benchmark checks be made?

31. What variants will initiate action?

32. How far are our promotional and personal contact activities deliberately intended to enhance our image?

33. Should there be a change of policy to intensify image development aspects of our promotion and personal contact?

34. Would image development be enhanced by the use of specialist agencies?

# Chapter 13. The referral (recommendations) system

The professions, constrained as they often are by the strictly policed rules of practice, have traditionally depended upon recommendations for the acquisition of new clients. It is a method which has never been criticized by any professional bodies or practitioners and indeed mostly they boast that recommendations or referrals are proof of the excellence of their work and thus no other form of promotion is required. It must be commented, however, that for a practice development method that has the approval of the collegial organizations of the professions, the enthusiastic support of individual members and the accolade of success, it is astonishing that the workings of the inter-personal network are not really understood and therefore not fully exploited. While the professions accept the inter-personal network as a method of business acquisition they have resolutely refused to examine the system in order that their individual members might operate an approved method more effectively.

In the qualifying professions estimates of all new business obtained from referrals range from 80 to 100 per cent. There can be few business activities wherein this overwhelming value of business is acquired through the effectiveness of a single marketing tool and yet so little knowledge exists of that tool or so few attempts have been made to establish whether despite its undoubted success it is nevertheless capable of further exploitation.

## Sources of information on professional services

Figure 10-1 in Chapter 10, 'How the individual practice is selected', gives the results of the study of 250 commercial concerns and 250 private individuals seeking information on how they located their professional advisers.

The professions included, apart from the more obvious ones such as solicitor, accountant, doctor, dentist, optician, architect, surveyor, veterinary, also covered a range of financial services such as stockbroking, pension consultants, insurance portfolio management, mortgages, which probably accounts for the inclusion of retail outlet merchandising, exhibitions and advertising.

It can be seen from the list in Figure 10-1 that many of the sources are likely to be inter-personal referees. For example, trade or social organizations and 'Advisers' in other professions probably provide guidance informally and not by issuing approved lists.

Organizations obviously represent an important and frequently mentioned source of information for professional referrals, but the advice, so often and so glibly given to professionals seeking to develop client contacts, to 'join a club' might have had some validity in the past but on its own is now of little value. The words of one American lawyer sum up the entire situation concerning involvement with communal, social, cultural and other organizations.

> Can you get clients from social, civic or charitable organizations? The answer to the question is simultaneously 'yes' and 'no'. If you join an organization solely to get clients, you will be wasting your time and money. The other members will see through you, and you won't get anything from them. On the other hand, if you belong to an organization because you sincerely believe in its purposes and you work hard for the organization, the other members will be impressed . . . and they will come to you with their legal work.[1]

## Non-client referral sources

From observation and research it is clear that the greatest number of referrals come from existing clients. The often repeated statement by professional firms that 'a satisfied client is the only requirement for a successful practice' is substantially true but it does require qualification in that clients have to declare their satisfaction to other firms and individuals seeking professional advisers. In other words referrals depend not just on 'satisfactions' but on statements of 'satisfactions' either sought or volunteered. This latter statement links directly with methods which can be adopted within the rules of practice which can be used to encourage clients to express satisfaction and which are dealt with below.

The research referred to earlier was directed to ascertaining how new clients arrived at the offices, chambers, surgeries, clinics or studios of practitioners and therefore did not concern itself with repeat usage. It can be safely assumed that the category 'friends and business associates' must have included a very substantial number indeed of individuals and firms which had had satisfactory experience with their advisers.

Both commercial and private client lists show that this category of referrers is the most important. However, the grouping 'own profession, business, trade, social or other organizations' also certainly contains individual referrers who fall into the first category and probably only in a minority of cases does an organization, as an organization *per se*, actually make the reference unless it is for its own professional advisers. The category 'associations of the professions concerned' probably, without exception, made no direct recommendation but sent any enquirers lists of members and thus their contribution must fall into the 'directory' method rather than the inter-personal network. In any event their importance was comparatively low as a source of introductions to professional advisers which may reflect the inadequacy of the associations, but more likely the restrictive nature of their rules which forbids individual recommendations.

Within the 'other professional advisers' category further enquiries revealed the dominant importance of bank managers to both individuals and to firms. After this for commercial firms accountants are the second most frequently used source of referral in this group with no perceptible difference for private clients between doctors, accountants and solicitors. Because of the infrequency of use and the sporadic nature of the demand for their services, architects and surveyors did not figure prominently but in fact they form a sub-system of some importance within their groupings. The estate agent, for example, for private clients appears to generate referrals for a number of professions and activities with a great deal of the flow only one way (see Figure 13-1).

There are of course sub-systems in other areas of business activity where the flow is reciprocal (see Figure 13-2).

1. Jay G. Foonberg. *How to Start and Build a Law Practice*. Law Students Division of the American Bar Association (Chicago, 1976), p. 33.

**Figure 13-1** Sub-system—estate agents referrals

**Figure 13-2** Sub-system—engineering referrals

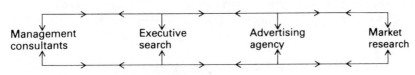

**Figure 13-3** Sub-system—management referrals

A similar sub-system might be found in the professions and businesses involved in servicing administrative and commercial management (Figure 13-3).

This is not by any means the end of the intricacies of the referral system. The research, based as it was on a small sample and not being specific, failed to pick up what must be important and frequent origins of recommendations which are totally unofficial and frequently deliberately obscured: for solicitors—magistrates' clerks, police or even jailers in criminal cases;[2] for accountants and tax advisers—civil servants in the Inland Revenue and Customs and Excise officers.

## Inter-professional references

Of course inter-professional referrals are of considerable importance for some professions although they tend to be one-way references: general practitioners to medical specialists, solicitors to barristers. Thus important practice development third party targets for medical specialists and barristers are their referrers without whom neither profession could practise

2. Quoted by Phillip Thomas and Geoff Mungham in 'Solicitors and clients: altruism or self-interest'. In *The Sociology of the Professions* (eds Dingwall and Lewis). Macmillan (London, 1983). See also, Chapter 6, 'Deciding the service offering of the practice' of this book.

because direct contact between them and the public as individuals or firms is forbidden. The opportunity or the occasion for medical specialists and barristers to make a reciprocal reference to a general practitioner or solicitor must be relatively rare and probably only occurring from social contacts.

Another form of inter-professional reference can be between practitioners in precisely the same discipline. Under-capacity, inconvenient location, lack of some specialization, availability, conflict of interest and cost could mean that a new client or even an existing client might have to be turned away on one particular occasion. A solicitor could not act for a husband and wife in a contested divorce, a veterinary surgeon's location may lead him to consider a lack of back-up which did not enable him to maintain a 24 hour service would be unsatisfactory for sheep and dairy farmers. In these circumstances it would be usual to suggest an alternative practice that has the skills, resources, availability, services and whatever else is required by the client or patient. The very professionalism of the practitioner would ensure that he did not offer his own services but that he recommended an alternative which he felt would be most suited to the client. Thus other professionals, both superiors—in a skill sense—and peers, are also legitimate referral targets and thus would or could form part of the segmentation strategy.

Many professions also generate references for professionals in other services, semi-professionals and traders which are not substantially one-way recommendations as in the case of barristers and medical specialists. Doctors recommend opticians and opticians doctors; architects recommend builders and builders recommend architects; accountants suggest stockbrokers and stockbrokers accountants. Thus a massive network of inter-personal, inter-professional relationships develop.

The importance of all this for practice development is to ensure that referral sources are as much part of the segmentation strategy and target as potential clients themselves.

## Encouraging referrals within the system

For most professions with both commercial and private clients serviced by the same practice there is always a potential new group of clients. Within commercial-client organizations there are individuals with personal needs for professional services; private clients are most frequently in employment and their employers represent potential clients.

There is no reason why a satisfied commercial client cannot make it clear that the firm's professional advisers would be willing to assist staff members with personal professional service requirements. There are advantages for all the parties involved. For the individual the fact that he is using the company's adviser gives him a leverage far greater than the value of his personal business and a sense of security in that the weight of the firm as a client stands between him and the professional in the event of any dissatisfaction; for the company, making available a professional facility to staff adds to the value of the total business generated for the professional practice and thus creates a useful countervailing power. Additionally, it demonstrates an interest in and care for individual members of the company and assists good industrial and personnel relations and staff welfare; for the professional practice a new client catchment is created which within it has further strong possibilities for a sub-system of referrals by the individuals served.

The converse is not so effective but nevertheless not without value. It is always possible that a private client is in a position to give a professional practice or practitioner with whom he has a satisfactory relationship the necessary 'visibility' at a time when the client's employers are considering appointing a new or additional practice.

Chapter 8, 'Professional services and the commercial client', explained both the concept of the decision-making unit comprising different people with different roles at different times in the choice process (Figures 8-1 and 8-10) and the explanation of the communication process in Chapter 3, 'Creating a client-centred practice', Figure 3-2, illustrates the importance of being known to decision makers during the decision-making process. The favourable mention of a practice at the appropriate moment could be critical in the ultimate choice, most particularly because other marketing methods are not permitted. The recommendation of a practice does not have to be from a member of the decision-making unit. Within firms there are individuals without authority but with influence, most particularly management outside the functional area concerned and support staff whose intervention one way or another could lead to the final choice or rejection.

Thus for the professional—individual or firm—there is the possibility of existing clients—commercial or private—representing an important referral source for new business. However, it should not be supposed that managers of client firms will automatically assume that their advisers are interested in serving private clients, particularly members of the firm or, conversely, private clients will assume that their professional firms would or could handle commercial business. Information to these effects must be communicated to the existing clients.

## Using the referral system methodically

Given that the most substantial part, if not all, of new business from private patients or clients, patrons or even cases arrives on the professional's desk through recommendations, then clearly it is important to know not only who the recommender might be, but also why he has made the recommendation. Obtaining such information is one fundamental activity in practice development (see Chapter 4, 'Preparing for practice development', pages 35–6.

It is only necessary where such an instruction does not exist already for it to be compulsory within the firm for all personnel without exception, to enquire from each new client or prospective client, who recommended him or suggested he made contact. If it was not through the inter-personal network how then did he become aware of the practice?

In some professions it is standard practice, if only for self-protection, to make this enquiry and in any event very often the client or patient volunteers the information when making an appointment or on the first interview. What professionals fail to do, particularly where they are not sole practitioners, is to tabulate this information so that a body of information is built up on sources of referrals by type of referrer, number and frequency of the references, types of clients or cases referred, and of course the name of the individual referrer. From this it will rapidly be seen which types of referrers and indeed which individual referrers are important to the practice. It will also reveal weaknesses in the referral structure. For example referrals from building society managers but not from insurance brokers would indicate, if appropriate, that more effort must be made to cultivate the latter. The patterning of the information is of the utmost consequence if the referral system is to be made to work effectively.

All referral sources should be tabulated and consolidated so that those concerned with practice development can identify who are the important third party targets. Centralization of the referral source list is needed because the value of any particular source or individual referrer may be disguised by the fact that new clients they have introduced have been dispersed through the practice and among different professionals.

The tabulation of referral sources must include a special category of inter- and intra-professional references since this enables a most powerful stimulant to be used—reciprocation. Wherever the opportunity for reciprocation occurs it should be used.

So far as inter-professional referrers are concerned the very process of compiling the dossier can be a powerful influence in encouraging inter-professional referrals. Contacting the referring firms or individuals to ask for more information on their own practice or services so that a reciprocal introduction can be made when appropriate, indicates to them the intention to at least attempt to offer something in return. It is obvious to all practitioners, a reference from another professional does not automatically imply that the referrer is a suitable adviser for any particular client. The fact of the referral is not the criterion for reciprocation. This can only be 'suitability' but and when all other things are equal, it is obviously sensible to recipro-cate introductions.

The compilation and centralization of a list of referrers is not likely to be effective unless there is encouragement to use it and a fairly frequent reminder of the existence of the list. Such a reminder could simply be in the form of an amendment to add or delete names. This draws attention to the existence of the possible reciprocation list in a very practical way.

For some professions it may be sufficient merely to list the names of inter- or intra-professional referrers but it is infinitely better if listings are also a dossier. Just what infor-mation on the individuals and their organizations which comprise the list should be included depends upon the referrers and on their professions. Location, specialization, size and avail-ability are basic to all types of professional reciprocation links but others will be more specific.

The dossier technique can be extended usefully to individual referrers in case the opportunity arises of being able to reciprocate on a non-professional basis. An accountant with a manufacturing and a computer software client might well have occasion to effect an introduction for the benefit of both parties. This would be an encouragement for the clients to recommend the accountant should an occasion arise. Accountants and bank managers and to a lesser extent, architects, surveyors and solicitors in commercial practice, are most likely to have information on clients' activities but those who largely serve individuals in their private capacity do not necessarily know the occupations or interests of their clients and patients. It would be unusual and indeed perhaps seen as impertinent for a veterinary surgeon to ask a pet owner about his business or other activities and yet this can be the basis of a simple but substantial and valuable information resource which can work for the benefit of everyone involved.

Compiling dossiers on clients is more a question of motivation than skill, most particularly when the information request is unusual as in the veterinary case. However, if practitioners and the referred appreciate that the information is to be used to develop an exchange of benefits and not for self-interest, then no favours are asked or given. It is neither to apply sales pressure nor is it mendacity to seek information and there is no reason to be inhibited in dossier compilation.


## Recognizing the referrer

It is unfortunately all too rare for referrals to be acknowledged by the referents. It is an act of common courtesy, if nothing else, to express thanks for introductions. This simple act has a value out of all proportion to the act itself. There are, if any, few individuals who do not enjoy recognition most particularly where they themselves are third parties to an introduction. 'The greatest pleasure I know is to do a good action by stealth and to have it found out by accident' wrote Charles Lamb. He was absolutely correct, acknowledgement gives pleasure and pleasure gives encouragement to repeat the action that generated the acknowledgement. There is no rule imposed by any of the collegial organizations which states that a referrer cannot be thanked and there is no control which can be exerted even if it was desired to do so, that can prevent this sort of acknowledgement giving satisfaction and encouragement. Thus, just as it has been suggested that it should be mandatory to identify the source of referrals, it should also be mandatory that a warm and quick acknowledgement is made to the referrer.

In contacts with the referrer it will never come amiss to suggest that the introduction will merit particular care in servicing the client and, if appropriate, that the person acknowledging the introduction will himself deal with the client assuming his rank represents an apparent 'benefit'. Referrers like to feel that their introduction is of special value and that the person referred will benefit because of the role and importance of the referrer. It is a very natural and basic human emotion to enjoy recognition whether it be from a waiter in a restaurant or a person of fame and repute in his own calling.

In some professions it is however very necessary to check with the client and receive his approval to acknowledge his contact to the referrer. There can be instances, particularly in the medical and legal professions, where the client or patient, despite the request for advice on the choice of a practice, does not want the referrer to know the advice has been followed.

Conversely, in some professions and in some instances it is possible and permissible to keep the referrer informed of progress, with the client's consent, even if it is only as innocuous a statement as 'we have had some limited success so far'. This type of contact creates an on-going communication and contact with the referrer and again is a reminder of the professional practice and its service. A progress report is another indication to the referrer that the role played in the introduction and value placed on it continues to be recognized, again meeting a human desire for appreciation.

Even when a consultation does not end with the result desired by the client, a progress report is still of considerable value. If the client or patient is displeased and has expressed his displeasure to the referrer, the professional at the very least has the opportunity of explaining, possibly in technical terms, what happened and why it happened.

Successful litigation, for example, can nevertheless leave the client substantially out of pocket and critical of the competence of the solicitor assigned to the case because of the outcome. The reality might be that the solicitor advised the client not to proceed with the litigation and explained the consequences of both winning and of losing but the client chose to go ahead, despite the fact that even if successful he could not recover his costs. This is a powerful defence for the solicitor against an actual or implied criticism of incompetence and one which will usually ensure that the referrer continues to regard the firm or individual as a suitable practice or practitioner to recommend.

Thus the progress report, whether negative or positive, is a valuable instrument in the effective use of the inter-personal network because the inter-personal network operates both ways. It can and is used frequently to deter people from approaching a particular practice. Not every enquirer asks 'can you recommend a good optician?' Some say 'what do you think of Bloggs the opticians?' This formulation can easily produce a negative effect and it is this negative response that the progress report goes a long way to mitigate.

## Identifying the reason for referral

The final step in the use of the inter-personal network is to ascertain, if possible, precisely the reasons why the referrer made the recommendation. This may well be the strength, an area of unique competence, facility or resource which was referred to in Chapter 3, 'Creating a client-centred practice', page 26. The differential advantage which every firm possesses distinguishes it favourably from all competing practices. It is not always easy for firms to isolate this differential advantage because they are too close to the practice, to the individuals within it and to the profession itself. Moreover, it is a difficult question to ask directly of clients (and likely to produce a somewhat facetious answer). Indeed even asking why a client chose a practice suggests an element of immodesty, the seeking of compliments or a sense of insecurity or disbelief in the practice itself. Asking a third party why he referred is not so difficult and the answer is likely to be less biased as a self-analysis of the situation.

Once it is known why referrers recommend the practice and the reasons will almost certainly be different for different situations, referrers, referents, professions and clients, then these are practice strengths to be built on, communicated and explained both to referrers and potential clients.

## Methodology

The referral system or inter-personal network is the single most important practice development tool available to most professions and as such it warrants very close study. Its use should be deliberate not fortuitous or reactive. The steps to be taken by each practice are simple and represent no more than an ordered methodology which avoids the mistakes of omission and commission.

- Identify sources of referrals.
- Acknowledge recommendations to the referrer (with clients' permission).
- Offer reciprocation where appropriate.
- Compile centralized list of referrers.
- Compile dossier on important referrers.
- Circulate list and dossier and check at frequent intervals who uses it, how it is used, how often it is used and why it is not used.
- Keep referrers (with clients' permission) informed of progress.
- Establish reasons for referral.

# Chapter 14.  The role of fees in practice development

It showed in the first place that this Thorne was always thinking of money . . . whereas it would have behoved him as a physician had he had the feeling of a physician . . . to have regarded his own pursuits in a purely philosophical spirit, and to have taken his gain which might have accrued as an accidental adjunct to his station in life . . . the true physician should hardly be aware that the last friendly grasp of the hand had been made more precious by the touch of gold.

*Dr Thorne* Anthony Trollope

Nowhere is the clash between the self-image of professions and the image of commercialism better demonstrated than discussion of the charges for service. The belief that 'one who performs a service for satisfaction not gain',[1] which permeates many definitions of professionalism, effectively removes 'price' from overt (if not covert) examination.

Nothing could illustrate this better than a publication issued by the Royal Institute of British Architects on what is purported to be marketing for architects. The importance of fees and fee structure and strategy within the practice development context is never mentioned, the contributors no doubt feeling happier confining themselves to minor marketing techniques such as press releases, photography and graphics—all good, safe subjects for architects.

Any discussion of the economic basis of professional practice starts with two anomalies. The first is semantic. A 'fee' is the price that the client pays for the service and yet the word 'price' is rarely used by professionals or practitioners. It has been pointed out[2] 'one does not ordinarily speak of the price of a semester of education, the price of a loan, or the price of a visit to the dentist'. Some 15 different ways can be identified of describing 'price' in the service sector of the economy. These range from the barrister's 'honorarium' to the consultant's 'retainer'. To some extent the nomenclatures used for price give an insight into a profession's own conception of its services while in other circumstances it is no more than a cosmetic embellishment to hide the reality of what in the final analysis is a commercial transaction.

The strategy of establishing soundly based charges for professional services is no more than the projection and direction of all issues within a practice in order to maximize profits, or achieve whatever other objectives are stated in the plan. It requires a realistic attitude to fees by those who are to establish them and this attitude must derive both from practice objectives and the personal aspirations of those who share directly in the success of the practice and those who hope to.

1. *Sociology of the Professions* (eds Dingwall and Lewis). Macmillan (London, 1983), p. 81.
2. John M. Rathmell. *Marketing in the Service Sector*. Winthrop (Cambridge, Mass., 1974), p. 72.

## Professional practice is not a business

The second anomaly is that the professions, despite what academic researchers may say to the contrary, are not a business in the accepted sense of that word. An example of professional thinking on this matter is summarized by one lawyer:

> Law is not a business; nor merely is it a profession, which is defined in the Oxford Dictionary as a vocation or calling especially one that involves some branch of learning or science but is one of three learned professions. Is it really suggested that it is in the best interests of the community that the proper approach to remuneration is purely on a time basis and supply, related to the question whether there are sufficient people practising. . . . Is the surgeon to be remunerated purely on a time basis? No profession worthy of the name has ever been impelled merely by the monetary reward. It expects, and has a moral right, to be paid properly for its skills and services.[3]

Such statements as 'the supply of professional services is very much more than a business transaction', 'all professional men always put their clients' interests before their own' would seem to take the professions outside the market forces of the business world.

Whether these views of professionalism are accepted or not there still remain other factors which separate services from conventional business activities. Some professions possess a monopoly of a set of widely demanded tasks so that the normal inter-play of market forces is inhibited. Reinforcing this is the fact, in many professions, for example law, medicine and dentistry, for work which is paid for out of public funds; the agreement on fees is reached by the governing bodies of the profession and there is no discretion the individual practitioner can exercise. In one profession at least, albeit a small one in numbers, it is actually the client who sets the fee. This is in the retention of a barrister by a solicitor.

These facts mean that the professional is placed in a less favourable position than the businessman who possesses greater opportunities to exploit a commercial relationship, possibly to the detriment of the other party.

While it cannot be denied that the revenues of a practice are vital for its continued existence and are one important measure of development, it is also true that the freedom of price flexibility which is available to businesses rules out many of the strategies which might be used and in any event the adoption of pricing strategies requires more than skill and knowledge. The reality of the situation is that practitioners will not involve themselves (even if their practice rules permitted it) in the more obvious methods of the market place and what they see as Levantine negotiations. Thus a pre-condition to the successful use of fees as part of the practice development strategy must be a change of attitude by practitioners to the whole subject.

Given therefore the situation as described, to compare a professional practice to business in so far as fee policies and strategies are concerned could lead to totally incorrect decisions. While the fundamental need of any organization must be to ensure that revenue at the very least covers costs, beyond this the peculiar position of the professions must be an important part of fee decisions.

- The belief (justified or not) that client interest supersedes self-interest.
- A predilection by professionals derived from history, education, training and osmosis to distance themselves from direct involvement in pecuniary matters.
- Legal interference in the mechanisms of the supply and demand position.
- In many instances fee scales are fixed by negotiation in which the individual practitioner takes no direct part.

The last two parameters indicate clearly that professional practices are a business only in a

3. *Conveyancer* 1972, pp. 81–82 quoted by Maureen Cain. 'The general practice lawyer and the client'. In *The Sociology of the Professions*. Op. cit., pp. 133–134.

somewhat restricted sense when, as is the case, there are legal and other mandatory controls on what professionals may or may not do, who shall be permitted to practise and what fees shall be charged. Thus some techniques which are effective in a business environment are of limited use or not applicable at all for the purpose of expanding a practice.

## Standard fees

The problem of establishing suitable fee levels did not exist when almost all the professions had standard scales or 'gentleman agreements' so far as their charges were concerned. Fees have only moved into the centre of the stage since price fixing has been increasingly condemned in most industrialized countries followed in some instances, for example the EEC and the USA, by this practice being made illegal. Even so there still remains a strong element of agreed fees in many professional services although some formal tariffs, as in the case of conveyancing charges, have been abolished. Nevertheless, chartered surveyors practising as estate agents operate a very similar range of charges (called commissions in this case). Architects have begrudgingly modified and under government pressure discontinued the 'obligatory status of minimum fee scales' while amending their rules to 'provide a satisfactory formula for flexibility over fees *but outlawing* the worst evils of irresponsible fee quotations'.[4]

In the United Kingdom at least, over 90 per cent of medical practitioners in all branches of private medicine accept the scale rates applied by the major insurance companies. The Stock Exchange for the moment continues to operate fixed commissions although de-regulation is now taking place following their total banning in New York and Toronto. The building societies' cartel has also disappeared.

Where such inter-professional agreements, whether official or informal, are reached or when fee levels are fixed by those who ultimately pay them (the State or insurance companies) there is neither a need for nor an opportunity to apply fee strategies unless some practices not constrained by professional rules wish actively to dissent.

If professionals believe that the profit maximization is incompatible with their status and their role in society and that it is unethical to charge 'what the market will bear', then the safe harbour of fixed or agreed prices will always be more comfortable.

Even so fee levels under the present economic and social conditions will never be wholly the result of the free play of market forces although the market will increasingly have a more pervasive influence. Given the restrictive monopolistic or oligopolistic arrangements that exist in certain professions which provide both 'market shelters' and restricted entry (supply) of services, the knowledge gap between many clients and practitioners which prevents the former from making any sensible assessment of 'value for money', and formal or informal fee level fixing, the development of a cohesive fee strategy as part of a total practice development plan is considerably restricted in terms of the available options and techniques.

Nevertheless within the constraints and motivations which have been explained, there still exists room for more profitable operations by the manipulation of fees as a practice development tool or weapon, depending on how the professional service firm regards its charges.

Before considering just what a professional practice can do to improve its performance through increasing the demand for its services and by obtaining a higher level of profitability or its concomitant, higher billable time utilization, one fact must be made abundantly clear. There should be no confusion between fee or price strategies and price cutting: they are not the

4. Royal Institute of British Architects Annual Report (London, 1982).

same thing. Indeed a fee strategy may demand exactly the opposite to reductions—that is increases. In every type of transaction and not just professional services, it is better for competition not to be based on fees. This can be, and usually is, destructive to the firm and may well be harmful to the purchaser of the service. But to say that fee reductions as a competitive response are usually destructive is not implying that they should not be flexible. The use of carefully designed and sensitively implemented fee strategies, designed for specific objectives and profit maximization, is an effective and indeed creative method of competing both within and external to a profession.

## Costing

If the use of fee strategies in professional services is virtually non-existent, it is in part due to the inadequacies of most costing methods for services which still operate on a 'faith, hope and 100 per cent' basis. The vagaries of costing the output of surveyors, veterinary surgeons, dentists, patent agents or actuaries' activities have caused many of them or their managements to adopt empirical and *ad hoc* approaches.

One result is that while professional service firms can usually determine the profitability of the practice as a whole, they cannot often calculate the profit or loss contribution of individual assignments, clients, individual professionals or even services. This, in turn, means that the development of a fee strategy is virtually useless because the components which lead to the subject for the strategy cannot be accurately identified.

Service firms' managements cannot be in full control of their operations unless they *do* develop a reliable system of 'service' or project cost accounting. Accountants and management consultants throw up their hands in horror when they find that their clients do not know with exactitude the cost of the products they are selling. Nevertheless, these and other professional service providers have often either neglected or ignored this problem in relation to themselves, relying on the total profitability of their operations to ensure continuing activity. Once more the *Sartor Resartus* syndrome shows itself to the detriment of the image of the professional service providers.

This situation is as inefficient as it is unnecessary, since a professional service firm can and should be able to identify costs. The reasons for the neglect are numerous and require study as a first step to rectifying the position.

Service firms continue to use traditional product cost techniques which are inappropriate when it is appreciated that 'product' of the service firm is usually difficult both to describe and measure; costs are primarily 'people' costs which will typically account for 70 to 80 per cent of total operating costs and perhaps 50 to 70 per cent of gross income; other costs are people related (e.g., occupation, travel, telecommunications); the output of personnel is both difficult to measure and highly variable in amount and quality and not just from day to day but from hour to hour and because the client participates in production the professional's output may be inhibited or extended by the quality of the client contact.

In relation to practice development a far more relevant approach is one which first divides costs between chosen activities designed to increase awareness of the firm and its services and to create favourable images. The second type are those incurred in presentations and negotiations with individual clients. These costs can be evaluated at three levels:

*Upper cost*—income sacrificed by the professional with a full work load plus expenses caused by the practice development activities.

*Lower cost*—for professional staff not otherwise fully occupied in their discipline. Only expenses are incremental items.

*Middle cost*—principally the professional's staff remuneration plus expenses.

The upper and lower costs seem to be relevant alternatives in the *short term* and the middle cost in the *long term*. In the short term the evaluation of the cost is a function of the work-load during a certain period. In the long term it is a matter of estimating the necessary marketing resources required to maintain the professional firm at a certain size. The professional firm can have a *high or a low work-load.* But the work-load can also be evenly or unevenly distributed on individuals. It can also be dispersed or concentrated in time. The volume of proposals can be low or high, the number of prospects can also be low or high.

In every individual case there may be present instead of the extreme of high or low, a particular level of operation, somewhere in between. Moreover, in any particular defined period of time, a particular and individual mix may provide optimum operating conditions.

In a situation where all the factors go in a positive direction it is reasonable in the short run to use the upper cost. In a negative situation the opportunity cost is zero. In the short run the lower cost should therefore be used. If positive factors keep prevailing it is possible for the professional firm to expand, if the negative ones prevail, it must contract. In a more balanced situation, the middle cost is reasonable, it is to keep a certain volume of work.[5]

The significance of these factors within the context of fee strategy is simply that no fee can be set or adjusted with any certainty of it successfully achieving whatever the objective may be unless the cost of the inputs to the service itself is known. The development of a fee strategy which has any real meaning is out of the question without basic knowledge of the nature of the firm's costs.[6]

## Considerations in establishing a satisfactory and acceptable fee structure

The moment the service firm or practitioner looks at the techniques which enable it to devise and operate a fee strategy, it finds itself faced with a dichotomy. These are the approaches offered by theorists engaged in developing a simplified model that helps to understand complicated reality and the approaches of marketing specialists discussing pricing on a descriptive level explaining what businessmen do, or say they do. Neither procedure is satisfactory. Any model is limited in use by psychological aspects—that is the psychology of service provider as well as the client. Either concepts or techniques alone are insufficient and probably misleading. A combination and balance is needed, but difficult to achieve. This situation should be recognized in considering the strategies suggested.

Fortunately commentators on pricing and fees have been more sensitive to the needs of service businesses than in most other marketing activities, so that the service provider does not find himself having to translate from tangible product to intangible service.

Developing fee strategies is an exercise which must be undertaken in two dimensions. First, it is necessary to think in terms of establishing the right fee and, second, of using the correct methodology to arrive at it. The latter is perhaps an even more crucial exercise in a service business than in most other enterprises. Correct fee levels for professional firms are perhaps more important than for product companies because of the economic structure of the service business. Employing as they do relatively little capital implies that pricing and time utilization are the primary elements of leverage in achieving profitability.

5. E. Gummesson. 'The marketing of professional services—an organisational dilemma'. *European Journal of Marketing*, Vol. 13 (5) (Bradford, 1979).
6. One approach for dealing with this situation called 'unique costs' is worthy of study. John Dearden 'Cost accounting comes to service industries'. *Harvard Business Review* (Cambridge, Mass., September/October 1978).

Although constrained by professional rules and the nature of markets, within the limited strategies and tactics which are relevant there remains a good deal of flexibility in setting fees and devising fee structures. Professional services despite, or perhaps because of, the knowledge gap between practitioner and client are in many instances far more 'value sensitive' than 'fee sensitive'. Fees, over an extremely wide range of services, are rarely the critical factor in deciding to appoint a professional firm or practitioner.

Six basic methods for arriving at fees have been identified:[7]

1. *Cost-based fees*   A conventional method of arriving at fees by summating the chargeable cost. The fee is arrived at for various levels of activity and time utilization which will yield the desired profit. Cost-based fees, although very commonly used, do have the disadvantage that cost does not necessarily lead to an effective and acceptable fee. Basing a fee on costs plus a desired profit takes no account of competition nor demand. The fee can impact heavily on itself since it can attract or inhibit demand at a level which affects costs.

2. *Competitive salary-based fees*   A variation of the cost–pricing system based on the average or competitive salary levels for the professionals involved and charged for the time utilized. This method means that fees are determined by the major cost centre which for the professional service firm is personnel, not materials, machinery or stocks.

3. *Contingency payment*   This is essentially the service equivalent of piecework rates in manufacturing or commission for salesmen. The fee for services performed is contingent upon a certain act being performed or by accomplishment. This is a method used by estate agents, some contract R & D, application engineering and operational research consultancy and in the USA by lawyers undertaking litigation work. A variation of contingency pay pricing is the *ad valorem* method of calculating fees—that is based on values involved in the service. The contingency and *ad valorem* it must be said is only a description of a method and does not describe just how the actual fee or percentage is calculated, which may be arrived at by the other methods listed.

4. *Fixed fees*   This is a uniformity within a profession achieved by a controlling or strongly influencing body. This body might be the government (fees payable to both its own professional advisers and those funded by the government such as legal aid), professional associations, insurance companies (medical fee rates). Fees may and frequently are fixed informally as in some types of consultancy fixed fees which, as Sibson points out, are the results of a fee decision not a method of reaching one and whatever the level fixed it may well have been set by one of the other techniques described.

5. *Contract fees*   This is a method of arriving at a fee by negotiation with a single firm; for example, rebates for insurance services such as reimbursable provisions on contracts covering group insurance. This method of fee setting is also common in some branches of management and engineering consultancy.

6. *Value-based fees*   Or what the market will bear. Other methods are only rough guides to value. Value pricing assumes that buyers will respond to fees in accordance with the value they place on the service. This is common practice in accountancy particularly for audit work (despite what is said to the contrary), some areas of research and again various branches of consultancy.

Since the Sibson categorizations were devised some deficiencies have been revealed but little that has been propounded has either advanced or improved the basic taxonomy because they do provide a useful basis for making the first decision in determining fees and perhaps subsequently adjusting them.

7. R. E. Sibson. 'A service'. In E. Marting (ed.) *Creative Pricing*. American Management Association (New York, 1968), pp. 147–152.

## Psychological factors

The deficiency of all the methods other than value-based fees is that the mechanistic approach ignores what is perhaps the most pervasive factor in client decisions relative to fees, that is their perception of the expectation being purchased. It is impossible to discuss fees without considering the psychology of the client. Indeed, as has been pointed out 'The price [fee] setter should therefore never forget that especially in the absence of previous experience, the potential customer [client] will frequently decide in favour of the more expensive quotation . . . [and will] seldom accept a low price [fee] as a valid excuse for shoddy work.'[8] Given little or no knowledge of the service, the firm or practitioner, the difficulty of competitive comparability, the client will use the fee level as a guide to expected quality and efficiency, however inadequate such an indicator may be. As with products, services perceived as under-priced are viewed with suspicion and the client will seek the safety of the middle to top range.

Clients for all professional services tend to have psychological blockages on many aspects of the service–fee relationship. While, for example, they are reasonably happy to pay for collateral evidence (see Chapter 10, 'How the individual practice is chosen', page 118) in the form of documentation there is a resentment of charges for 'advice' in the form of telephone conversations. Consequently the wording of invoices takes on a considerable importance in making fees acceptable and thus in client retention and in stimulating referrals. The essential requirement is to notify the client on the invoice of everything that has been done. That 'no invoice can be too long' is an over-statement but it contains a great deal of truth so far as fee acceptance is concerned.[9]

## Fees and the non-client public

Before going on to consider how the specific fee or fee structure can be arrived at it is as well to appreciate that although the fees should be set to satisfy both the client and the practice, there are other publics to consider who may not have a direct or immediate pecuniary interest yet whose involvement can be crucial to the professional firm.

Most of the approaches to fee strategies either view the situation purely from the standpoint of the professional practice or practitioner or the client or there is an uneasy attempt to reconcile widely different interests.

In Chapter 12, 'The importance of images and perceptions', it was stated that the professional firm has many publics besides the client. Page 140 listed 13 such publics all of whom, where applicable, must be considered in the setting of fees. This is an important sensitivity which it is unwise to ignore.

## A multi-stage approach for setting fees and fee structure

It is at this stage that an inexorable rule has to be considered no matter how much information, how much skill and how much science go into establishing what the fee will be.

High fees = opportunity for high profit = low chance of success.
Low fees = risk of low profit or loss = high chance of success.

8. Andre Gabor. *Pricing*. Heinemann Educational Books (London, 1977), p. 175.
9. There are many useful hints and guidelines on obtaining fee acceptability in Jay G. Foonberg's *How to Start and Build a Law Practice*. Law Students Division of the American Bar Association (Chicago, 1976), particularly pp. 29, 64, 73 and 85.

More than anything else the practitioner requires a methodology for arriving at fees which are acceptable to the firm, to clients and will not influence third publics (possible referrers) adversely. It has already been remarked that the firm that is at the mercy of its clients deserves sympathy and nothing else.

Some methodologies comprise a multi-stage process which leads towards the final fee but such mechanistic approaches fail to account for the interaction between the different stages. To be effective the multi-stage process must be reviewed as cyclic and reiterative rather than a one-way flow from start to finish. The stages are:[10]

- **Objectives**  Just as with the total practice development strategy an early step must always be to decide and to obtain agreement on fee objectives. These can be as variable as the objectives of the total strategy; a given level of profitability, return on investment, achievement of specific growth rates, high cash flow, optimization of special skills and resources, attracting new clients/higher level of repeat consultations or instructions.

- **Designation of targets**  This stage will have been completed in the preparation of the practice development strategy referred to in Chapter 5, 'Devising a practice development strategy and plan', pages 55–7. Clearly, the fee structure must fit the target market and it may well be that having arrived at the fee structure either because of the nature of costs or of demand, it may be necessary to reconsider the market targets in the total practice development plan.

- **Demand estimate**  The next step must be an estimate of the demand which will be generated at a particular fee level. Because it would be impractical and unprofitable to undertake marketing research for every occasion, but by no means impractical to arrive at general level of acceptability, this must be best judgement.[11] The teleological nature of pricing decisions is nowhere better illustrated than at this stage where fee level can generate or inhibit demand and where high or low demand has an immediate favourable or adverse impact on costs and thus fees. Nevertheless, those responsible for setting fees cannot sit on the fence. A view must be taken on assumed demand at given fee levels.

- **Fee–image relationship**  There is a direct correlation between fees and image. As has already been pointed out a professional service just like a product can be suspect if the fees are perceived as so low as to affect the quality or delivery of the service. Conversely, high fees will frequently indicate a high level of qualification, experience or ability.

  It is unwise to an extreme to attempt to arrive at a fee level without first considering what image the practice wishes to convey both overall and in the specific transaction under consideration.

- **Selection and use of communication techniques**  Again reverting to Chapter 5, 'Devising a practice development strategy and plan', in which the communication tools were listed, the decision which now has to be taken is which of these will generate the demand estimated at the fee level proposed. This again must be a judgemental decision towards which not even the most advanced thinking on marketing can contribute. No matter how sophisticated the marketing of any company may be and no matter how many protestations to the contrary are made, the communication 'mix' is still decided much more by empirical than methodological means. Just because there is unlikely to be any multi-million pound budget to juggle with the problems are no less severe. Indeed they are probably greater in having to

---

10. The author is indebted to Professor Alfred Oxenfeldt for his permission to adapt for professional service purposes his 'Multi-stage approach to pricing' and its modification in *Pricing Strategies* AMACOM (New York 1975), pp. 162–165.
11. An interesting technique devised by the DuPont Corporation related to products, but which is applicable to professional services, is the 'Price and the perception of performance' method. This is described in a critique by Aubrey Wilson 'How to tell when the price is right'. *Campaign* (22 September 1979).

work within a very limited budget and in a market where there is little record of client reaction to any given fee level and perhaps no market information whatsoever. Yet again the practice developer has to take a posture even with minimal information.

- **Decision on fee policy**   The practice will have to make a decision on the basic policies relative to fees. How far will fees be flexible to meet particular circumstances or to secure and retain particularly desired clients? What will be the policy relative to keeping the fees above, level with or below competitive fees? Is there to be some provision for fee incentive for perhaps continuity, forward commitment or use of the full or fuller range of services available? It is even possible that reciprocity with clients whose products or services can be utilized by the professional practice would be considered and encouraged.

- **Selection of a fee strategy**   It is useful to distinguish fee policy from strategy. Policy might be said to apply to the predicated situation, most particularly those situations that are recurrent. However, demand is never wholly predictable and is subject to many fluctuations caused by the impact of the forces of change which are largely uncontrollable—social, economic, political and technological. Changes whatever their cause may well demand a change in fees. Strategy is the formulation of the guidelines in setting fee levels to meet any special situation not envisaged or allowed for within the policy principles. It is in fact the contingency fee plan and the trigger for implementing it would be any situation which the price policy could not encompass.

- **Choice of fee tactics**   Surprisingly, some of the pricing techniques adopted in parts of the consumer goods industry are applicable for professional services but their very names will usually lead to instant rejection as examples of commercialism at its most brash and therefore totally inapplicable. This is quite wrong. Whatever nomenclature and however they are used in consumer goods and services' markets their applicability is clear. The main methods which are relevant to professional service pricing tactics are summarized in Figure 14-1.

If the titles and techniques of fee tactics appear totally divorced from professional practice it is only necessary to see how many of them are in current use. 'Offset' fees can be found in dentistry where a low examination fee may be combined with high cost ancillary services, for example X-rays or supplies such as prophylactics; 'discount' offers are commonplace in computer services, engineering and management consultancy; 'service flexibility' is not unknown, indeed is commonplace, in many forms of financial services most particularly insurance; 'inducement' (or loss leading as it is known in commercial parlance) is an extreme taken by solicitors offering free first interviews to private clients who may be involved in accident claims.

Precisely how each tactic is used is totally dependent upon the service involved, the target client group, and what might be termed the 'ambient conditions'. Whatever the circumstances, the use of any of these tactics to be effective, requires a knowledge and understanding of clients and in the case of commercial clients a knowledge of the selection and decision-making process also.

Any discussion of fees in professional services is surrounded with a type of taboo typified at its extreme by the barrister who receives not a fee but an honorarium, and all financial arrangements are negotiated through his clerk. (Barristers still carry in their gowns the vestigial remains of the pocket into which the fee was placed to avoid their actually having to receive the money from the instructing solicitor.) Thus fee tactics are frequently seen, not as they are—a legitimate and efficient tool of practice development—but as a somewhat devious means of separating the client from his money. Nothing could be further from the truth. If the nomenclatures and connotation of fee tactics create a semantic blockage to their utilization, then there is a case for changing the titles. However, whether it is called 'loss leading' or 'development fees', or a 'sprat to catch a mackerel', the tactic remains the same and is wholly applicable to professional service marketing.

When policy, strategy and tactics have all been decided and agreed there still remains the final step which the whole multi-stage process is leading to, the selection of the fee or fee structure. The interactive nature of these stages and re-cycling, which will lead to the selection of the actual fee, is best illustrated on the same basis as the total practice development strategy,

| Title | Description | Effect |
|-------|-------------|--------|
| 'Offset' | Low fee for 'core' service but recouping on 'add ons' (see Figure 2-3, Chapter 2, 'Understanding service businesses') | Psychologically favourable at the quotation stage, but can easily lead to difficulties on implementation. Advantages in some cases of client being able to control extent of commitment |
| 'Inducement' | Fee charged produces sub-standard profit or loss but attracts new clients or helps retain existing clients, used on the basis it will be possible to recoup fees on later transactions | Successful with unsophisticated clients but tends to give a fee ceiling which is difficult to penetrate later |
| 'Diversionary' | Low basic fees on selected services to develop image of value for money which transfers to total practice | Generally effective so long as the client does not feel obligated or that he has been persuaded to use more realistically costed elements in the total service offer |
| 'Discrete' (for commercial clients) | Fee level brings the decision into an area of authority of a DMU favouring the firm. A lower fee may take decision to lower management; a high fee to the board. This tactic necessarily requires an intimate knowledge of the prospect firm | While the decision can be moved into the DMU responsibility area favouring the firm better able to appreciate the offer, all fee adjustments upwards or downwards have associated risks |
| 'Discount' | Quotation subject to discounts on a predetermined basis, e.g., time schedule, extent of commitment, magnitude of transaction | Positive encouragement to client to structure transactions on mutually favourable basis |
| 'Guarantee' | Fee includes an undertaking to achieve certain results—the undertaking surpassing that of competitors | Moves competition from consideration of fees to consideration of values and places high quality service in most favourable position to compete with lower quality services |
| 'Service flexibility' | Quality of service hence costs varied to enable fees to remain unchanged | Removes fees as major negotiating point, substituting the service but note effect above for 'diversionary' fees |
| 'Conditional' | Fee is conditional on the purchase of other services | Tied in service has to be attractive in itself or else potential for the basic service is reduced. This method is illegal in some countries |
| 'Predatory' | Fee set well below competition as means of removing them. Realistic fees applied later | Requires accurate assessment of competitive resources and policies. Can be self-destructive and also illegal |
| 'Skimming' | Fee set high when demand is inelastic or capacity short and gradually reduced as situation becomes competitive | Gives extra profitability and a hedge against later sub-standard profit. Enables the firm to keep an edge over competitive firms so long as the original high fee has been maintained long enough |

**Figure 14-1** Fee tactics

namely as a planetary system (see Figure 14-2). This system has final price as the 'sun' and the various stages arriving at price moving around on an eccentric course depending both upon the circumstances of the practice and the changes in the environment in which they operate.

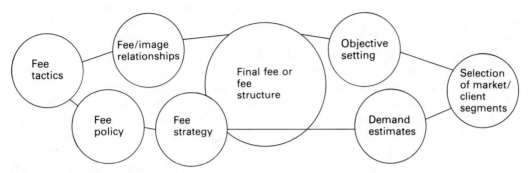

**Figure 14-2**  Selection of fee or fee structure

For the decision on the final fee the practitioner will be limited in his options by the various factors which impact on fees. Nevertheless, there will be a range of possibilities that will be consistent with the various stages of the fee-setting procedure.

The two key points are that fees charged must cover direct costs and carry a reasonable margin of profit; the arithmetic of pricing must not be ignored; that is a study of the costs and the revenues generated by alternative fees within the range which is circumscribed by the different stages passed through in moving towards the selection of the specific fee. By approaching the final fee on the basis of each different consideration the risks of deciding what this fee shall be, based purely on 'cost' or 'values', are avoided and a more rounded view which improves judgement is obtained.

Although the multi-stage approach is claimed as practical as opposed to the elegant theories which are frequently offered, the practicality is often limited by lack of information on which to base each incremental decision. It is here as much as anywhere that the information resource referred to on pages 34–5 of Chapter 4, 'Preparing for practice development', and the control information in Appendix B of Chapter 5, 'Devising a practice development strategy and plan', make a real and calculable contribution. The multi-stage approach will have the virtue for each firm, no matter how lacking it is in information, of at least indicating the data it requires to achieve, as time progresses, better and better fee bases and structures that are both practice and client orientated.

Fees may be a key decision factor when services are undifferentiated while in other circumstances they will be of little or no consequence within the restraints imposed by the client's resources. In the first instance when identical services charge identical fees the fees are not part of the decision-making process. This could apply to payment of doctors, dentists and other professional personnel employed in state health services. The opposite circumstance is medical assistance in an emergency where it is the existence of the assistance and not its cost which is all that matters. Between these limits, fees will play a variable role in the range of factors considered deciding both on the use of a professional service and the provider of that service.

The multi-stage approach suggested will narrow down the options and range of fees from which the choice must be made. It is a considerable aid to judgement but does not replace it. There is no certain way to arrive at an optimum fee and the multi-stage approach is an attempt at systemization and avoiding the excesses which on over-reliance on rigid methods can produce at one extreme or allowing emotions or history to shape the final decision at the other.

The problems and rewards of effective techniques for setting fees or devising fee structures as a vital part of the total practice development plan have been treated only superficially. It has been more an introduction to the subject than a detailed explanation of its mechanics. The purpose has been to ensure that the question of fees is not allowed to occupy a less important place and command less consideration within the practice development plan than its all pervasive impact on results justifies. All professional firms should examine their policies (or lack of policies) to ensure that methods of setting fees which have been used in the past are still relevant in today's conditions and will remain so in the foreseeable future.

Fee setting at the correct level is of considerable consequence both for the individual and for the survival of the firm. Fees are a weapon, or a tool, to obtain and retain clients as well as to ensure the profitable continuance of the firm. The two objectives are inter-related and lend themselves to a variety of strategies for their successful achievement. Those concerned with practice development, faced with increasing professionalism in marketing professional services, need an understanding of fee-setting techniques if they are to have any chance of success.

# Chapter 15. Guidelines for the choice of practice development methods

There is little argument in the professions about the use of any practice development tools just so long as they are appropriate to the profession and to the audience they address. It would, for example, be totally antipathetic to most professionals and counter-productive in its effect to adopt in-store demonstrations as a means of stimulating demand for their services. But setting aside such an extreme as this there is in fact a very wide range of techniques which can be used in their standard forms or adapted, for most practice development purposes. The problems facing any particular practice are to obtain a knowledge of all suitable methods, to decide which ones will be cost effective and then to use them with skill, creativity and above all with sensitivity. Page 60 in Chapter 5, 'Devising a practice development strategy and plan', and Figure 17-1 in Chapter 17, 'Non-personal methods of practice development' list a number of techniques and demonstrates that the choice may well be wider than appears at first sight, even with the mandatory constraints within which most professions operate.

## Internal/external influencing factors

A number of factors require consideration in arriving at the correct selection of the effective methods to be considered and used:

- How are enquiries usually generated and received? The inter-personal network (referrals) will certainly dominate but media references, site signboards such as architects use, public forums, communal, social, professional or business involvement or sponsorships might also, but only by way of examples, make contributions to the generation of enquiries and conversions to clients.
- The strategic objectives of the practice relative to those segments of the community—business or private—they wish to service will be of considerable significance in the choice of methods. Whichever methods are chosen, they have to be capable of reaching the target audiences.
- The degree of expertise of the prospective clients in both the choice process of the correct profession for their needs and in the subject matter of their enquiry will also affect choice of methods. This factor conditions the form the 'message' must take and therefore the way which the 'message' is carried. The communication method and message have to be compatible.
- For commercial clients the stage at which the choice process can be intercepted and the classification of that choice make some methods of practice development preferable to others. (See Figures 8-4 and 8-6 in Chapter 8, 'Professional services and the commercial client.)

- The creation or reinforcement of awareness of the practice may be the over-riding need. Techniques which have a degree of longevity will be more effective in reinforcing 'visibility' than those which are ephemeral. Examples of the former are the distribution of diaries, calendars and usable, but not consumable, small gifts while the latter might be personal contacts, media advertising.
- Extent of resources available for practice development is a very obvious arbiter of choice. The cost of different methods varies widely both relative to the method itself and the strength and frequency with which it is used. Choice of methods needs the most careful alignment with the availability of resources.
- Since surrogates are always required in communicating information concerning any service, methods of communication with the clients and prospective clients must be capable of using the surrogates effectively. The greater the augmentation of a service with a physical component the simpler it is to communicate with its market and the wider becomes the choice of tools. Essential evidence[1] is always easier to use in any communication than the intangibilities of a service.
- The extent to which the method chosen can be controlled will be a significant factor because of the inability to stock services. An unexpectedly high response rate may embarrass both the practice developer and the professionals in that enquiries cannot be handled expeditiously or work commenced quickly. Direct mail dispatches can be aligned to response rates; a media advertising campaign or a conference once underway does not lend itself to either acceleration or limitation.

If these factors are related to the choice of methods to be adopted it will ensure at best a totally effective 'mix' and at worse it will limit the risks and consequences of failure.


## Practice development policy

'Effective', however, is somewhat loose in meaning but it does imply that the methods selected assist the practice to achieve its objectives whatever these may be on the time scale required and economically. To reach these desiderata there are some clearly defined rules. It should be noted here, however, that whereas reference has been made frequently to 'objectives', in considering the tactical use of different methods, their purpose is better described as goals.'Objectives' might best be defined as 'general aims' while 'goals' are very specific for each method and each occasion. There are six rules to be followed.

1. *Setting goals* Whatever techniques are adopted both the overall objectives of the practice development strategy and the purpose for which a particular method is used must be clearly defined, and in this case it goes beyond the segmentation objectives referred to earlier. Throughout practice development, failures are constantly ascribed to the methods used rather than to the fact it was never clear precisely what they were intended to achieve.

    Any one practice development activity might be viewed by those in the practice as having many different purposes. The senior partner may regard the efforts as designed to obtain enhanced personal and practice esteem; the practice developers may understand the goals to be the acquisition of new clients; the partnership secretary's belief is that the intention is to attract the brightest of the current year's graduates, while the financial controller sees it as contributing to an improved cash flow. Typical goals for practice development techniques can comprise many of those listed in Figure 15-1.

1. Lynn G. Shostack. 'The importance of evidence'. *The American Banker* (New York, 25 March 1981). See also Chapter 10, 'How the individual practice is selected' of this book.

Image development of the whole firm

Image development of the service

Promote the service irrespective which firm provides it (concept promotion)

Concentrate on firm's services

Develop an atmosphere conducive to the acceptance of the service

Offer a cluster of supporting services not the basic service (see Chapter 2, 'Understanding service businesses', page 16)

Improve the level of client knowledge of the service

Promote size/reputation/experience of the firm

**Figure 15-1** Goals

The list can be endless but the point is that if there are different views within the firm as to what is being attempted by the use of the methods which have been adopted, there will also be major areas of disappointment at the results. If the effort succeeds in any one objective it will be said to have failed in all the others when it was never the purpose to encompass so wide a range of sometimes conflicting objectives.

2. *Defining targets*   The 'targets' must be defined, identified and practical. The segmentation technique described in Chapter 5, 'Devising a practice development strategy and plan', can become over-elaborate and impractical if in the end of the characteristics of the segment are not identifiable in terms of commercial concerns or private clients. It is after all one thing to draw a segmentation profile, for example, 'management buy-out situations in early stages of consolidation and regrouping' but quite another to find such situations. Another example might be 'wealthy individuals with private pension arrangements'. In these cases it would be difficult to do more than generalize as to what type of media and communication methods such people are exposed to.

3. *Effective messages*   The 'message' conveyed has to be effective in terms of being relevant to the recipient, 'benefits' or problem-solving orientated, comprehensible and believable. The communication method itself is only a vehicle for delivering the 'message'. The practice developer must know precisely what it is the message is designed to achieve. The achievement of the steps of the communication process in Figure 3-2 in Chapter 3, 'Creating a client-centred practice', could all represent suitable goals. Within the 'action' level comes of course 'increasing revenue', 'higher profit', 'improved old to new client ratio' and a contribution to all the other possible objectives some of which have been set out in the strategy.

For 'messages' to be successfully conveyed it is necessary to consider timing too. This is important. The best constructed and targeted 'messages' delivered at an inappropriate time will not achieve their purpose. For some types of professional services there will be a high seasonality factor—auditing, loss assessing and adjusting, a range of medical and education linked services—while others may be also sensitive to timing but on a more unpredictable basis. This itself is one reason why those involved in practice development must scan both the immediate and the outer environments within which the firm operates.

4. *Co-ordination*   Co-ordination of activities is the fourth rule for effective application of practice development methods. An analysis of failures in all marketing shows that in a very significant number of cases the cause of failure has been lack of co-ordination not just between the use of different methods but between marketing departments and the rest of the organization. While there are no recorded instances of substantial failures from these causes in professional services, it is only because there has, until very recently, been no major practice development activity. The lessons to be learned from both the consumer and

industrial goods and services industries are particularly valuable. Thus, before any practice development effort is launched, the firm must be sure that success will not, for example, create an embarrassing shortage of capacity or require expensive inputs or less effective services to meet demand. Equally, all the methods used to develop the practice should be synergistic rather than just neutral in relation to each other. Co-ordination means total co-ordination, within practice development and within the firm as a whole.

5. *Feedback and benchmarks*   In Chapter 3, 'Creating a client-centred practice', the term 'the marketing concept' was used as another way of describing and defining practice development. The sub-concepts, which together comprise the overall approach embrace, albeit in a slightly different form, all the rules given in this chapter but particularly call for continuous feedback and for benchmark checks on progress. It is certain to be wasteful to undertake any practice development unless feedback occurs from the clients, prospective clients and third publics (referrers and others who influence decisions) to whom the message is directed. In the simplest terms the continuum of the communication process can be checked. Are we more or less 'visible' than we were? Is our message better understood? Is it more believable? Does it have relevance?

These are all easy factors to check, but if, for example, the tactical goal is an improved image for the practice, then to evaluate this requires skills of a different and higher order. Nevertheless to launch an image improvement or correction campaign, without being prepared to devote resources to assess the results would be, in business terms, feckless. Simple systems for obtaining feedback can be developed both using marketing research and by internal checks—tracing sources of new business and enquiries, comparing the conversion rate for enquiries to business before and after the use of a particular practice development method. Market research can be self-conducted or commissioned and either way should not be confused with major national studies undertaken by large companies and running into thousands of pounds of costs. The feedback system and data are very much part of the information resources referred to in Chapter 4, 'Preparing for practice development'.[2]

6. *Evaluating results*   The last of the rules is to ensure that whatever methods are used it should be possible to evaluate, if not measure, their effectiveness in terms of the resources they absorb and the results they produce. It is alas true for all marketing that no method exists for pinpointing the outcome of the use of any one method or any one 'message'. The market place is not a laboratory and it is not possible to measure the result of the introduction or change of any variables since the control of others is not within the capability of any firm, no matter how large. It might be thought that the achievement or non-achievement of the objectives or the goals indicates success or failure, but it is always possible that the activities of other practices will induce or reduce business for competitors. Press reports and books on do-it-yourself, conveyancing and attacks on solicitors for over-charging for these services substantially cancelled out the efforts of the Law Society on behalf of its members to promote conveyancing by solicitors. If the Law Society failed it is unlikely any individual practice would have fared any better and might well have attributed failure to the incorrect selection of practice development methods or their inadequate use or a weak 'message'. Nevertheless with all the problems and hazards of seeking to evaluate the impact of individual and combined practice development methods, some guidance can be obtained, sufficient to ensure that resources are not wasted and that major mistakes are avoided. Thus what is being sought is a usable indicator that a particular method or particular 'message' is having a positive or negative effect.

2.  A check list summarizing key feedback information will be found in Appendix B, Chapter 5, 'Devising a practice development strategy and plan'.

## Budget setting

One of the guidelines suggested above to ensure cost effective use of practice development methods is the alignment of resources available with objectives and goals desired. The problem of resource allocation was touched in Chapter 5, 'Devising a practice development strategy and plan'. Resources, of course, comprise more than money but the availability of finance is a key issue because little can be achieved without money or the equivalent, that is time. Having said that, however, there are many low cost, indeed very low cost, techniques which can be adopted by a professional practice and the idea that large sums are involved can be dismissed as incorrect and unnecessary.[3]

There are again unfortunately no precise rules which can guide a firm or individual on precisely what level of resources should be devoted to the practice development activity. So much depends on individual variables; strategic and tactical objectives and goals, the local and national circumstances, the professional service itself, the life cycle position of the firm or the service. There are many others. However, it is useful to review some of the alternatives so that those who are responsible for practice development can consider them to see which ones either as they stand, combined with others, or modified in some way are most appropriate. All systems for arriving at budgets are inadequate when the effect of any individual method is not traceable. The selection must be based on the least inadequate alternative which most closely meets the three requirements for:

- Least wastage.
- Least risk to the firm.
- Best estimate of results.

Figure 15-2 summarizes the major conventional methods and lists their principal advantages and disadvantages. The inadequacy of all budget-setting techniques is perhaps exemplified by the extent of the disadvantages as compared to the advantages.

So far as the individual practice is concerned an eclectic approach is required but modified by a goodly mixture of empiricism and judgement. Together these are just as likely to achieve the best results as a slavish adherence to the theories and techniques of budget setting.

As an indicator in percentage and actual terms American experience for at least one profession is worth quoting (see Figure 15-3).

The one advantage that professional services have over other activities in relation to budget setting is that the disposal of the budget is across a far more limited range of choices than must be considered by non-professional services and some of the most costly techniques are not usually applicable, most particularly distributive networks, financial incentives and aids and many types of sponsorship.

## Guidelines for the use of personal contact techniques

There is one more guideline which can be used to assist the practice developer in the choice of the appropriate methods to adopt and this relates to the inclusion of a planned system of personal contact. Personal contact is frequently the most effective method of practice development but can also be the most costly. There are, however, in the case of this tool some

---

3. Christopher West (ed.). *Marketing on a Small Budget.* Associated Business Programmes (London, 1975) and Aubrey Wilson and Christopher West, 'Effective marketing at minimum cost'. *Management Today* (London, January 1982).

| Method | Advantages | Disadvantages |
|--------|-----------|---------------|
| Percentage in financial or time input terms of previous year's income | Always affordable so long as earnings are constant | No provision for growth or exploiting opportunities |
| Percentage in financial or time input terms of expected income | Allows for growth<br>Encourages stability in practice development | Appears to cause practice development activity<br>Can lead to over- or under-spending in growth or declining markets<br>Treats practice development as a constant factor, irrespective of service position on a life cycle |
| Percentage in financial or time input terms of profits or profit excess | Extra profits invested in practice development can be offset against tax therefore subsidized | Profits appear to cause practice development activity<br>Plan will be unstable and can vary widely from year to year<br>Risk of practice development appropriations being cut can cause premature allocation |
| Matching competition | Stabilizes competitive activities<br>Creates a sensitivity to competitive situations | Competition appears to cause practice development activity<br>Comparable expenditure difficult to estimate<br>Expenditure level and quality of practice development not correlated<br>Time lag to respond |
| Objective and task method | Forces detailed consideration of objectives | Problems in attributing results<br>Difficulty in establishing weight and form of practice development to reach objective |

**Figure 15-2** Setting practice development budgets—principal methods

| Annual fee income | Practice development budget | |
|-------------------|------------|----------------|
| £100,000 | 8–12% | £8,000–12,000 |
| £250,000 | 7–10% | £18,000–25,000 |
| £500,000 | 6–9% | £30,000–45,000 |
| £750,000 | 5–8% | £38,000–60,000 |
| £1,000,000 | 4–7% | £40,000–70,000 |
| £2,000,000 + over | 3–5% | £60,000–? |

**Figure 15-3** Architectural practice budgets (USA)[4]

very precise criteria which can give accurate guidance on whether it should be included in the 'mix' of methods adopted. Personal contact is most effective when:

- Prospective clients—commercial or private—are concentrated or limited in some way.
- The service has to be adjusted to the client's precise needs.
- The flexibility and comprehensiveness which personal communications possess to a far greater extent than any other tool, in addition to the attitude and manner of the representative of the practice, are needed to build up confidence and to establish rapport.

Using these criteria it can be seen that, for example, it is likely to be very effective in the

4. Quoted by Christopher Ratcliffe. 'Expanding the architect's practice'. A paper given at a joint conference sponsored by the Royal Institute of British Architects and the Institute of Marketing (London, May 1982).

barrister–solicitor connection, patent agent–inventor and surveyor–developer. It would be far less appropriate for veterinary surgeons and pet owners or opticians and the public where other techniques such as 'retail outlet merchandising' are more cost effective.

If the guidelines set out in this chapter are used it will provide a mesh which will certainly assist the practice developer in both narrowing down choice to the most appropriate methods and incorporating them in a cost-effective way. The four screens which should be adopted and which have been described are:

- Internal/external influencing factors.
- Practice development policy.
- Budget setting methodology.
- Conditions for the use of personal contact techniques.

If each method to be considered is examined for its likely level of cost and for the various factors incorporated into each set of guidelines, a sensible, practical and hopefully profitable combination of techniques will emerge which will materially assist the practice towards its strategic objectives.

## Guidelines for use of non-personal communication techniques

The non-personal communication methods in all marketing and certainly in practice development are often the subject of misunderstanding by firms which attempt to use them, by organizations which create and operate them and by the recipients of the message they convey. This is because of the confusion which frequently exists between methods and media and the lack of precise agreed objectives for each promotional activity.

The range of methods and media is nothing like as constrained for professional services as is usually thought and as the list in Chapter 17, 'Non-personal methods of practice development', shows. Such limitations as there are stem substantially from the constraints of self-image and the image of the profession as being incompatible with non-personal practice development methods (already referred to in Chapter 1, 'Why practice development?'). Many professionals argue that neither personal nor non-personal methods are necessary since high quality service is the best technique for practice expansion. At the same time, however, they assert that the knowledge gap between the professions and their clients is too great to allow the clients to make a technical assessment of 'quality'. It has been stated 'the recipients of expert services are not themselves adequately knowledgeable to solve problems or to assess the service received'.[5]

While this may be true in a largely technical sense, it does not mean that users of professional services do not assess 'quality' using other criteria. That these criteria are neither relevant nor sensible in the eyes of professionals is of no consequence. It is the reality which has to be considered in practice development, not what professionals may regard as 'ideal' or 'sensible'. In this respect the Gronroos view on how quality is evaluated by users is the one that must prevail (see Chapter 2, 'Understanding service businesses', page 17).

Whether arguments on users' abilities to assess and evaluate the services they receive are spurious or not, if professionals can accept that the many methods open to them are an effective means for improving their practices and that these should be used for all the reasons given in Chapter 1, 'Why practice development?', then there is a case for consideration of each and every one of them.

5. Eliot Freidson. 'The theory of the professions state of the art'. In *The Sociology of the Professions* (eds Dingwall and Lewis). Macmillan (London, 1983), p. 41.

Thus, among the early questions which require answers are:

- What coverage is needed?
- What frequency must be adopted?
- What continuity is necessary?

If objectives and targets are precise the co-ordination of these three aspects will ensure that practice development is not undertaken on a hit-or-miss or reactive basis. Indeed, one of the commonest failings of professional service firms is the sudden termination of all development activities in response to their success. That is, a high work load leads to reduced or cancelled activity.

Reference to Figure 3-2 in Chapter 3, 'Creating a client-centred practice', shows that the process of achieving a favourable decision is a continuum taking the prospective client from a condition in which he is ignorant about the service or practice to knowledge of it, an understanding of the message, an appreciation of its relevance to him, a belief in its accuracy and finally to a favourable decision. The more acceptable the method to the client and the stronger the message then the quicker will be the move from unawareness to action. Conversely, the stronger the countervailing forces shown in Figure 3-2 the more difficult it will be to achieve a favourable decision and the longer it will take.

In considering guidelines for the use of non-personal promotion and practice development techniques, the need for precise unambiguous objectives for each method adopted is an important element in ensuring cost effectiveness. The planning format given as Figures 5-10 and 5-11 in Chapter 5, 'Devising a practice development strategy and plan', breaks down each activity, media/method and relates them to the objectives. Using this format will encourage systematic consideration of each method chosen. Figure 17-2 in Chapter 17, 'Non-personal methods of practice development', illustrates examples of a range of objectives, methods, media and audiences. Obviously not all alternatives and combinations are listed nor are all those which are necessarily applicable to professional services. A sufficient number is included to suggest that horizons can be safely widened and that the alternatives open for presenting a professional service are both wide and sensible.

# Chapter 16.   The use of personal contact

Certainly, the most important single method of developing a practice is through personal contact if only because professional services are totally 'people' based. The decisions on the use of a service or a particular practice are made substantially on the basis of the client's or patient's reaction to the practitioner, perhaps combined with the source and strength of any recommendation. Because, without exception, the professions are people not machine based no matter how far the mechanization of services may go, they will always involve people in their provision. The manufacturers for the most part have little direct contact with the ultimate users of their products, whereas professional services, as was pointed out in Chapter 2, 'Understanding service businesses', always involve the client and indeed the prospective client in their production. This presents opportunities, not available to anything like the same extent to the manufacturers of goods, to develop and strengthen loyalties through the use of personal contacts which are necessarily part of the production of the service itself.

A profession must have personal contact with its clients and potential clients and no single profession even hints at the desirability of any other type of link. In terms of practice development the problem of using personal contacts only arises when it originates from the professional and not from the client. Such professionally initiated contacts are usually described pejoratively as 'touting'. While most professionals would willingly concede that salesmen who service their own practices and their own personal needs follow a respectable and indeed useful, if sometimes irritating, occupation, selling is nevertheless considered not to be an occupation for a professional to indulge in.

In examining individual methods of practice development that can be used by professionals, it is necessary to make a distinction between existing clients and the acquisition of new clients. There is little if any objection to using personal contact in seeking to retain clients, extend the use or frequency of their uptake of service, strengthen loyalties and encourage, even if only passively, referrals, inform and explain the service, the practice, its skills, resources, facilities, interests and in fact everything that has relevance to the client's actual perceived or even covert needs. The dichotomy appears when the subject is a non-client who has not voluntarily approached the practice. Because, for most professions, 'cold calling' is unquestionably not permitted, it is better to leave the approach to new clients to the other non-personal methods discussed in Chapter 17, 'Non-personal methods of practice development', and to confine the description of the use and technique of personal contact to existing clients or those who have approached the firm on their own volition or have been stimulated by some other practice development method to make the approach.

There has already been reference to the low status of marketing among many professional men and women, and their disdain and distaste for both the methods of marketing and the market place. The semantic road block which was so ably defined and described many years ago[1] has not noticeably diminished in most professions and has prevented many professionals who most certainly have inter-personal skills from exercising them for practice development purposes. It is worth making the point again that practice development will never be conducted effectively so long as professionals feel that it is incompatible with professionalism.

However, once an acceptance is achieved and a decision is made that the professional firm *will* actively present its services, then a further series of decisions must follow in relation to the method to be adopted. In consideration of precisely which method will or will not be included, personal contact will tend to dominate.

## Advantages of personal contact

Personal contact has some very distinctive advantages over all other methods which might be used for practice development. Moreover, these characteristics are particularly relevant for professional services.

- Because demand for professional services is always highly selective and at any one time limited, individual rather than mass communication is feasible and efficient in terms of coverage and cost.
- As a professional service has to be adapted to a client's individual needs, even in the most routine of activities, personal contact can make the adjustment rapidly and effectively in terms of the information that is to be provided and the questions to be asked from the client. This flexibility is perhaps the most important attribute of personal contact.
- Because professional services of all types are complex and the knowledge gap between the practitioner and his client or patient may be wide there has to be a range of information tiered for different levels of receptivity and understanding. Personal contact enables the message to be adjusted to the appropriate level of client knowledge or need and to be totally comprehensive or simplistic while all the time concentrating on the substantive issues.
- Personal contact is attention getting. It obtains and maintains a far higher level of concentration and interest than can be achieved by any other method of communication.

However, there is a negative aspect that cannot be ignored. Personal contact is costly, being labour intensive and of generally the most expensive kind. But for this restraint there might perhaps be no decision to make, since all practice development with existing clients could be undertaken in face-to-face encounters. The question is one entirely of cost effectiveness.

The positive attributes listed above must be weighed against the cost disadvantages and related to the conditions each practice faces in the segments selected for practice development. If it can be seen they have a particular value, then the decision to include personal contact as a formal and structured part of the practice development methods, is easily taken.

Every member of the firm who interfaces with clients at any level is capable of making a positive or negative contribution to practice development. The professionals' efforts will be supported or diluted by the image projected by others. A client-orientated practice is one which is directed to presenting the firm and its services in the most favourable light at all times. It is however the personal link with the client which provides the best opportunity for this presentation and will in any event most usually be an early screen in the client's decision process.

The responsibility on the professional in his role as practice developer or part of a practice

1. Warren J. Wittreich. 'Selling—a prerequisite to success as a professional'. (A paper presented at a conference in Detroit, Mich., 8 January 1969.)

development team with this objective is considerable and calls for a high degree of empathy and understanding. However, to suggest in professional services that personal contact is or should be confined to those allotted this role would be to circumscribe this activity unnecessarily.

Clearly the practitioners are highly potent, positive and negative influences but to allow any personnel irrespective of rank, seniority or function to meet clients when they are not instructed in at least the rudiments of inter-personal business techniques may well be disastrous for the practice development effort and for the practice itself.

For professional service firms more so than for those offering other intangibles or products, there will always exist a core of 'backroom boys', 'academics', 'practitioners', for whom nothing other than the elegant solutions of problems and application of sophisticated techniques will count. Their job satisfaction is in the efficient completion of the task in hand, irrespective of clients' changing needs, attitudes, perceptions and on-going developments. These are the professionals who will never, by inclination and by personality, be good at inter-personal business relationships and it is useless to try to train or persuade them to be other than they are. What must be done, however, is to eliminate the negative aspect of their approach and to convince them of the over-riding requirement for 'satisfaction engineering', since the firm depends upon a flow of old and new clients to continue to exist.

There is an old adage which says that no one ever won an argument with a customer. This is increasingly true of clients if only for the reasons enunciated in Chapter 1, 'Why practice development?', namely an increasingly knowledgeable and vocal public no longer in awe of the claimed superior knowledge and intelligence of the professions. More questioning clients will increasingly choose the practice they perceive as meeting their needs and feel no obligation to tolerate arrogance, lack of involvement or any of the other less complimentary criticisms levelled against the professions.

Thus a major task in developing inter-personal approaches is to ensure that the base is not eroded by bad client relations created at any level within the practice. The whole organization must be aligned to a policy and *must believe* that the client comes first. If personnel using direct contacts for practice development are not to be perpetually looking over their shoulders to ensure that their position is not undermined by others in the firm, then it is obviously important that these 'others' must have some familiarity with the skills and methods of inter-personal activity.

It has already been indicated that the professional who is motivated and who enjoys personal contacts is the ideal person to represent the practice and to undertake the work of introducing a systematic programme of using this technique. Irrespective of his qualifications, experience or abilities in his discipline, to succeed he has to possess certain qualities. The use of personal contact as part of the practice development activity requires that those whose task it is have drive and personality, are good listeners, possess a determination to go on trying despite the outmoded view that 'a professional is a person gentlemanly enough to take "no" for an answer', are conscious of the client's professional and human needs and have a 'feel' for situations. While the extent of these requirements will vary depending on the situation, they are never absent. It is, however, the exploratory capabilities which will distinguish the most successful users of inter-personal methods from all others. Without this explorative interest the practitioner will fail to demonstrate just how the service and his firm will meet the client's needs. He will, with commercial client companies, fail to identify the decision-making unit and his lack of interest in the client will show through as a barely concealed disdain for the whole process.

In professional services the representatives of the practice must take on a managerial as well as a communication role. Because services cannot be successfully offered without deploying a whole array of the professional firm's resources—human and infrastructure—the practice representative must be capable of explaining and demonstrating them and ensuring that expectations of quality, punctuality and results are met.

Moreover, he must be capable of taking the initiative and of organizing and progressing an enquiry through to its successful consummation. Because every professional service offers efficiency and increased certainty for the client it cannot, least of all firms, afford to make mistakes, appear dilatory or disinterested and unreliable.

Thus, the representative of the professional service has to be both managerial and entrepreneurial—to have and to be seen to have the stature to deal at an equal level with the client with whom he must negotiate.

## Techniques for the face-to-face meeting

There are far more ways of offering a practice or a service by personal approaches than those which are commonly associated with the more aggressive types of presentations. There is, for example, the very gentle 'concept' approach which is to provide information on a type of professional services and its benefits but not suggesting that the firm necessarily undertakes the activity. At the other extreme there is the more aggressive 'free trial' most usually found on the outer fringes of professional services and certainly some financial services have not distinguished themselves by their techniques or by the dignity in the way they present themselves.[2]

The method to be adopted will be dependent upon a number of factors:

- How the enquiry originated—client stimulated or firm stimulated.
- Extent of the information the client can and is prepared to provide.
- Degree of selection expertise of the client.
- (*For commercial clients*)   Type of buying situation encountered; new task, modified re-purchase, repeat purchase.
- (*For commercial clients*)   Stage of the decision-making process reached; anticipation or recognition of a problem; determination of the requirements the service must meet, specification or description of the service and service firm, search for and qualification of the individual or practice, obtaining offers and presentations and analysing them, evaluation of the offers, selection of most suitable practice or individual, designation of the methods for carrying out the service, performance feedback and evaluation.[3]

A careful examination of the approach of those professionals who are consistently successful in their inter-personal relations will show that their merit lies in the use of the approach inherent in the principles enunciated in Chapter 7, 'Professional services and client needs', namely, reducing uncertainty, understanding problems and total professionalism in the discipline involved and the way it is presented.

The actual decision process so far as the client is concerned is a five stage continuum. The client has to agree:

1. The need exists.
2. The service offered is the correct one to meet it.

2. However, and perhaps exceptionally, as referred to in Chapter 14, 'The role of fees in practice development'. The Law Society has approved a scheme whereby clients involved in possible accident compensation claims can have a first free interview with a solicitor.
3. The full description of the decision-making continuum is contained in Chapter 8, 'Professional services and the commercial client'.

**3.** The service firm is capable of providing the required service.

**4.** The fee or fee structure is acceptable or is thought will be acceptable.

**5.** The time for completion is satisfactory.

Unless these five points receive five affirmations the decision goes against the service firm. There have to be five 'yesses'. One 'no' and the negotiations inevitably end unfavourably.

If compared with Figure 8.6 in Chapter 8, 'Professional services and the commercial client', it can be seen that in a straight repeat purchase all these points will be agreed. In a modified re-purchase or a new task the onus is heavily on the representative of the practice to convince the actual or prospective client that all the bulleted items above will meet his requirements.

Because professional personnel in personal contact situations usually stress the features of the service to be offered, that part of the meeting which is concerned with achieving a favourable decision to use the service firm, tends to be unstructured and reactive.

Just as it is possible to identify the major points with which agreement between the client and professional must be achieved before a favourable decision will be made so it is equally possible to define the various steps which the practice representative can take to help achieve these objectives.

- Pre-approach: preparation and planning of the meeting.
- Approach: introduction, greeting, appearance, attitude, poise and mood. A show of enthusiasm and a businesslike manner will favourably impress all clients.
- Attention: obtaining undivided and favourable attention. The prospective client needs to be convinced that there is a message of importance to him.
- Interest: communicating what the practice has to offer in terms of the client's interests and the benefits to the client.[4]
- Need: presentation of benefits (with proof) in a deliberate, clear, relevant and skilful manner.
- Favourable decision: logical summarization of the most convincing arguments, partly developed from the preceding dialogue.

## The use of intrinsic and extrinsic methods

In Chapter 7, 'Professional services and client needs', pages 85 and 86, a reference was made to 'intrinsic' and 'extrinsic' methods of offering or describing a professional service. These are fundamental distinctions which must be considered in devising the approach and technique for offering the service. The desideratum is always to offer the service intrinsically if the situation will permit this. Most but not all prospective clients will respond to such an approach because they appreciate its inherent value over the extrinsic method. In many situations, however, there will be a mix of both the intrinsic and extrinsic and only the sensitivity and understanding of the professional for the situation and the personalities of the people involved will tell him the correct balance.

There may, of course, be no decision to make if the client wishes to know what the service firm can do for him without volunteering what he wants it to do. Equally, the decision as between intrinsic and extrinsic approaches may be made unconsciously and in response to the dialogue which ensues between the professional and the client. There are no set formulae that

4. The skills of problem identification are referred to in Chapter 7, 'Professional services and client needs', most particularly the organizational framework devised by Avrom Sherr has some features which are relevant to the presentation situation.

can be adopted, even if the precise situation is known. An understanding of how the decision is reached will provide an accurate guide for deciding the optimum method.

The use of extrinsic messages is of course less than satisfactory but may be forced on the professional by the refusal or the inability of the client to give the practitioner the material on which he can base an intrinsic approach—that is dealing with the substantive problem. However, as soon as it is decided, whether consciously or unconsciously, what combination of the intrinsic and extrinsic is required then a second series of distinctions require consideration. An extrinsic approach will rely on one or a combination of three themes:

- Emphasis on the **methods** which the practice or professional adopts.
- Emphasis on the **reputation** of the firm or individual in terms of skills, experience, qualifications, facilities, resources, interests and contacts.
- Emphasis on past **success**.

These three approaches should be used to open up a situation which enables the professional to initiate or move to the more efficient intrinsic message. The three extrinsic dimensions are thus routes to a dialogue from which the main personal contact effort can be made.[5]

The first of these, **emphasis on methods**, is a technique in which the characteristics of the service are presented rather than the outcome. Logically, problem solving should come first and the methods second. In professional services precisely the opposite often occurs and as a result situations are often distorted to meet the techniques available. For example, in a business situation, a decline in sales can be interpreted in all good faith as a management problem, a financial problem, an R & D problem, an industrial relations problem, an information problem. Each interpretation may well unconsciously reflect the special expertise of each service firm consulted.

Nevertheless, emphasizing the methodological approach, provided it is stress on flexibility and not a fixation on methodology, is at least a starting point for coming to grips with substantive problems. Every instinct in the professional would be to make it clear that the methods to be adopted are dependent on the nature of the situation. The client must then describe the problem if there is to be a realistic basis on which to assess the service being offered. This has the dual advantage of both helping to identify the problem correctly and the professional who can recognize the limits of his knowledge and skill.

The second technique adopted in an extrinsic approach to clients is the **emphasis on reputation** of the professional service firm and its personnel. These are major assets but unless the client can understand how a solid reputation will translate into specific benefits, it has little real relevance other than providing a certain level of credibility. Moreover, when a client is not talking directly with the personnel whose services are being offered, he has little opportunity of assessing for himself those whose reputation is supposed to impress him.

There are, of course, a number of circumstances in which emphasis on the reputation of personnel makes sense. Although outstanding knowledge of the client company's technology, techniques or organization is not always required to solve a problem the presence on the staff of the practice of acknowledged leading experts contributes not only to credibility, but also towards the removal of some of the initial uncertainties. The same situation, of course, applies to private clients where the equivalent of an understanding of a company's technology might be an understanding of the social or cultural milieu of the client's ethos and environment. However, even in these circumstances, the representative of the practice must have a demonstrable, if not necessarily outstanding, knowledge, skill or experience in the claimed area of competence or experience.

5. Warren J. Wittreich. 'How to buy/sell professional services'. *Harvard Business Review* (Cambridge, Mass., March/April 1966).

The third technique of emphasizing **past successes** is the one most likely to produce results if handled tactfully and purposefully, but more often than not it defeats itself beause the analogy is not appropriate. This is usually because the client situation is not really understood. The stress must be less on the success story than on the substantive nature of the problem which was successfully solved. Explaining a success does not necessarily convince the client that an element of luck did not exist on that occasion, that the situation would have resolved itself anyway, that a combination of factors besides the activities of the professional service firm were at work. By stressing the substantive nature of the problem and the specific skills used to interpret and solve it rather than the success itself, two things are achieved:

- The client is able to assess the professional's capabilities in recognizing a unique aspect of a given situation.
- An evaluation is permitted of the professional's capabilities in coming to grips with the problem.

In other words, in the use of an analogy, the client must be capable of identifying himself with the situation being described.

In a summarizing diagram, Figure 17-4, Chapter 17, 'Non-personal methods of practice development', the inter-relationship of the intrinsic/extrinsic approach with client needs and other methods of practice development has been illustrated. It will be seen that the extrinsic method is phased out as quickly as possible, but while it is used the three techniques described above will be involved.

## Timing the use of personal contact techniques

Realistically it is the decision-making process not the decision itself that governs the speed, timing and sequence of the personal interview directed to obtaining business for the practice. Practice development is both an on-going and multi-activity process and there is in fact no single point in the course of a relationship with a client where favourable decision occurs, but there are many points in the relationship where effective presentation is required.

The decision-making process for most professional services involves a series of'incremental choices, each of which eliminates certain alternative solutions from further consideration. The decision process, as delineated in Chapter 8, 'Professional services and the commercial client', Figures 8-4 and 8-5, is along a continuum. This, so far as the commercial client is concerned, is the 'creeping commitment' rather than 'the moment of truth' and to a more limited extent the private client's move towards the decision is also phased. For all clients the presentation of the services and the professional service firm at a personal meeting must follow the same progression as the decision making. This is illustrated in the encapsulation of the interface between the decision process and the practice development methods in Chapter 17, 'Non-personal methods of practice development', Figure 17-4.

From this it will be seen that personal contact, unlike all the other practice development functions, can be, and usually is, involved during the whole of the course of the decision-making progression. The sequence depends on whether an enquiry is client- or service-firm-induced since in the former case the first stage—anticipation or recognition of a need or problem—will already have taken place, and in all probability views will have been formed on the second stage—determination of requirements the service must meet—and the third stage—specification or description of the service and service firm.

The actual timing of personal selling activities can be considered under six separate, but interlinked, activities which are roughly chronological in order.

1. *Identification of opportunities*  The whole of Chapter 11, 'Identifying potential clients', has been devoted to this subject. Both client-generated and service-firm-generated enquiries demand that the opportunity, once identified, should be related to the ability of the service firm to meet the real needs of the situation. This, in turn, requires that the practitioner's ability to interpret the needs of the prospect must be of a high order of professionalism and integrity.

2. *Group communications*  This is an on-going process which entails exposing prospective clients as a group to the services provided by the professional firm. Although this is frequently achieved by non-personal methods, there is a very definite place in group communications for personal contacts. Because, as has already been noted, inter-personal communication is flexible and comprehensive, it is possible to refine the message to meet the needs of a particular group. In-house and public seminars, luncheon meetings, presentations, both at the service firm and where clients gather, are all forms of group communication techniques.

   Although in group communications there must be a larger element of the extrinsic approach than in individual communication, it is still perfectly feasible to narrow this down to encompass the interest of any cohesive smaller concentrations of common activities or problems of individual clients within the group.

3. *Individual communications*  This is obviously the critical contact because it is only in the one-to-one situation that the professional can be specific about client problems and needs and professional solutions. It is in the one-to-one situation the practice representative can deploy his inter-personal and discipline skills to accomplish the necessary steps to a favourable decision.

   Personal contact to obtain business which occurs at the invitation of the prospective purchaser is never regarded with the same degree of antagonism and dislike as when the contact is made on the initiative of the vendor. For most professions 'cold calling' (non-invitation by client) is viewed as impertinent, undignified, aggressive and, most importantly, inappropriate for the professional services. Such a view is not, of course, necessarily justified since it is based on the personal selling techniques sometimes adopted in the aggressive sectors of industrial and consumer markets. Nevertheless, 'cold calling' is better avoided even if permitted.

   Instead, the practice developer, so far as stimulating the attentions of prospective clients is concerned, should use the wide range of non-personal promotional methods (which are described in the next chapter) and then let personal contacts nurture the interest which has been expressed.

4. *Presentation of the service offer*  If there were a 'moment of truth' in the purchasing of professional services, it would be at this point. Personal meetings and presentations require skill which most certainly can be learned if the will to acquire them is there. This, of course, is a question of motivation. The technical and mechanical aspects of presentation demand as much care as the message to be conveyed. Thus, the presentation must follow a logical pattern: perhaps the background to the enquiry, a statement of the problem or original situation analysis, re-statement in terms of the problem identified, detailed description of the approach and methodology, the total expected yield or result from the application of the service to the situation and expression of the solution in terms of personal and/or corporate benefits to be obtained.

   Possibly even at this early stage some indication of fees may be needed but perhaps not asked for directly. It must be emphasized yet again that the client is listening for only one message, the one that tells him precisely how the service will benefit him.

   The presentation must be at a level which is compatible with the state of knowledge of the listener and this obviously affects the form and content of the presentation. The less familiar the listener is with the subject matter the greater the uncertainty he will experience although not necessarily exhibit. Thus, the practice representative needs to develop a mental scale of the 'state of knowledge' or knowledge gap between practitioner and client:

- Ignorant (of the subject matter)
- Below average
- Average
- Above average
- Expert

A presentation which has misjudged the knowledge gap by more than one category has every likelihood of failing both as a presentation and in its objectives to achieve some pre-determined action. Thus, if a presentation is pitched at 'average' level to an expert, it will be largely wasted and will result in impatience, aggression, and even ridicule. An above average level of presentation to a below average audience will not achieve an understanding and without understanding clients would be foolish to take any action. Moreover to expose, however unwittingly, the lack of knowledge of the audience, is hardly likely to produce a favourable atmosphere.

A further check[6] developed for a post-interview performance evaluation between a lawyer and client does in fact give some useful guidelines for presentations to any client of any type of professional firm (see Figure 16-1).

One of the obvious and fundamental differences in service as opposed to product selling is the lack of anything tangible to show or demonstrate. But while it is not possible to show a professional service, it is certainly possible to develop visual material to illustrate the outcome of the application of the service to the situation or to use relevant surrogates.[7]

Indeed, it is more important in presenting an offer of professional services to produce visual material than in a product selling situation where even if the product cannot be shown at the meeting, it can be produced at some time or in some location. Thus visual means of demonstrating services should be used but they must not be contrived. A check list for the use of visual material might be:

- Is the point worth making?
- Can it be adequately verbalized—if so, what purpose would visualization achieve?
- Does the visual aid supplement the verbal medium rather than replace it?
- Does the visual achieve unity?
- Are the symbols acceptable?
- Is it visually fluent?
- Is it visually honest?
- Does it utilize suitable techniques to improve its effectiveness?
- Is the visual for the benefit of the audience or the presenter?
- It it readable by all those present?

Not everyone is capable of developing his own visual aids for presentations. There are however, within many service firms, particularly accountants, architects and surveyors, departments and individuals who can supply this facility, and in any event, there are firms and individuals specializing in the preparation of visual aids. At the presentation the

6. Avrom Sherr. 'Developing and improving your practice'. A paper presented to a Law Society Conference (Coventry, 1983).
7. The reader is referred to Chapter 10, 'How the individual practice is selected'. The importance of evidence, pages 116–18. Also the work of Lynn Shostack.

| |
|---|
| Giving recognition to client |
| Offering observation |
| Broad question or opening |
| Encouraging |
| Reflecting |
| Exploring |
| Answering client question |
| Seeking client ideas |
| Accepting client ideas |
| Using client ideas |
| Offering of (the professional's) feeling |
| Acceptance of feeling (understand what the client feels) |
| Using silence |
| Summarizing to re-open |
| Reassuring |
| Indicating understanding |
| Pre-directional probing (hypothesis testing) |
| Terminating (indirect) |

**Figure 16-1**   Client-centred behaviour

professional is faced with showing the relevance of the service he offers to the specific problem identified and its cost effectiveness. He must ensure that the client is satisfied that the correct service is being offered and that the most suitable professionals will be allocated to the work. The total offer must meet, to the maximum extent possible, the fundamental needs of the client: reduction of uncertainty in both the situation to be resolved and in the selection and instructing of the service; confidence that the problem has been understood and can be solved; and assurance that the professionalism of the service firm is of the highest order.

5. *Monitoring*   During the execution of the service, there should be a constant feedback to clients on the progress and results. Although this may well be a function of the professionals actually conducting the work there is a strong case for it being undertaken by the person who obtained the instructions either alone or in co-operation with the professions. Because service projects will sometimes change during their execution, without good communication and feedback the areas of uncertainty can widen and become more, not less, intense. Expectations have an unpredictable habit of moving out of line with reality. By monitoring the situation, client disappointment and frustration at the end of the project can be avoided and continuing goodwill ensured.

Monitoring can be successfully achieved only if both good working relations and good communications are established between the client and the service company. These desiderata call for a clear understanding of the role of each party, something the practice representative can help to achieve, standing as he does between the professionals who do the work and the client who will be the recipient of the result. Agreement is needed as to whom letters, communications and reports must be addressed, and with whom meetings can be held. A large part of setting up an effective communication system will be the responsibility of the professionals assigned to the project, but the practice representative has a role to play in ensuring that a system is indeed set up and maintained. Such a system *must* include the practice representative, so that he is always aware of the situation and can report back knowledgeably to the client. Bearing in mind that the practice representative will, by choice, be a professional with inter-personal skills and will thus have the confidence of both the professionals working on the assignment and the client, he is, in an ideal position to monitor and report on progress.

It is an interesting reflection on the communication problem that of 1913 charges of misconduct brought against American lawyers in 1981 about 25 per cent were directly attributed to 'lack of communication' and a further 33 per cent were related to this. Thus well over half of all misconduct could be attributed to lack of communication.[8] The equivalent figures for England, Wales and Northern Ireland in the late 1970s were 12 per cent and 30 per cent respectively. If this situation is, as is more than possible, replicated in other professions, the value of monitoring to ensure good communications needs no further advocacy.

6. *Follow-through* Just as the delivery of a product is not necessarily the end of the supplier's responsibility, neither is the end of the service assignment the end of an involvement. Suppliers of professional services are strategically placed to watch the outcome of their work but frequently fail to do so. Setting aside the fact that interest shown in a commercial client's performance or a private client's activities and life, following completion of a service, is an affirmation of the practice's faith in its own work, it is also indicative of commitment and acceptance of responsibility. Moreover, 'follow-through' is yet another characteristic by which professionalism is identified. At the same time it provides opportunities for appraising new needs for existing or new services. Thus the practice representative can achieve the double objective of continuing to reduce uncertainty and inspire confidence in his client while having the opportunity of assessing new potentials for business among clients.

These six phases, although parallel with the decision phases, are not mutually exclusive. Thus the 'follow-through' process contains many of the elements of the 'individual communication' activity.

Appendix A of this chapter is a business communication check list which will provide guidelines for personal contact techniques.

## Telephone contact

Personal contact, of course, does not have to be face-to-face. The telephone is also an important and appropriate medium. The first contact with the firm may well be by telephone so that the manner in which such a discussion is handled, both in its mechanics and content, will have an influence in a decision by the client to proceed further. The contribution which good telephone techniques make to the firm's image was dealt with in Chapter 12, 'The

8. Kathryn S. Marshall. 'The client interview—a marketing opportunity'. A paper given at a Law Society Conference (Leeds, February 1983).

importance of images and perceptions'. This includes a check list for evaluating the quality of telephone response.

To maximize the benefit of telephone contact it is a *sine qua non* that those who intervene between the client and professional must understand their role and its contribution in creating an atmosphere which is conducive and encouraging to developing both the discussion and the relationship. It is however not sufficient for support staff to handle the telephone well; it is equally incumbent on the practitioner to develop appropriate skills in the use of a communication method that is all too often taken for granted.

A policy decision of the individual practitioner or the firm is whether to handle all enquiries as far as possible or whether this is to be left to non-professional support staff. It cannot be gainsaid that when a client telephones a professional practice the desire is almost invariably to speak to a professional member of staff although he will often accept substitutes. Good practice development would include a policy of easy access and direct contact, but it must be accepted that this is by no means always possible.

There is nothing novel, unusual or execrable in the use of personal contact techniques to develop a practice. Historically this has always been the major method by which firms acquired and retained clients. Because the collegial organizations ban direct unsolicited approaches or, where they do not, make it incumbent on a member of a profession to withdraw when a colleague already has a relationship,[9] this is not a reason why personal contact techniques should not be used in appropriate circumstances. If the firm's mission is 'satisfaction engineering' then personal contact can be the most effective of all methods for achieving this.

9. Typical of this situation is 'It is appreciated that instructions are obtained as much by representation as by recommendation but a member on arriving at a case and being informed by the client that another member has already received firm instructions to act shall forthwith retire'. *Code of Conduct, Professional Ethics and Practice of the Institute of Public Loss Assessors*, Rule 3(c).

# Appendix 16A[10]

The main advantages of telephone over letters, telex and facsimile are its immediacy and ease of use. The first of these is self-evident; the second can be a trap. Just because the telephone offers the easiest means of communication (for some temperaments even easier than face-to-face conversation), that does not necessarily mean it is the most effective. Hence the checklist to help make that first judgement, then to help use the telephone to best advantage.

## 'Go-ahead' checks

1. A call in response to a request to call back is an automatic 'go-ahead'.

2. Is it necessary to impart/obtain information/ideas/options/requests right away?

3. Is an exploratory dialogue needed to determine the information to be imparted/obtained?

## 'Follow-through' checks if 'yes'

4. If respondent is known, should you:
   - Call direct on outside line?
   - Get secretary to call?
   - Get switchboard to call?

5. Do you know, precisely, respondent's:
   - Name?
   - Telephone number?
   - Organization?
   - Department?
   - Function/occupation?

6. If respondent is not known, what single, simple question is most likely to:
   - Be understood by respondent's switchboard?
   - Lead to speaking to the right respondent?

7. Is there any information you need to absorb, or have by you before making the call?

8. Is your telephone call preliminary to a more formal communication? If so, it can help to jot down points on which you expect to obtain agreement or which need amendment.

10. From *A Book of Business Communications Checklists.* John Bittleston and Barbara Shorter. Associated Business Press (London, 1981), pp. 42–44.

9. When in contact with respondent, ensure respondent understands:
   - Your name.
   - Your organization.
   - Why you are calling.

10. Have you thought out the right questions/statements most likely to produce a quick and useful response?

    It may take a moment or two for the respondent to switch on to your subject, so structure your call like a formal communication, working from the general to the particular, e.g.,

    'I am calling about XYZ contract' (Subject)

    'Second draft, dated whenever' (Definition)

    Stop there. The respondent may not have the reference handy. This is his switching on time anyway. Continue:

    'The section dealing with so and so' (Detail)

    Pause again, then raise the point of discussion (Issue).

11. Bear in mind:
    - Most people make notes.
    - Few have shorthand, so slow down when giving critical reference information.
    - Stick to key points only; if appropriate, offer to confirm main points and cover supplementaries in writing.
    - It often helps to open by asking respondent if he has a moment to spare on the telephone; he may have a room full of people or other matters to attend to.
    - 'Body language' signals of incomprehension, disagreement, or eagerness to interject, are absent during a telephone conversation; learn to listen for their audible equivalents: brusque monosyllables, inappropriate changes of subject or aggressiveness, evasiveness, filibustering, hesitancy.
    - Do not use the telephone to persuade a respondent into giving an immediate response without good reason; the quality of response invariably suffers.
    - If the line is bad, offer to ring off and re-call; do not waste effort in frustrated inaudibility.
    - Ensure that the respondent repeats back essential points.
    - Use electronic facilities (like automatic call back) to the full.
    - Time differences can apply to many overseas calls; this consideration often argues the alternative use of telex or facsimile—which can often save more time in total telephone calls.
    - When possible, delay more remote calls until cheap rates operate.

# Chapter 17. Non-personal methods of practice development

Chapter 5, 'Devising a practice development strategy and plan', listed methods which could be considered by most professions for incorporation into the communication 'mix' and this included even those disciplines where there are strict rules of practice which appear to prohibit all direct forms of exposing the practice to its publics.

The nature of these constraints and the rigidity with which they are applied vary considerably from one profession to another and many are currently liberalizing their rules or at least considering the question of relaxation. In accountancy, ophthalmics, law, surveying and architecture changes have already been agreed.[1] Thus the choice for the practice developer is rapidly widening.

It must be said again that although it is possible to develop a framework within which decisions can be made as to the selection methods to be used this does not give any precision. In the final analysis the choice of which techniques, when to use them and the weight with which they will be applied will be a matter of judgement on the part of the professional. This will be based on the profession's rules, culture and history, the practice's objectives, the nature of the markets in which they wish to operate, cost, the appropriateness and acceptability of the methods to the audience they are intended for and, of course, good taste, inasmuch as their adoption will not demotivate either the practitioners or their clients.

It is little consolation but even in the most sophisticated of marketing organizations, judgement will always take precedence over mathematical models, test marketing and the other approaches used to decide the 'mix' of methods and to maximize the effectiveness of techniques.

## Cross-fertilization

It is always possible that there may be some cross-fertilization of ideas for practice development both from other professions and from outside the professional field. If a professional service can be classified by its characteristics and then a comparison made with the methods adopted by firms not operating under conditions of restraint but whose services share the same characteristics, there may be the opportunity for creative imitation. This may

1. For example, in mid-1982 the Quantity Surveying division of the Royal Institute of Chartered Surveyors was given permission for its members to advertise and some 20 per cent of members of the Architects' Registration Council, but who are not members of the Royal Institute of British Architects, are also free to advertise and members of the Royal Institute of British Architects can advertise in printed publications only. In late 1983 the Institute of Chartered Accountants recommended the complete abolition of restrictions on publicizing individual practices and even investment trusts, restricted from advertising by the Prevention of Frauds (Investment) Act, have found means of publicizing themselves through advertising. Early in 1984 The Law Society permitted individual advertising by solicitors.

(The inter-personal network, fee strategies and personal contact techniques have been dealt with in depth in Chapter 13, 'The referral (recommendations) system', Chapter 14, 'The role of fees in practice development' and Chapter 15, 'Guidelines for the choice of practice development methods'.)

| Title | Description | Relevance and examples |
|---|---|---|
| Media advertising | Print, radio and TV (including teletext) | Permitted for surveyors, some architects and some parts of private medicine. Increasingly likely to be acceptable in other professions |
| Public relations | Techniques which establish and maintain a mutual understanding between an organization and its various publics | Used formally by some accountancy and legal practices and by all the qualifying associations themselves |
| Merchandising | Activities directed to creating an atmosphere conducive to purchase of goods and services at the point they are available | Waiting areas of most professional service firms have some relevant literature which is an example of a merchandising technique |
| Support services | Satellite services which strengthen the core service and provide more and better facilities for clients | All professions |
| Marketing research | Systematic study of characteristics of demand and its configurations | All professions |
| Competitions | Reward for the best performances of some activity (e.g., company accounts presentation) | Usually used on the edges of professional services, e.g., management consultancy |
| Inward visits | Organized invitations to firms to meet personnel, view facilities and other relevant matters | Commonplace in contract R & D but frequently used in most professions dealing with commercial clients and a few with private clients |
| Directories and year books | Listings which increasingly include specializations | All professions |
| Educational campaigns | Explanations of methods and use of a professional service, but not necessarily specific to any one firm | Usually undertaken by qualifying associations, but also commonplace in all professions. Speakers are sent to schools, universities, clubs, etc. |
| Exhibitions | Displays usually with a common theme or interest and usually in a venue away from the firm | Often used for consumer professional services, particularly financial, but not permitted by most professions as yet |
| Business gifts | Practical, low value 'visibility' items such as calendars, diaries, jotter pads, pens | Accountancy, surveying, architecture, veterinary, patent agents, loss adjusters, and many other types of non-medical consultancy |
| Franchising | Licence to allow an independent second party to use the name and carry on the business of the franchiser under strictly controlled conditions | Only used so far on the edges of professional services; management and marketing consultancy, financial services |

**Figure 17-1** Communication methods for practice development

| Title | Description | Relevance and examples |
|---|---|---|
| Financial incentives and aids (not to be confused with fee strategies) | Provision of facilities to make purchasing possible or to provide an extra reason for a favourable decision | Law but tends to be used substantially as a multi-client approach whereby costs are shared between clients with linked but non-competitive interests. An alternative is the availability of financial incentives as part of a wider offer in which inter-professional disciplines are involved. The obvious example is the developer–construction company architect/surveyor loop |
| Reciprocal arrangements | Arrangements between organizations whereby their roles as vendors and purchasers are interchangeable. (Most commonly used within a group either as 'arms length' or favourable trading transactions.) As professional services firms are labour intensive the opportunity to trade reciprocally with suppliers is limited | Accountancy, architecture, design, computer services. Although intended more as a courtesy than a practice development method, interchange of services by doctors both for themselves and their immediate families is a form of unorganized and non-commercial reciprocal trading |
| Guarantees and warranties | Undertaking to accept liability under stated circumstances for default in the service | Generally implied in all professional services, but rarely specifically stated. Professional negligence and association coverage for default are always available but rarely promoted |
| Direct mail | Mailing of informative literature to individuals or firms, sometimes as newsletters | Accountancy, law, estate agency activity of chartered surveyors, financial services |
| Distribution network | Either owned branch offices, hospital clinics, surgeries, studios or intermediaries offering the services | All professions for owned branches, including a relatively recent development of medical, dental and ophthalmic facilities in department stores. Intermediaries used in financial services, architects' shops |
| Joint approaches | Linking of disciplines to provide clients with a 'turn key' offer | Particularly used in the professions associated with construction, chemical plant and civil engineering |
| Co-operative promotions | Joint publicity either by one profession or linked professions, but usually undertaken nationally by associations although can be mounted locally | Most professions but particularly law and accountancy |
| Lead time | Period between placing of instructions and either initiation or completion of the instructions | All professions but particularly law, veterinary and medicine because of the element of emergency which may exist with clients and patients |
| Sponsorship | Financing, underwriting or subsidizing events, books, academic research or departments | Accountancy, financial services, consultancy of different types |
| Vehicle livery | Vehicles marked to give information on a practice | Not common but used by some firms on small inter-office or client delivery light vehicles |

be particularly true for the satellite services of professional firms. For example, executive search services of an accountancy practice share many of the characteristics of advertising agencies and as such the latter may have some interesting pointers which can be adopted or adapted.[2]

In looking at the individual methods of practice development there are definitional problems in that some could well be parts of other techniques, for example 'sponsorship' could be logically included in 'merchandising' and 'competitions' in 'public relations'. Similarly, there is no generally accepted boundary between some methods and some media and a few might justifiably be interchanged. An example of this is 'exhibitions' which could be viewed as a technique in its own right or a medium for 'display'. The decisions on categorization are recognized and are arbitrary in some respects (see Figure 17-1).

While a number of these methods are at present only used on the edges of professional services—that is those activities which are not subject to the same controls as in the qualifying professions, they have very strong implications for all professions in the future under increased governmental and public pressure to liberalize their rules.

## Media

It will be self-evident which media are appropriate for many of the methods listed, e.g., directories, but others may not be so obvious and there may also be alternatives. The media for consideration will be among those shown in Figure 17-2.

| For advertising and PR | National, regional, local press, TV and radio: technical, commercial, professional and commercial publications; films, video, audio tapes; catalogues, programmes, office and site signs |
| --- | --- |
| For merchandising, inward visits, client training, brochures, conferences, secondments | Own or appropriate other premises including rooms specially designed for presentations |
| Brochures, newsletters, small gifts | Mail |
| For sponsorship | National, local, regional events, books, academic, charitable and cultural activities |
| Off premises display | Exhibition venues, sites or other relevant locations |

**Figure 17-2**  Media choice

It can be seen from all that has gone before that there is a considerable cross-mesh of objectives, audiences, methods and media which would appear to give a totally impractical number of possible combinations. Fortunately, many combinations are either obviously inappropriate or impractical. For example, a target audience comprising officials in local government could not be approached cost effectively by media advertising in journals not devoted to local government matters. Conversely, PR in the local press and on local radio and perhaps direct mail might well succeed in conveying whatever message is desired to this group.

## Inter-relationships

The mesh and permutations nevertheless still remain considerable as can be seen if the situation is illustrated (see Figure 17-3).

2. A system of classification and illustrations of its practical use is given in Aubrey Wilson's *The Marketing of Professional Services*. McGraw-Hill (London, 1972), Chapter 1.

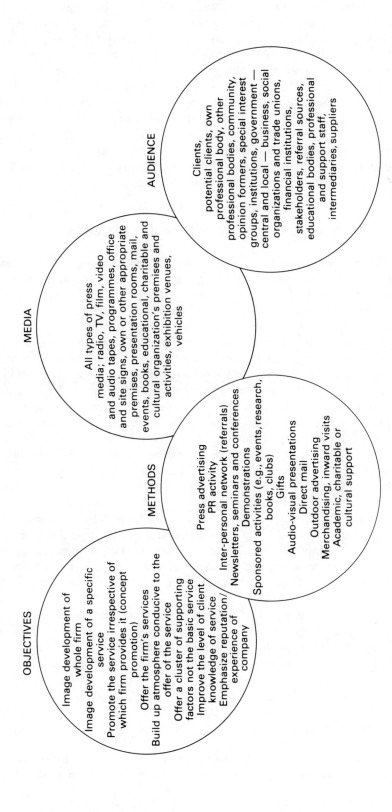

**OBJECTIVES**

Image development of whole firm
Image development of a specific service
Promote the service irrespective of which firm provides it (concept promotion)
Offer the firm's services
Build up atmosphere conducive to the offer of the service
Offer a cluster of supporting factors not the basic service
Improve the level of client knowledge of service
Emphasize reputation/experience of company

**METHODS**

Press advertising
PR activity
Inter-personal network (referrals)
Newsletters, seminars and conferences
Demonstrations
Sponsored activities (e.g., events, research, books, clubs)
Gifts
Audio-visual presentations
Direct mail
Outdoor advertising
Merchandising, inward visits
Academic, charitable or cultural support

**MEDIA**

All types of press media; radio, TV, film, video and audio tapes, programmes, office and site signs, own or other appropriate premises, presentation rooms, mail, events, books, educational, charitable and cultural organization's premises and activities, exhibition venues, vehicles

**AUDIENCE**

Clients, potential clients, own professional body, other professional bodies, community, opinion formers, special interest groups, institutions, government — central and local — business, social organizations and trade unions, financial institutions, stakeholders, referral sources, educational bodies, professional and support staff, intermediaries, suppliers

**Figure 17-3**  Communication mix

Achieving the right 'mix' of methods and media to achieve the objectives is perhaps one of the most difficult tasks facing, not just practice developers, but everyone engaged in marketing. While only limited help can be given to firms or individuals in respect of selection of appropriate methods and media, by presenting a comprehensive list such as this and using the pointers both in this chapter and Chapter 15, 'Guidelines for the choice of practice development methods', the basic errors of omission and commission can be avoided at the outset. Experience will contribute to improved judgement and decision making as the plan develops. This, however, will only occur if, as has been emphasized in Chapter 3, 'Creating a client-centred practice' (The marketing concept steps 8 and 9, page 27) and Chapter 5, 'Devising a practice development strategy and plan' (Evaluation and control, pages 61–3), there is on-going monitoring of the plan and the elements which comprise it, an evaluation of the effects of the various activities and controls for adjustment.

## Communication methods and the decision process

Given there is no formula which can be applied to determine which communication technique would be most effective in any particular circumstance or at any particular stage of the decision-making continuum used both by commercial and private clients, it is useful to illustrate just how the interface might occur. It is emphasized, however, that any picture which purports to show timing can only be a 'snapshot' of a particular situation.

The purchasing sequence in Figure 8-10 in Chapter 8, 'Professional services and the commercial client', brought together the three dimensions of the commercial purchasing process. The fourth component is of course the communication methods which could not be illustrated on the same diagram. However, using the same sequence, which to a modified degree will be adopted however informally and unconsciously by private clients, it is possible to relate technique to decision stage as well as to the personal contact approaches which have been described. This is illustrated in Figure 17-4. Its value does not lie in the situation it depicts so much as indicating a way in which each communication method which is permissible can and should be related to the decisions being taken at any given point in the whole process.

From the diagram (Figure 17-4) it will be observed that in the hypothetical situation illustrated and as was pointed out in the previous chapter, the extrinsic approach is phased out quickly and personal contact is relevant through almost the whole sequence whereas 'merchandising techniques', 'inward visits', 'educational campaigns' and the 'inter-personal network' are not applicable until stage 4 of the continuum. A totally different situation could apply in different circumstances where perhaps these particular methods would be introduced in earlier or later stages. The position is dynamic and Figure 17-4 is intended only to illustrate an example.

The key techniques, the inter-personal network (referrals), fee strategies and personal contact have each had one chapter devoted to them because they are methods which are vital and commonly used in all professions although in varying ways. Three further tools are however sufficiently ubiquitous and important to warrant some explanation, if not a whole chapter.

## Public relations (PR)

Even the most enthusiastic writers on PR admit that it and its practitioners are not well regarded in business. Inevitably *sartor resartus* springs to mind. If the practitioners of this

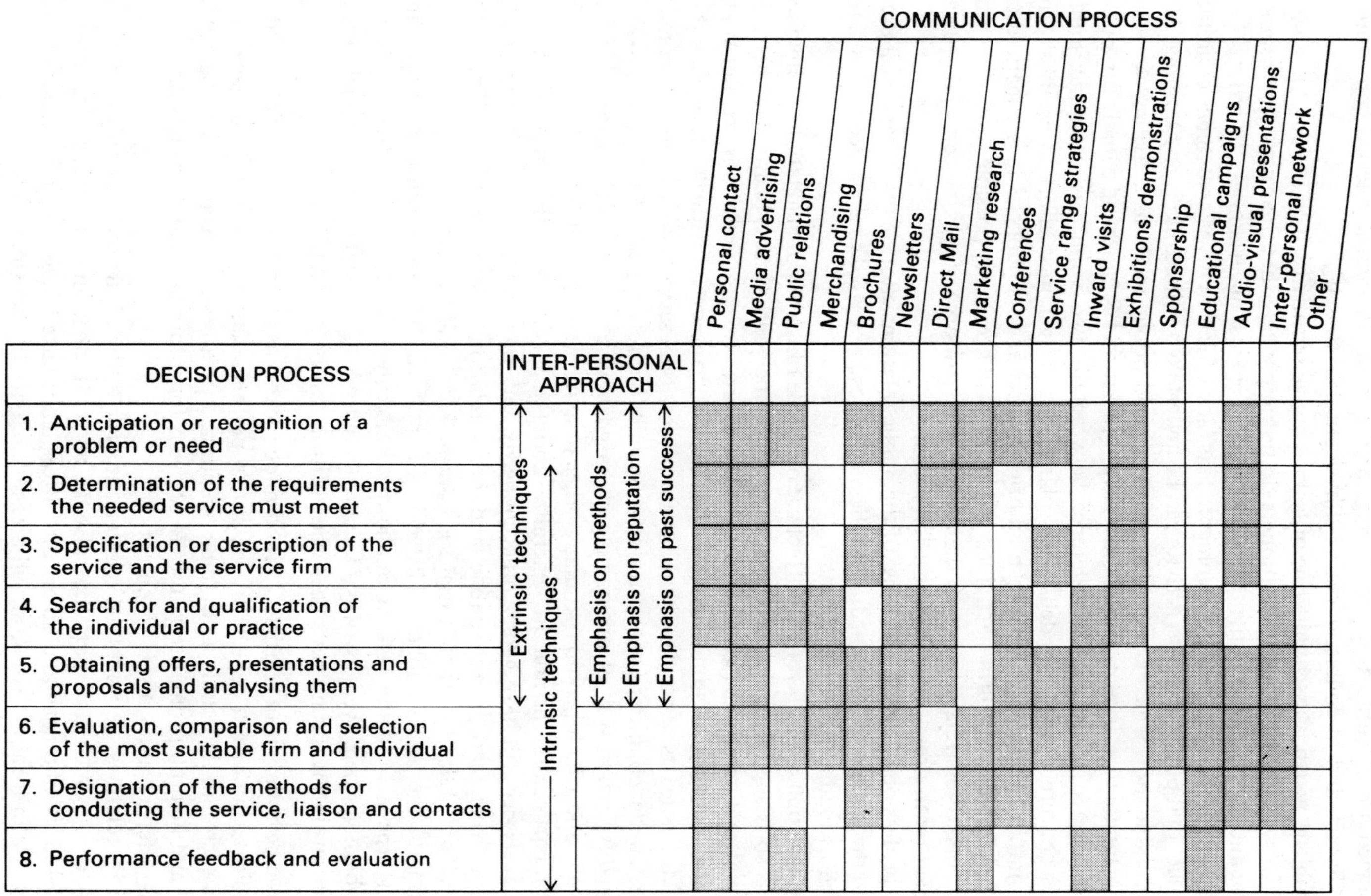

COMMUNICATION PROCESS

Communication methods (columns):
- Personal contact
- Media advertising
- Public relations
- Merchandising
- Brochures
- Newsletters
- Direct Mail
- Marketing research
- Conferences
- Service range strategies
- Inward visits
- Exhibitions, demonstrations
- Sponsorship
- Educational campaigns
- Audio-visual presentations
- Inter-personal network
- Other

INTER-PERSONAL APPROACH
← Emphasis on past success →
← Emphasis on reputation →
← Emphasis on methods →

← Extrinsic techniques → ← Intrinsic techniques →

DECISION PROCESS

1. Anticipation or recognition of a problem or need
2. Determination of the requirements the needed service must meet
3. Specification or description of the service and the service firm
4. Search for and qualification of the individual or practice
5. Obtaining offers, presentations and proposals and analysing them
6. Evaluation, comparison and selection of the most suitable firm and individual
7. Designation of the methods for conducting the service, liaison and contacts
8. Performance feedback and evaluation

**Figure 17·4** An example of communication methods and the decision process

particular service are unable to produce a satisfactory image and acceptance for themselves, how can they produce them for others? But the same criticism can be made of architects in badly designed and decorated offices, management consultants whose internal communications are chaotic, and of course, doctors—'Physician heal thyself'.

This problem, which is essentially one of lack of image sensitivity, is to be found in almost all professions but only because practitioners do not appreciate that their own performance, appearance and attitudes can mitigate or contribute to clients' uncertainties, the reduction of which is a vital part of practice development. This lack of sensitivity is sometimes combined with the belief that public relations activity can be undertaken without skills and training. This is a toxic combination which ensures the death of good public relations activities.

It is unfortunate that, in marketing terms, the abbreviation PR can stand equally for 'public relations' or 'press relations'. The difference between the two is not just semantic: public relations is concerned with the deliberate, planned, and sustained effort to establish and maintain mutual understanding between an organization and its publics.[3] It is a methodical attempt to promote all the firm's activities and interests in every way possible (excluding paid advertisements). Press relations covers the relatively narrow area of seeking editorial or news column mention in press, radio or television media.

For the professional service firm most of the public relations effort tends to centre on press relations to the neglect of other media and the mechanics are geared to press needs. Thus, the publicity effort is inhibited from the start.

Practice development calls for the correct use of a wide range of public relations techniques. That this is so is supported by the undisputed dominance and success of the inter-personal network in attracting clients (see Chapter 13, 'The referral (recommendations) system'). The inter-personal network is stimulated by exposure of firms or individuals through public relations. Moreover, its particular suitability for professional services which must use practice development under conditions of constraint, rests on its indirect appeals. These appear to offer one reasonably certain way of overcoming embargoes which are maintained for ethical or other reasons and which prohibit so many other practice development methods.

It is not particularly helpful to generalize about the communication 'mix' since each professional service will have widely differing needs, but, by and large, it would appear that professional firms tend to use public and press relations more intensively than other techniques. That is not to say that usage is always skilful and elegant.

In looking at the firm's publics as listed in Chapter 12, 'The importance of images and perceptions' (page 140), the task of public relations can be more clearly observed and its differing objectives perceived. By way of example and taking a number of key publics or, in public relations terms, prime audiences, the position can be summarized thus:

- **Client and potential client relations**   Good public relations apart from the obvious need to communicate important aspects of the firm's performance, activities and achievements includes such minute details as training telephone operators and secretaries to be polite, friendly and helpful, prompt responses to requests for information and prompt thanks for business, referrals and outside co-operation.
- **Community relations**   Community relations links activities of the firm not only to the local community of which it is part, but also to its total environment. The secondment of personnel to sit on official and other committees, assistance to educational establishments, participation in local activities, are all areas of activity for consideration.
- **Staff relations**   These are concerned internally with personnel factors and externally with recruitment. Well-conceived public relations can do much to enhance employees' sense of

3. Institute of Public Relations (London).

pride in the organization's ideals, achievements, growth records and concepts of service to its clients. In the same manner good public relations will considerably aid recruitment of personnel. A high level of awareness concerning the firm will have a partial screening effect in attracting applicants conforming more closely to requirements than if knowledge of the organization is lacking or incorrect.

- **Referral source relations**   Perhaps more than most groups it is important to maintain good communications with those individuals and organizations who can influence business and clients. Keeping them informed on existing and developing interests, expertise and experience as well as achievements, changes in personnel and locations are typical subjects for public relations among this group.
- **Professional relations**   This involves the interaction of the service firm within its own and linked professions. It includes participation in their own professional activities such as working parties, study groups, inter-firm comparisons and conferences which may contribute to the state of the art or the profession's well-being. Perhaps as important is the provision of speakers at and participation in activities of other groups—professional and non-professional—in which the firm may be interested.
- **Stakeholder relations**   Every firm has to be financed whether the funds come from individuals such as equity partners, outside investors or financial institutions. Stakeholder relations are directed to developing satisfactory links with stakeholders, potential investors and those who influence investments. The task is not only to keep these audiences informed of the firm's achievements and plans, but to ensure that the policies and activities of the firm are correctly interpreted.

The opportunities for public relations for most professional service firms are myriad but wasted. This is because what are essentially extremely good news stories are not always identified. When they are, the do-it-yourself propensity of professional service firms is never exhibited to worse effect than in clumsy efforts to obtain press or other media coverage, and in presenting the item either as a document or perhaps an interview.

The major faults have been identified and their antidote suggested.[4]

*Personal reasons*

- Fear or scorn of simple language.
- Failure to distinguish between the written and spoken word.
- Hiding behind a protective screen of clichés and jargon.
- (*in personal interview*)   Accents.
- (*in personal interview*)   Physical peculiarities and disadvantages.

*Social reasons*

- Too specialized environment (business incest).
- Inability to stand back from own firm or from self.
- Circumscribed and specialized thinking.
- Supposed need to maintain the 'official line' language.
- Fear of criticism particularly from own profession.
- Cocooning over a long period from uncomfortable reality.

While a great many of these faults can be cured by simply appreciating that they exist and others can be eradicated by skill training, professionals ought never seek to avoid the

4. Kenneth Hudson. *The Businessman in Public*. Associated Business Programmes (London, 1976), Chapters 3 and 4.

- Analyse special expertise of firm and individuals which subsequently can be used for external communication purposes
- Conduct inventory of outside activities of partners and other professional and support staff in the firm to determine community penetration and to identify areas where firm might consider participation
- Analyse positioning of the firm through external and internal audit. Self-image and peers' perceptions
- Exposure in the professional and general press on matters of professional expertise
- Professional advice, counsel and service on relevant professional matters and other activities which necessitate dealing with the media
- Stimulation of professional articles by the firm's professionals which can then be used for direct mail purposes
- Printed materials about the firm (brochures and leaflets)
- Consideration of educational activities and seminars to gain recognition for the firm among prospective and present clients, referral sources and future staff
- Speaking engagements and subsequent publicity, which can then also be used for direct mail contacts with clients and others
- News releases on diverse subjects—new partners, mergers, successful activities, innovations or changes in the profession or its disciplines, special honours to firm members, outside activities
- Interviews on radio and television—palens, interviews on professional subject, timely discussions related to matters of current interest that reflect the firm's special experience

**Figure 17-5**  Check list for public relations

employment of the specialists to undertake activities in which they have no ability or only a limited proficiency.

A suggested list of activities[5] in the public relations field which was developed for law firms and has been generalized for all professions is the check list comprising Figure 17-5.

Good public relations should be a channel, not a barrier, between the service firm and its publics. It is a regular continuous programme of sensitive response to the various publics served. It is not a posture of goodwill assumed in order to solve current problems and given up when those problems are removed. Of the many elements in the marketing mix, public relations perhaps is the most applicable and powerful available for practice development.

This check list is action orientated and calls on firms to devise and implement a consistent programme and not wait for any particular communication media to seek them out. Features and interviews for press, radio and TV should always be offered and it will be found they are very frequently taken up. Just as it is absolutely necessary for a practice to be 'visible', so for public relations purposes it is equally necessary for it to be known that the firm or individual can provide features, interviews, comments or even just letters. A build-up of these types of public relations material will quickly identify a firm as 'newsworthy', 'expert', 'co-operative' and the approaches will be made by the media. Given that on a random basis editors, journalists and producers can locate many sources of information on a particular profession, activity or circumstance, then high 'visibility' is more than likely to ensure that the practice will be invited to contribute.

## Direct mail

It has always been recognized that one of the most valuable forms of media for small business

5. Adapted and reproduced by permission of Harshe-Rotman & Druck Inc. (Chicago, USA).

is direct mail and since most professional firms tend to be small, this is a technique which should find favour with them.

The major advantage of direct mail is that it is possible to target the message accurately to the clients and, indeed, to individuals within companies.

The second benefit is the control which can be exercised over the rate and timing of mailings. If response reaches a level which places too great a strain on the firm, the mailing quantities can be reduced or stopped or if the response is low it can be increased. The third advantage of direct mail is that dispatch can often be timed at a favourable or propitious moment to parallel some event, conditions or circumstance. One of the most ubiquitous uses for direct mail is by the accountancy profession where many firms send their clients information on changes in taxation on the day following the budget.

The question of reliability of sources of addresses is of prime importance. A firm's own client and prospective client list ought to be the most accurate one available, but the reality is that these are often out of date. An example of this is a solicitor who wrote to every client for whom he had made and held a Will but with whom he had had no contact for the last five years, suggesting that the will be looked at in the light of the client's present situation and current conditions. Among the replies were several from personal representatives which indicated that later Wills had been made which the solicitor did not hold nor had he any knowledge of them. The only interpretation that can be placed on such a situation is that the firm could not distinguish between inactive and lost clients and thus their own mailing list was inaccurate.

For those professions where it is possible to contact prospective, as opposed to actual, clients it is necessary to consider the development or acquisition of names and addresses other than clients. It is unfortunately more the rule than the exception that many compilations on which direct mail plans are based are taken from directories and other sources which can be as much as 40–50 per cent inaccurate. This is caused by, for example, removals, deaths, changes of occupation, status, home ownership in the case of individuals or discontinuances, re-locations, mergers, start-ups and a wide range of other reasons among commercial concerns. However, such a high order of inaccuracy does not have to be accepted if direct mail users take care in ensuring that sources are relevant, of a reasonably recent date and that lists have been 'cleaned' and monitored regularly.

Membership of organizations, shareholders' registers, attendances at conferences, are likely to be accurate at the time of the compilation, which is more than can be said for journal circulation lists and many trade directories. A large number of tabulations begin on a false basis in that they claim or imply they are exhaustive when, in fact, an individual or firm appears in them only by virtue of having bought the entry.

The question of topicality is equally important. Local rating and electoral roles are said to be 10 per cent out of date at their time of publication and this is certainly true of yearbooks and other annual publications. Thus, a three-year-old directory could be as much as 30 per cent inaccurate.

With a good base list it is possible to undertake a certain amount of 'cleaning' from knowledge within the firm of the locality or community. For example, in *The Times* and *Fortune* publications showing major companies by various criteria, size being the principal one, it is possible, without difficulty, to identify the significant mergers not accounted for in the compilations. Similarly, anyone knowledgeable about advertising could without difficulty separate in any of the many directories, agencies which concentrate on consumer markets from those that specialize in industrial markets.

Once a good base source is developed then monitoring should occur as a routine process. This enables identified changes to be recorded; for example, the appointment of new personnel, changes of address, acquisitions and divestments and other corporate activities in the case of commercial firms and births, marriages, deaths, removals, house ownership in the case of private individuals. A useful check on 'bought-in' lists is to retain returned envelopes noting 'gone-aways' or unlocatable addresses. This will highlight the validity of any claims of accuracy and currency.

Given these checks and actions the direct mail lists can be accurate and, therefore, at the very least the mailing begins with the possibility of success enhanced.

For the three dominant reasons given—accurate targeting, control of timing and topicality, but also other, reasons, direct mail can be one of the most economic methods of practice development but can also be one of the most extravagant. With control over the target audience and timing, economy can be ensured, but if the message itself is unremarkable the mailing will be totally wasted. The mailing piece is unlikely to go further than the wastepaper basket. Everyone receives a plethora of direct mail of one sort or another, some on such a regular basis that it is possible to discard many of the pieces without opening since the label or envelope is recognizable.

At any moment in time there are a finite number of individuals and firms considering the adoption of particular services. If a mailing piece arrives at that moment, it will stimulate a reply. For all others it will be wasted as an immediate practice development effort, but might contribute to longer-term prospects. If this is so, it justifies the expense of large coverage and clearly it must be profitable for some firms to do this since they persist in their particular approach. However, for most practices a policy of ensuring penetration to the right person at perhaps a higher cost per piece mailed is generally the best one.

This means that the contents themselves must be attractive and in the case of commercial recipients of apparently sufficient importance to pass through the screening personnel of postroom, secretaries, assistants and others. One of the most effective ways of doing this and ensuring attention is to address the prospect by name and to personalize the message as far as possible.

The usual form of direct mail adopted by professional service firms is that of a letter setting out the services available combined with a brochure, but even this somewhat conservative approach is regarded by many firms as brash. Nevertheless, there is a strong case for the use of attention-getting devices which are not themselves incompatible with the firm's image. A wristwatch strap calendar sent month by month through the year, each time accompanied by news items on the service company's activities, is an example of a continuous mailing programme. The calendar was habit-forming and was missed if not received. A light touch can be adopted for perfectly serious services. A regular mailing of wire puzzles to clients and prospective clients by a firm of ergonomic consultants emphasizing their problem-solving capabilities in relation to physical forms of objects proved to be highly effective in terms of response and recall.

Direct mail gives the service firm more opportunity to explain its 'product' than many other methods of practice development. If the effectiveness of direct mail is to be assessed, it will always be necessary to return to first principles and to know clearly what the direct mail campaign was intended to achieve. The importance of precise goals can never be overemphasized.

Thus, if the objective of the mail piece is to persuade recipients to send for further details, its effectiveness should not be measured in terms of business achieved, but in terms of responses for more information. Similarly, if the mailing is to open the way for a personal meeting, the measure of its success is not requests for more information by mail (however useful this may be), but the number of appointments requested. However, even with such narrow goals it is still not possible to make a totally accurate assessment of success achievements since many elements other than the mailing may contribute to the action being measured. For example, a service firm may be known to have successfully undertaken work similar to that which the prospective client is considering, but this information came from the press not a mail piece. Under these circumstances, the attribution of a new client to direct mail would only be partly accurate. However, even if total accuracy cannot be achieved, a measure of relative success is still more than worth while, since it gives at least some criteria for comparison of effectiveness.

## Check list

The following steps should be observed in designing and implementing a direct mail programme:

1. Decide objective of mailings.
2. Identify the target audience.
3. Locate or construct suitable mailing lists.
4. Test check a random sample from the list to ensure they fit the criteria on which the compilation was made and information in the lists is current.
5. Identify names of recipients where possible.
6. If lists are bought or any agency used check origin and date of last revision of lists.
7. Decide the number of mailing pieces to be sent.
8. Decide copy, illustrations, inclusion of any attention-getting devices.
9. Copy test mailing piece on typical respondent types.
10. Decide initiation date, rate of dispatch.
11. Decide if follow-up mailing is to take place and if so after what period or on what type of response.
12. Devise mechanics for removing responses or failed contacts' names to avoid wastage in follow-up mailings.
13. Test mail a limited number of pieces.
14. Note speed and quality of response and revise mailing piece or lists as results indicate.
15. Decide elapsed time at which results will be evaluated.
16. Evaluate results against objectives and assess cost effectiveness.

## Market research

Traditionally, marketing research has been seen as a process by which facts concerning the sale and transfer of goods and services are gathered, recorded, analysed and reported on. Ideas and data are collected from many sources and form the basis for action founded on logical analysis and judgement. Research properly conducted is an organized, highly methodical and planning procedure to increase knowledge and understanding of the subject under review as a basis for informed decision making.

For most professions the immediate needs are usually for information relating to their own clients rather than the wider environment in which the firm operates. However, for practice development purposes the first step in the plan is to undertake a situation analysis. For this certain data will be required and whether these are obtained by formal marketing research or informally they are still needed. Chapter 5, 'Devising a practice development strategy and plan' (page 48), and Chapter 6, 'Deciding the service offering of the practice', page 74 listed some key information objectives all of which could be obtained by the use of marketing research. However, the individual practice can gain enormously from what is in effect a micro-study of its own clients.

Such an enquiry will reveal many aspects of the way the practice is conducted and perceived and which normally remain hidden. Apart from identifying the image of the practice it will also reveal such things as communication failures, the attitudes of staff to clients, convenience or effectiveness of facilities, the desirability of changes in the composition of the range of services offered, and a host of major and minor matters that can usually be either corrected or further built on to enhance the position of the practice.

Appendix A(i) of this chapter shows part of a questionnaire used by a legal practice to identify its perceived (by clients) strengths and weaknesses. Appendix A(ii) is a short American enquiry form. A very detailed questionnaire designed for US accountancy practices is also available.[6] Studies such as those listed in Chapter 5, 'Devising a practice development strategy and plan', can be extended to embrace many other objectives and the cost of such enquiries does not rise proportionately with the extent of the questioning although there is a point of diminishing returns in terms of information yield.

An examination of possible research objectives will quickly reveal that there are more objectives than practicable applications for the use of the information obtained. However, it is always sensible to compare any research objectives with a check list to ensure no important ones are omitted.[7]

## Is research needed?

While a plea for more information can always be made, it is nevertheless necessary to test whether, in any given circumstances, research is indeed required in order to make decisions and to devise a course of action. If the cost-to-yield ratio is not satisfactory, then it is imperative to consider whether to do research at all.

Precisely what marketing research can do for the professional service firm will depend upon its ability to conceptualize a market situation, to conduct the survey, and to act on the results. Targets for research are more numerous than profitable and care is therefore needed in selecting topics to be sure that they are actionable, rather than just interesting; profitable, rather than just useful.

In deciding if research is needed, the use of criteria will assist a decision:

- Why is information needed?
- What information is needed?
- What resources will be required to obtain it?
- What will be accomplished by its acquisition?
- When can the results stemming from its acquisition be obtained?
- What conditions must be met?

The answers will give a positive indication as to whether research should be initiated.

Research for professional services will be less to monitor the course of the practice development activities than to influence their outcome—a totally different philosophy from that which prevailed in the past on the rare occasions when research was undertaken by professional service companies.

6. S. G. Webb. *Marketing and Strategic Planning for Professional Service Firms.* AMACOM (New York, 1982), pp. 98–107.
7. Aubrey Wilson. *Marketing Audit Check Lists—a guide to effective marketing resource realization.* McGraw-Hill (London, 1982).

The information resource, as was pointed out in Chapter 4, 'Preparing for practice development', makes an important contribution and there is every reason to build up information not just from the internal records of the firm but also by enquiries among actual and potential clients. Practice development to be successful will rely heavily on information which is recent, detailed and accurate.

For some professions and some practices methods besides those described in some depth and perhaps not listed will be more appropriate. The practice developer might best consider these against a background of more information than has been possible to include in this chapter. The bibliography at the end of the book has references to publications in which many of the techniques have been examined in depth. Although, almost without exception, these books have been written for those involved in the marketing of goods and services which are not subject to the constraints of professional services, they all contain adaptable information. The practice developer should not be deterred by their commercial presentation and should keep firmly in mind that every method that itself is permitted by the profession can be performed within a manner completely compatible with the status and dignity of the professional and the practice.

# Appendix 17A(i)

Part of a postal questionnaire used for commercial clients. The major sections included questions under the following headings:

- Finding and choosing a legal practice.
- Making an appointment.
- Visiting the practice.
- Meeting the solicitor.
- Progress and communication quality.
- Completion (including assessment of 'value for money').

The following extract is taken from the section 'Meeting the solicitor':

8. Did you see the person with whom the appointment was made?  YES/NO

9. If not, was the substitution acceptable?  YES/NO

   If a substitute, was the person a partner
                   qualified solicitor
                   legal assistant
                   other member of staff?

10. Is it usual to deal with the same individual for every matter
    your company consults the practice on?  YES/NO

11. If not, would you prefer this type of continuity?  YES/NO/NO PREFERENCE

12. How did you perceive the attitude and knowledge of the solicitor
    and his support staff?

|  | Excellent | Good | Fair | Poor |
|---|---|---|---|---|
| Legal knowledge concerning the particular matter | ☐ | ☐ | ☐ | ☐ |
| Knowledge of your firm's circumstances or business | ☐ | ☐ | ☐ | ☐ |
| Ability to respond quickly to your requirements | ☐ | ☐ | ☐ | ☐ |
| Ability to explain complex legal matters | ☐ | ☐ | ☐ | ☐ |
| Ability to set out options/alternatives/ consequences of any given course of action | ☐ | ☐ | ☐ | ☐ |
| Quality of advice | ☐ | ☐ | ☐ | ☐ |
| Punctuality of completion | ☐ | ☐ | ☐ | ☐ |

Other comments  _____
                _____
                _____

13. Do you feel the solicitor understood the problem your firm
    was consulting him on?  YES/NO

14. Did you ask for an estimate of the likely level of fees
    and other charges?  YES/NO

15. If so, was the solicitor able to meet this request?  YES/NO

16. Did you leave the meeting with a clear idea of the subsequent
    sequence of events and actions for both solicitor and your company?  YES/NO

17. In general how do you feel your firm was treated by the solicitor
    who handled your matter?

    _____
    _____
    _____

# Paul N. Luvera & Associates

**LAW OFFICES**
917 SOUTH THIRD STREET – P.O. BOX 427
MOUNT VERNON, WASHINGTON 98273-0427
206-336-6561

**SEATTLE OFFICE**
TELEPHONE (206) 223-0870

**MAILING ADDRESS**
P.O. BOX 427
MOUNT VERNON, WA 98273-0427

LITA BARNETT-LUVERA

JOHN G. KAMB, JR.

A PROFESSIONAL CORPORATION

Thank you very much for consulting our office regarding your legal
problem. We appreciate very much your trust and confidence. We
are interested in improving our legal services. We would appreciate
your assisting us by completing this questionnaire and returning it
in the stamped, self-addressed envelope enclosed. Your response
will be kept confidential.

Yes No

___ ___ 1. Did you feel our office personnel were friendly and treated
you courteously?

___ ___ 2. Why did you select our office originally?_____

_____

___ ___ 3. Did our office keep you adequately informed regarding your
legal matter? If not, do you have any suggestions on how we
might improve on this?_____

_____

___ ___ 4. What was the nature of the legal work we did for you?_____

_____

___ ___ 5. Did you feel the lawyer spent sufficient time with you on
your legal matter?

___ ___ 6. Did you feel that sufficient attention and time were devoted
to your legal matter?

___ ___ 7. Were your telephone enquiries answered to your satisfaction?

___ ___ 8. Were you satisfied with your dealings with the office staff?

___ ___ 9. Do you feel that our fee for services was reasonable for the
work performed?

10. We would appreciate any comments that you might have that will
help us to improve our service to our clients. Please use
the reverse side of this sheet if necessary.

Thank you very much for your time and courtesy in filling out
this questionnaire.

# Conclusion

Neither this book, nor indeed any single book, could communicate to professionals seeking to develop a practice development policy all that needs to be known about the subject. It has, at best, provided an introduction to the subject and hopefully a logical ordering and methodology for devising and implementing a strategy to ensure the profitable and satisfying development of a practice. It has not sought by artfulness or guile to find ways of avoiding the rules of the profession but to indicate what can be done within both the spirit and the letter of practice, laws or guidelines as they are at present time. It is also an overview of what might be permissible in the future as different professions relax their constraints.

The task of what for many will be a completely new activity and way of thinking might appear daunting, most particularly when it has been one theme of this book that successful practice development will depend on the professionals themselves. Marketing experts, while they have a role to play in the provision of some specialist advice and services, are not appropriate. In fact acquiring the skills for practice development is far from difficult. What is harder to generate is the necessary motivation to acquire these skills and to use them. In many respects everything is against acquiring motivation: tradition, training, the rules of practice, the attitude of colleagues and even of clients all combine to make the practitioner doubt both his own capabilities and whether the whole activity can be accomplished and, if accomplished, whether it is worth while.

The answers clearly rest in the first chapter, 'Why practice development?'. It is perhaps appropriate to end this book where it began with a re-statement of the reasons why practice development is necessary now or, if it is not, will be in the not too distant future:

- Survival.
- Competition.
- Inflation.
- Technology.
- Changing public attitudes.

All are combining to remove the protection and to reduce regard which the professions have traditionally enjoyed and in some ways to attack the basis of the relationship between them and their clients.

More pervasive perhaps will be increasing public and governmental pressures, world-wide, for relaxation of the restrictions which prohibit a more obvious presence in the market place. The book has not sought to advocate changes in professional practice rules. This is a socio-political issue and irrelevant to objectives which the author set himself. What it has attempted to do is to show how practices can flourish in the new ethos which is developing and all the advantages which will ensue:

- Increased profitability and thus realization of personal and practice aspirations.
- Greater work satisfaction with its concomitant intellectual stimulation and the opportunity of greater self-expression.
- Better career opportunities which will attract the highest calibre recruits.
- Improved service to clients by bringing as close together as possible their needs and the firm's output.

No techniques of practice development can change the course of events and it would be absurd to suggest that they could or that they should be used in this manner. Every firm and every individual professional must decide their own posture and attitudes for whatever future is predicted for their profession. The reality of the market place will not go away any more than the cold winds of competition—inter- and intra-professional—will cease to blow because they are ignored.

Perhaps the extent and speed of change will not be as great as some observers have forecast but in any event, preparing for alternative scenarios is the only prudent course for anyone with a concern for the future. This book offers the raw material for one scenario to meet unfamiliar and possibly even unpleasant changes. It has been said that the only good thing about the future is that it comes one day at a time . . . but come it will.

# Bibliography

The bibliography of practice development is sparse to an extreme. Those charged with practice development will have to be prepared to adapt from the important, useful and highly practical work that has been undertaken for products and commercial services.

By far the most complete bibliography on services' (as a whole) literature is that compiled by Christian Gronroos, Swedish School of Economics and Business Administration. Helsinki.

## Professional practices

F. A. R. Bennion. *Professional Ethics*. Charles Knight (London, 1969).
A. M. Carr-Saunders and P. A. Wilson. *The Professions*. Associated Business Press (London, 1980).
R. Dingwall and P. Lewis (eds). *The Sociology of the Professions*. Macmillan (London, 1983).
P. D. V. Marsh. *Business Ethics*. Associated Business Press (London, 1980).
G. Millerson. *The Qualifying Associations*. Routledge & Kegal Paul (London, 1964).

## Marketing (general)

C. Gronroos. *Strategic Management and Marketing in the Service Sector*. Swedish School of Economics and Business Administration Research Reports (Helsinki, 1982).
E. W. Wheatley. *Marketing Professional Services*. Prentice-Hall (Englewood Cliffs, NJ, 1983).
Aubrey Wilson. *The Marketing of Professional Services*. McGraw-Hill (London, 1972).

## Market strategy and planning

W. Goldsmith. *Forward Planning in the Service Sector*. McGraw-Hill (New York, 1977).
H. Jones. *Preparing Company Plans*. Gower Press (Farnborough, 1974).
J. Stapleton. *How to Prepare a Marketing Plan* (3rd edn). Gower Press (Farnborough, 1983).
S. G. Webb. *Marketing and Strategic Planning for Professional Service Firms*. Amacon (New York, 1982).
J. Winkler. *Winkler on Marketing Planning*. Associated Business Programmes (London, 1972).

## Marketing in specific professions

H. Bachner and K. Hosin. *Marketing and Promotion for Design Professionals*. Van Nostrand Reinhold (Wokingham, 1977).

L. Berry and L. Capaldini. *Marketing for the Bank Executive*. Leviathan House (London, 1975).

J. G. Foonberg. *How to Start and Build a Law Practice*. American Bar Association (Chicago, 1976).

Insurance Institute. *Modern Techniques in the Marketing and Merchandising of Insurance*. Insurance Institute (London, 1971).

G. Jones. *How to Market Professional Design Services*. McGraw-Hill (New York, 1973).

S. Kennedy. *Marketing of Professional Information Services*. MCB (Bradford, 1981).

E. J. Ornstein. *The Marketing of Money*. Gower Press (Farnborough, 1972).

P. Tisdall. *Agents of Change: The Development and Practice of Management Consultancy*. Heinemann (London, 1982).

R. J. Williamson. *Marketing for Accountants and Managers*. ICMA (London, 1972).

## Publicity and public relations

W. Howard. *The Practice of Public Relations*. IM/Heinemann (London, 1982).

Kenneth Hudson. *The Businessman in Public*. Associated Business Programmes (London, 1976).

E. Kopel. *Financial and Corporate Public Relations*. McGraw-Hill (London, 1982).

J. E. Marston. *Modern Public Relations*. McGraw-Hill (New York, 1979).

L. Nolte. *Fundamentals of Public Relations*. Pergamon Press (Oxford, 1979).

Public Relations Consultants' Association. *Public Relations in Practice: Some Examples of Consultancies' Work*. PRCA (London, 1978).

M. Williams-Thompson. *PR in Practice*. Pergamon Press (Oxford, 1968).

## Pricing

A Gabor. *Pricing, Principles and Practices*. Heinemann (London, 1977).

A. Marshall. *More Profitable Pricing*. McGraw-Hill (London, 1979).

E. Marting. *Creative Pricing*. AMA (New York, 1968).

A. R. Oxenfeldt. *Pricing Strategies*. Amacon (New York, 1975).

J. Winkler. *Pricing for Results*. Heinemann/IM (London, 1983).

## Advertising

S. Broadbent. *Spending Advertising Money*. Business Books (London, 1979).

M. Davis. *The Effective Use of Advertising Media*. Business Books (London, 1981).

T. F. Garbett. *Corporate Advertising*. McGraw-Hill (New York, 1981).

W. Haight. *Retail Advertising*. General Learning Publications (London, 1976).

N. Hart. *Industrial Advertising & Publicity*. Associated Business Programmes (London, 1978).

I.P.A. *Getting the Most Out of the Advertising Budget*. Institute of Practitioners in Advertising (London, 1979).

F. Jenkins. *Advertising Made Simple*. W. H. Allen (London, 1973).

## Miscellaneous

The following books all include a number of issues relevant to the practice development for professional firms.

H. Heaton. *Productivity in Service Organizations*. McGraw-Hill (New York, 1977).

P. Kotler. *Marketing for Non-Profit Organizations*. Prentice-Hall (Englewood Cliffs, NJ, 1982).

M. Mokra. *Marketing the Arts*. Praeger (Eastbourne, 1980).

E. J. Ornstein and A. Nunn. *The Marketing of Leisure*. Associated Business Press (London, 1980).

# Author index

# Subject index